S0-BJP-088

Studies in British Art

St Mary's, Tadcaster, Yorks. Chancel east window, 1878.

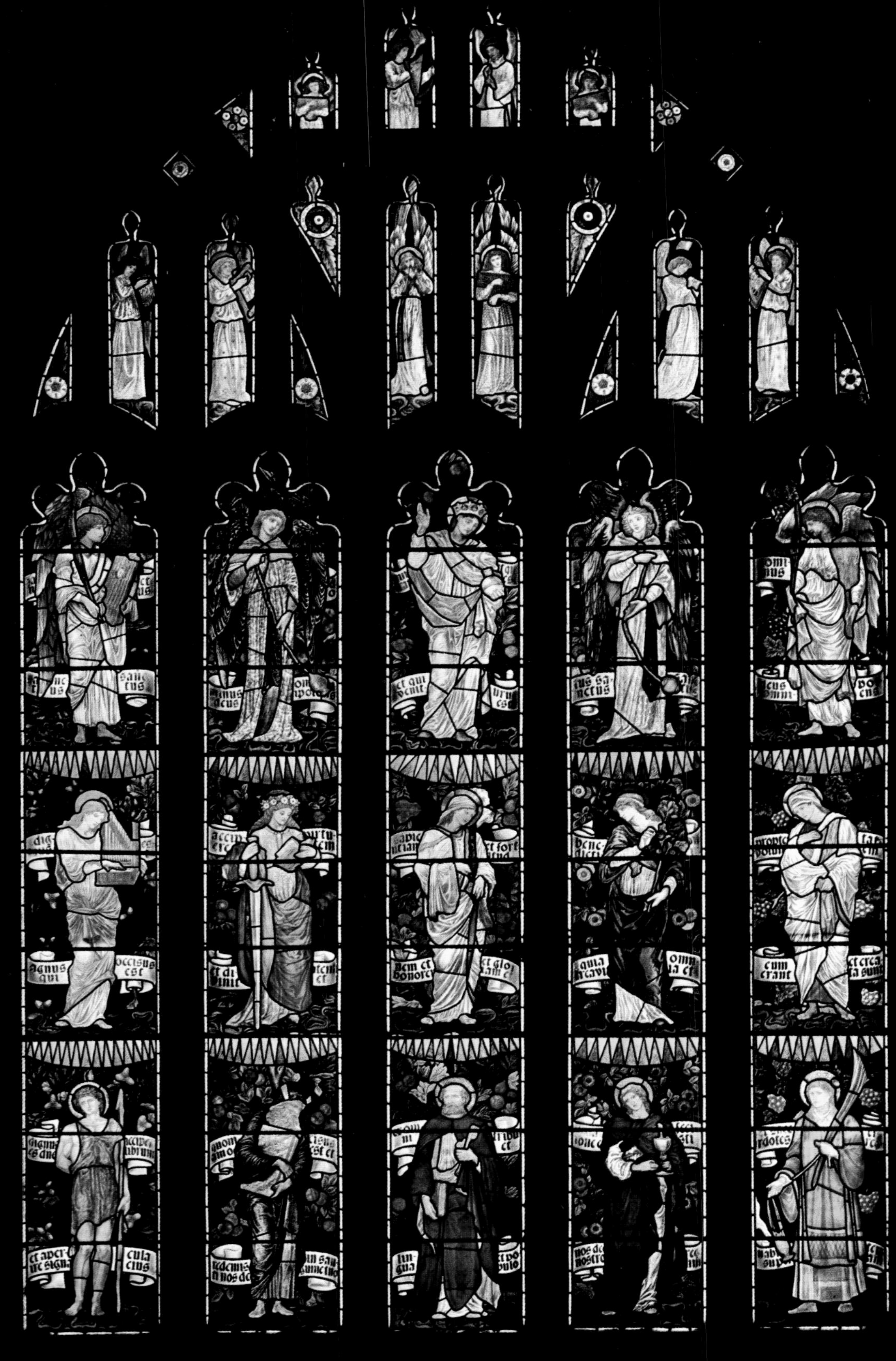

THE STAINED GLASS OF WILLIAM MORRIS AND HIS CIRCLE

A. Charles Sewter

•

PUBLISHED FOR
THE PAUL MELLON CENTRE FOR STUDIES IN BRITISH ART (LONDON) LTD
BY
YALE UNIVERSITY PRESS
NEW HAVEN AND LONDON · 1974

Library of Congress catalog card number: 72-91307

International standard book number: 0 300 01471 6

Designed by Sebastian Carter and set in 14 point Ehrhardt type.

Printed in Great Britain by The Curwen Press Ltd., Plaistow.

Colour plates printed in the Netherlands by Joh. Enschedé en Zonen, Haarlem.

Published in Great Britain, Europe, and Africa by
Yale University Press, Ltd., London.
Distributed in Latin America by Kaiman & Polon, Inc., New York City;
in Australasia and Southeast Asia by John Wiley & Sons Australasia Pty. Ltd., Sydney;
in India by UBS Publishers' Distributors Pvt., Ltd., Delhi;
in Japan by John Weatherhill, Inc., Tokyo.

Contents

Acknowledgements

In the course of preparing this study I have received help of various kinds from so many people that adequate acknowledgements to all of them are quite impossible. I should like, however, to record my special thanks to the Trustees of the Leverhulme Research Fund for grants in aid of expenses for the years 1956 and 1957; to the British Academy; to the former Vice-Chancellor of the University of Manchester, Sir William Mansfield Cooper; and to the Faculty of Arts Publications Committee of the same University, for generous contributions towards the costs of publication. Hardly less profound is my sense of gratitude to Mr Basil Taylor and his colleagues formerly of the Paul Mellon Foundation for British Art, for the care with which they considered the problems of organizing and rendering as easily usable as possible the mass of information contained in my typescript.

At early stages in the research, I was greatly indebted to Mr S E Overal and Miss Bridget Goshawk of the William Morris Gallery at Walthamstow; to Dr Mary Woodall, then Director of the Birmingham City Art Gallery, who afforded me special privileges in the use of material belonging to the Gallery; to Mr John Brandon-Jones, who lent me the Philip Webb account-book, sketch-book and letters in his possession; to Mr Ronald Briggs of the William Morris Society, who provided me with microfilm of Burne-Jones's account-books in the Fitzwilliam Museum, and photocopies of the Morris sketch-books in the British Museum; and to Mr Joseph R Dunlap, American secretary of the William Morris Society, for information regarding certain windows in the United States.

It is a pleasure also to record my appreciation of the help received from many art gallery and museum officials, who gave me facilities for studying works in their charge; from innumerable clergymen who allowed me to study and take photographs in their churches, and who carefully answered my many postal enquiries; from vergers who willingly unlocked churches and chapels at a minute's notice; from many private owners, principals and headmasters who admitted me to their houses, colleges and schools; from many Post Office and Police officers who helped me to find out-of-the-way churches; and from the History of Art Department of the University of Manchester which provided some of the photographs necessary for study.

I wish also to thank my former wife Margarita Medina, my sister Mrs Dorothy Davis, my two sons and my students who patiently accompanied me on tours or excursions, and helped in the taking of notes and the reading of inscriptions; Professor Sir Nikolaus Pevsner, who was the first to recognize a number of Morris windows, and whose continued interest has been a tremendous encouragement; Professor Ellis Waterhouse, who supplied several pieces of information which had eluded me, and who scrutinized and corrected a number of my Latin transcriptions; and Professor Andrew McLaren Young, whose unfailing kindness and hospitality made my researches in and around Glasgow especially pleasant. Information and help of other kinds has been most gratefully received also from Miss Mary Bennett, Miss P Butler, Miss Catherine Hall and Lady Mander; from Mr Peter Bird, Mr F W Challenger, Professor Peter Collins, Mr A R Dufty, Mr Cecil Farthing of the National Buildings Record, Mr Colin Franklin, Dr W E Fredeman, Professor Ken Goodwin, Mr John Gordon-Christian, Mr David Gould, Mr A L Hasker of Hammersmith Public Libraries, Mr R R Langham-Carter, Mr John Lowe, Sir Edward Maufe, Mr Stephen Otto, Mr E Penning-Rowsell, Mr J A Ross, Mr A E Simpson, Mr Nicholas Taylor, Mr H Whittaker, Mr Geoffrey W Wood, and Mr Kenneth Yeates. Mr Alfred Fisher of the Whitefriars Stained Glass Studios at Edgware was generous with his time on the occasions of my visits to his premises. Two of my former students gave me very practical help: Miss Ann Clements by reading an early draft of chapter 1, and making many valuable suggestions for its improvement; and Miss Mary Steel by patiently checking innumerable points and eliminating a number of inconsistencies.

In the last stages of preparation, after the text of this volume was already in the publisher's hands, I have received a great deal of most valuable and welcome help from Mr Sanford L. Berger, who most generously sent me photo-copies of his unrivalled collection of original documents, drawings by William Morris, and sketch-designs by Morris and Co., and by Duncan Dearle; and from Mr Martin Harrison, whose researches have disclosed a number of early Morris windows which I would not otherwise have known about, and whose findings he has most generously communicated to me. The full fruits of these new sources of information will not be apparent, however, until the publication of the catalogue of windows in the succeeding volume.

A very special tribute is due to Mr Dennis Frone, whose beautiful photographs add immeasurably to the usefulness of the book. And finally I owe the profoundest thanks to the officials of the Yale University Press for the sympathy, patience and tolerance with which they have translated a dense and difficult typescript into elegant print; most especially to Miss Robin Bledsoe, the editor on whom the heaviest burden fell, for her ready understanding and constructive criticism, and to Mr Sebastian Carter, the designer.

If there are others whose names I ought to have mentioned but have omitted to do so, perhaps they will forgive me for including them collectively in the category 'too numerous to mention'. Without such ample and generous cooperation from many quarters a compilation such as this would have been a hopeless undertaking from the start.

Even with so much help, however, I remain only too conscious of the limitations of the book which is here put before the public. Without doubt, Morris windows and designs and cartoons for them will continue to be discovered for many years to come. The windows made for churches and other buildings in India, South Africa, France,

Australia and other foreign parts clearly deserve detailed study which I have been unable to give them. And many aspects of the subject, such as the iconography and the technique, call for further investigation. One could well spend another decade in research, and still not exhaust the possibilities of the field. The book, however, is in some ways a pioneer effort, for no other monographic study of any firm of nineteenth-century stained-glass artists yet exists. My hope is that this work may serve to induce other students to explore the field further; there is certainly a great deal more that is worthy of description, record and analysis.

Altrincham
March 1973 A.C.S.

Sources of Illustrations

Unless otherwise stated the photographs were supplied by the owners of the works, as acknowledged below. The exceptions are:

Columbia University, Department of Art History, New York: 478
'Country Life': 329, 410
F. H. Crossley (© National Buildings Record): 5, 354–57, 498–500, 509
F. Dobinson: 327, 631
S. Eost and **P. Macdonald**: 13–15
Dennis Frone, ARPS (Paul Mellon Centre, London): 3, 19, 22, 28–30, 33–35, 40, 43, 46–48, 52, 53, 64, 67–69, 73, 76, 77, 97–100, 102, 103, 143, 146, 167–69, 171, 173, 204–09, 212–16, 222, 225, 229, 230, 249, 257–62, 275–77, 279, 282, 294, 309–19, 324, 326, 330–32, 335, 337, 338, 340, 342, 348, 350, 353, 372, 374, 391–95, 397, 403, 424, 428, 435, 443–45, 447, 450, 453, 454, 471, 475, 477, 494, 495, 497, 505–08, 517–21, 530, 544, 548, 557, 559, 560, 567, 568, 572, 577–84, 610, 611, 616, 619, 620, 625, 628, 636, 640, 645, 657; Frontispiece, II, III, V, VI, VII, VIII, IX, XI, XIII, XV, XVI
Hartnoll & Eyre Gallery, London: 127, 514
F. M. Hueffer, *Ford Madox Brown: A Record of His Life and Work*: 12
A. F. Kersting: 108–10
H. C. Marillier, *A Note on the Morris Stained Glass Work*: 89, 563, 587
G. A. Oliver, DA (Paul Mellon Centre, London): 612, 615, 646
H. Rathbone, *The Cartoons of Ford Madox Brown*: 185, 186, 266, 281, 336, 339, 427, 452, 462
A. Charles Sewter: 1, 4, 6–9, 11, 16–18, 23–25, 27, 54, 55, 79, 80, 86–88, 101, 106, 107, 116–18, 131, 136, 138, 139, 148–50, 153, 177–80, 217–21, 231–35, 239, 240, 245, 250–55, 263–65, 280, 284, 285, 288, 289, 295–99, 303–06, 308, 320, 322, 325, 358, 375, 379–87, 398–401, 406, 413, 431, 432, 437, 456, 457, 459–61, 463, 466–70, 472–74, 483–92, 503, 504, 510, 523, 527–29, 531, 532, 535–38, 541, 547, 555, 556, 558, 561, 569, 575, 576, 596–98, 603–06, 613, 614, 621, 622, 624, 629, 630, 632–35, 638, 639, 641–44, 647–56, 658, 659; X, XIV
University of Manchester, History of Art Department: 2, 333, 334, 402, 440; XII
Emery Walker: 660
C. H. Wood (Bradford) Ltd: 174, 190

Photographs are reproduced with the kind permission of the individuals and institutions listed below. Acknowledgements are also due to the owners of all windows, drawings, sketches and cartoons who have permitted the reproduction of works in their possession, and whose names are not specifically included.

Churches and Cathedrals
The Vicar of All Hallows, Allerton, Liverpool: 508, 544, 577–84
The Vicar of Amington: VIII, 169, 171, 173
Canon Bryan Green, Rector of Birmingham: 519–22
The Vicar of Bishop's Tachbrook, The Reverend T. C. F. Mander: 143
The Vicar and Churchwardens of St Peter's, Bournemouth: 168
The Provost of Bradford Cathedral: 174, 177–80, 190
The Vicar and Churchwardens of Bramley Parish Church St Peter's: 505–07, 560
The Minister and Kirk Session of Brechin Cathedral: 649
The Rector and Churchwardens, St Nicholas, Bromham, Wilts.: 319
The Vicar and Churchwardens, St Anne's, Brown Edge, Staffs.: 471
The Rector and Parochial Church Council, Catton with Stamford Bridge, Yorks.: 262
The Vicar and Churchwardens of the Parish Church of St Edward the Confessor, Cheddleton, Staffs.: X, 167, 249, 288
The Rector and Churchwardens of St Mary's, Doddington in the Diocese of Ely: 216
The Rector and Wardens of All Saints, Elton: 645
The Vicar and Churchwardens of St James' Church, Flockton: 372
The Vicar and Churchwardens of Forden, Monts.: 454
St Stephen's Parochial Church Council, Gateacre, Liverpool: 567
The Kirk Session of Belmont and Hillhead Parish Church, Glasgow: 612
Canon B. H. Kemp, The Vicar of St Stephen's, Guernsey: VI, 204–08
The Vicar, All Saints, Harrow Weald, Middlesex: 568
The Rector, The Reverend Canon N. S. Baden-Powell, St Deiniol, Hawarden, Flints.: 636
The Vicar and Churchwardens, St Margaret's Church, Hopton-on-Sea: 559
The Vicar and Churchwardens, St John the Baptist, Knaresborough, Yorks: 450
The Vicar of St John the Evangelist, Knotty Ash: 350
The Dean and Chapter of Llandaff Cathedral: 265, 284, 305, 306, 463, 466–68
The Vicar and Wardens, St Martin's, Marple, Cheshire: 395
The Mill Hill Chapel Committee: 494, 495
The Kirk Session, St Rule's, Monifieth, Angus: 527
The Wardens of High Pavement Chapel, Nottingham: 647
The Rector and Churchwardens, St Mary's, Old Swinford, Worcs.: 657
The Deans and Canons of Christ Church, Oxford: III, 19, 22, 324, 353–57, 497–500, 529–32
The Vicar and Parochial Church Council of St Wilfrid's, Pool-in-Wharfedale: 258–60
Canon H. Knightingale, FSA, Vicar of Rochdale: 397
The Vicar and Churchwardens of St Margaret's, Rottingdean: 616, 619, 620
The Vicar and Churchwardens, St Martin's-on-the-Hill, Scarborough: VII, 64, 67–69, 73, 76, 77, 391–94
The Rector and Churchwardens of Speldhurst: 444, 445, 447, 503, 504
The Vicar of Christ Church, Southgate: 101–03, 517
The Rector and Wardens of St Peter's, Woolton, Liverpool: 475, 477

Public Collections

Aberdeen Art Gallery: 20
The University Court of the University of Aberdeen: 633
Ashmolean Museum, Oxford: 41, 42, 344–47, 409
Birmingham City Art Gallery: 10, 21, 26, 31, 32, 38, 39, 44, 45, 51, 56, 60, 70–72, 78, 81, 85, 111–15, 119, 120, 123, 124, 126, 129, 132–35, 137, 147, 151, 152, 154–59, 161, 163, 175, 181–83, 191, 195, 196, 200–03, 224, 226–28, 241–43, 247, 248, 271–74, 278, 286, 287, 290–93, 302, 307, 349, 376, 414–23, 430, 433, 434, 436, 438, 451, 464, 465, 479–82, 511–13, 526, 542, 543, 545, 546, 564–66, 601, 602
Brighton Art Gallery: 631
Bristol City Art Gallery: 522
The Trustees of the British Museum: 50
The Master and Fellows of Jesus College, Cambridge: 413, 424, 428, 431, 432, 435, 437, 443
The Master and Fellows of Peterhouse, Cambridge: 325, 326, 329–32, 335, 337, 338, 340, 342
Carlisle City Museum and Art Gallery: 493, 549–51, 554, 562, 570, 571
Art Institute of Chicago: 351, 352
The Syndics of the Fitzwilliam Museum, Cambridge: 84, 121, 122, 223, 533, 534, 661, 662, 664, 665
The University Court of the University of Glasgow: 613–15
The Trustees of the Lady Lever Art Gallery, Port Sunlight: 617, 618
Leeds City Art Gallery: 36, 449
Letchworth Museum and Art Gallery: 609
University of Manchester: 334
William Morris Gallery, Walthamstow: 37, 58, 62, 65, 66, 82, 104, 125, 128, 130, 144, 145, 162, 165, 166, 170, 176, 184, 187–89, 192–94, 238, 256, 283, 301, 368–71, 373, 388, 389, 407, 408, 442, 458, 524, 525, 553, 626, 627
National Gallery of Ireland, Dublin: 607
Municipal Gallery of Modern Art, Dublin: 573, 574
National Gallery of Scotland, Edinburgh: 83, 172
National Gallery of Victoria, Melbourne: 476, 585
The Principal, Fellows and Scholars of St Edmund Hall in the University of Oxford: 225, 229
The Master and Fellows of New College, Oxford: 3
Stanford University Museum of Art, California: 127
Tate Gallery, London: 57, 59, 425, 426
Toledo Museum of Art (Gift of Edward Drummond Libbey): 244
Victoria and Albert Museum, London: 49, 61, 74, 75, 91–96, 105, 140, 141, 160, 197–99, 210, 211, 236, 237, 267, 269, 270, 323, 341, 343, 359–67, 390, 396, 429, 439, 441, 446, 448, 496, 515, 516, 588–95, 599, 600, 608; I, IV
Walker Art Gallery, Liverpool: 328
Whitworth Art Gallery, University of Manchester: 404, 405, 455, 501

Private Collections

Mr Sanford L. Berger, Berkeley, California: 63, 164, 300, 663
Bradfield College, Berks.: 16, 17
Brook Street Gallery Ltd, London: 623
Castle Howard School for Boys, Welburn, Yorks.: 536
The Lord Provost of Dundee: 603
Leger Galleries Ltd, London: 637
London Borough of Hammersmith Public Libraries (Cecil French Bequest): 268
J. S. Maas & Co Ltd, London: 552
Manchester College, Oxford: 629
Mrs Roderic O'Conor, Oxon.: 246, 377
Queen Elizabeth's Grammar School, Blackburn: 643
J. A. Ross, Esq, Bieldside, Aberdeen: 411, 412
P. A. Snow, Esq, MA, FRAI, JP, the Bursar and Clerk to the Governing Body of Rugby School, Warwicks.: 640
Mr Spencer A. Samuels, New York: 514, 516
Stone Gallery, Newcastle-on-Tyne: 378
St Mary's College, Strawberry Hill, Twickenham: 1
The Duke of Westminster (Saighton Grange, Cheshire): 634, 635

The Stained Glass of William Morris and his Circle

I

The Victorian Revival of the Art of Stained Glass

Writers in Victorian times devoted a great deal more attention than in any previous period to the description, analysis, criticism and propagation of the arts. Most especially, they were concerned with the question of the relationship between the 'fine' arts of painting and sculpture, and the 'applied' or 'minor' arts, many of which had acquired a new importance in the national economy as a result of the development of industrial or semi-industrial methods of production. The artistic qualities of manufactured goods, it was realized, could have an important influence upon their salability in the market, and hence upon the prosperity of the nation. It therefore became a matter of national concern to encourage good design and to improve the education of artists, designers and craftsmen. A great deal of effort was directed towards researches into the techniques and processes of the arts of earlier periods, towards the organization of exhibitions, the foundation of museums and art galleries, the establishment of art schools, lectures, classes and mechanics' institutes. Much of this effort was perhaps misguided, and there can be no doubt that the Victorian period produced a phenomenal quantity of ambitious pseudo-artistic monstrosities, based upon totally false notions of the relationship between form and ornament. Many of the products shown in the Great Exhibition of 1851 seemed to express the belief that the more the craftsman and designer elaborated their work, the more they tried to make it look like something other than what it really was, the better it must be as a work of art.

But the path towards a sounder taste was gradually discovered, mainly as a result of the operation of two factors of prime importance: firstly, the enthusiastic study and discussion of the art of earlier periods, and the discovery of the principles of design implicit in it; and secondly, the development among the craftsmen and designers of an appreciation of the actual materials in which they worked, and a feeling for the treatments and processes which best exposed the qualities of those materials, whether of wood, metal, glass, textiles, or whatever. These two factors operated, so to speak, at opposite ends of the art-producing sector of society, the first in the intellectual world, the second in the workshop; and their full effect depended upon their meeting in those all-too-rare persons who were capable of understanding theoretical principles, and at the same time were either skilled and experienced in workshop practice, or at least possessed a quick and intuitive responsiveness to workshop materials, tools and processes. This was the situation which gave such importance to men like Augustus Pugin and William Morris.

The art of stained and painted glass itself required a similar conjunction of the imaginative faculties of the painter-designer and the craft skills of the cutter, glass-painter, kiln-man, assembler and glazier. The revival of this ancient art in the Victorian period, which became one of the most spectacular phenomena of the century's art, was brought about primarily by an enthusiasm which was capable of fusing together the imaginative, intellectual and practical raw materials. Characteristically, one of the best expressions of this enthusiasm was written by Francis Wilson Oliphant, a man of some education, 'an artist well skilled in drawing the human figure', and a glass-painter of considerable experience.[1] In his pamphlet, entitled *A Plea for Painted Glass* (1855), he wrote:

> The power of glass . . . to convey colour is quite unique; no kind of painting can at all come up to it. It is true, we cannot have the infinite gradations of our great oil colourists; we cannot round one tint imperceptibly into another, as it is given to them to do; so much we grant; but for power and brilliancy, or even harmony and sweetness, glass well-made and skilfully used has a scale of beauty which no gradated pigments laid on an opaque surface can hope to equal. Glass . . . is a luminous material, full of points which catch the light like the facets of a diamond; and it is this which accounts for the gem-like lustre of old windows. Always light, because always suspended against the day, they yet respond with indescribable sympathy to every change in the heavens, answering one by one, sweet vassals of the sunbeams, according to place and aspect, to the inspiration of the light. In the north and east, they proclaim the sun's rising with a flush of radiance, which gradually melts into repose, as the great exhibitor passes round the south to glow there in the splendour of noon, and finally blazes and sinks behind the glorious western window, which waits all day for that beatitude of sunset, with which its beauty is identified.[2]

This rhapsodic appreciation of the inherent qualities of the medium represents a fresh discovery by the awakened sensibilities of the period, and it was this which underlay all the efforts of the revival, and provided its motivation.

Of course, among the vast quantities of stained-glass windows produced in the nineteenth century, a great deal is artistically negligible or deplorable, produced by artisans in commercial workshops simply as an article of trade, and as devoid of good drawing, imaginative design and profound feeling as of true understanding of the materials. But the best Victorian windows, among which some of those produced by Morris's firm must take the pre-eminent place, were the finest stained glass made in at least three hundred years. The wilfully blind attitude of the older historians who, after subjecting the structure, decoration and fittings of a church to scrupulous and detailed description and analysis, could conclude by remarking that 'the stained glass is entirely modern', leaving it at that, will no longer do. As long ago as 1937, the late Dean Milner-White remarked that 'one day it will fall to the historian to write the full story of the revival of glass-painting in the nineteenth century.'[3] That day must now be very near. A re-assessment of Victorian achievement in many spheres of artistic activity is, indeed, needed; but in no field is a fresh investigation so urgently required as in that of stained glass, which is unfortunately being lost or destroyed almost daily as a result of ignorance, prejudice, the shifting of residential areas and the demolition of redundant churches.

At the present stage of research, however, no thorough and systematic survey of the whole field is yet possible; there are too many unanswered questions, too many important names to which it is possible to attach only a very few actual surviving examples. The productions of some of the best studios vary disconcertingly in both style and quality over a period of time, and these variations are often unintelligible unless one can discover who were the designers. Information of this kind is often elusive, and in its absence generalizations are extremely risky. What is required above all is a series of monographic studies of the most interesting individual artists and firms, based upon such archive materials as are available, identifying windows and designers, and supplying reliable dates, so that chronology and development can be understood. This is what I have tried to do for the firm of Morris and Company. No other firm's output is more worthy of this detailed attention.

Before describing the windows made by this firm, and defining the characteristics of their style and development, it is necessary to sketch in something of their historical background. Perhaps the greatest difficulty in appreciating the nature of the Victorian achievement in stained glass arises from the very considerable obscurity which prevails on the subject of stained-glass work in the preceding generations.[4] There are, of course, close connections between the revival of interest and activity in stained glass and the Gothic Revival in architecture. It is significant that Horace Walpole, one of the first architectural neo-Gothicists, was also among the first collectors of early stained glass. Some of the glass which he collected fortunately still remains in the windows of his villa at Strawberry Hill: a number of small medallions and panels from Swiss, Flemish and other sources, and mostly of late-sixteenth- or seventeenth-century date, decoratively arranged and supplied with borders and in-fillings by William Peckitt (1731–95) (*1*).* Such medallions and panels, however, usually of domestic application and generally painted in enamel colours on single pieces of more or less clear glass, gave little indication either of the structure of mediaeval and Renaissance church windows as mosaics of variously coloured pot-metal, or of their principles of composition. Peckitt and a few of his contemporaries such as James Pearson (born 1750) and Francis Eginton (1737–1805) did, indeed, make a number of church windows, sometimes utilizing the mediaeval figure-and-canopy type of design, and incorporating some coloured pot-metals: as, for instance, in the window of 1769 by Peckitt, originally in St John's, Manchester, and now, rather clumsily cut down to fit its new situation, in St Mary's, Hulme, Manchester (*2*). But the variety of coloured pot-metals available was very limited, the quality of the glass itself was poor, a heavy reliance on painting in enamel colours was general, and the part played in the design by lead-lines was not clearly understood.

These eighteenth-century men tended to think of stained glass simply as painting on a transparent support instead of on canvas, and to ignore the special demands of the medium.

***Arabic figures refer to the black-and-white illustrations, Roman numerals to the colour illustrations.**

In matters of design, they relied to a great extent upon copying paintings by admired old masters such as Raphael, Rubens or Guido Reni, intended for totally different purposes, and usually known by them only through the uncoloured translations of engravings; or they copied paintings by contemporary artists such as John Hamilton Mortimer, Benjamin West or Sir Joshua Reynolds.

The most important windows executed in England during the second half of the eighteenth century, those made by Thomas Jervais in 1777–83 for New College Chapel, Oxford, are typical of the whole period (*3*). The designs consist of an adaptation by Reynolds of Correggio's *La Notte*, and a series of allegorical figures of Christian Virtues by Reynolds himself. The colouring relies almost totally upon opaque enamels; the neo-Gothic canopy-work above the Virtues, which was the work of Jervais, lacks all architectural sense; cutting is reduced to the simplest possible lines, and the general effect is of a series of painted rectangular panes separated by a crude grid of bar-lines. At this period, indeed, the ancient technique of the mediaeval and Renaissance glaziers was in decay, if not entirely lost. Because of the obscuring effect of the enamel colours, men like Jervais chose to use thin and clear glass, and good quality pot-metals tended to disappear from the market. The 'really important glass, "flashed" ruby (that is to say, clear glass coated with a thin layer of red glass), was apparently unobtainable. Glass as nearly red as possible was produced by staining the glass several times by the old "yellow-stain" process.'[5]

Between this period and the opening of Morris's stained-glass studio in 1861, a great deal happened, both technically and artistically, in the recovery of a proper understanding of the art. The man who probably did more than anyone else to re-establish the mosaic principle was Thomas Willement (1786–1871), whose first windows were made in 1811. A distinguished expert on heraldry and a Fellow of the Society of Antiquaries, he devoted much scholarly attention to mediaeval ornament and design. Unfortunately, he was a poor designer of figures. An important window which he made in 1843, the east window of the Lady Chapel at Wells Cathedral, typically consists of a structure of strong, well-designed Decorated canopy-work, with archaistic figures derived from a variety of mediaeval sources, inserted somewhat incongruously in the openings (*5*). A little later, as in his Maria Bethune memorial window of about 1850 in the south transept at St Nicholas, Worth, Sussex, his figures become less deliberately archaic and take on instead an academic Raphaelesque look which does not accord well with their setting. He is seen at his best, perhaps, in purely heraldic work, such as the really splendid Grantley window of 1840 in the north nave aisle at Ripon Cathedral.

But Willement's use of the mediaeval method of constructing a window out of a mosaic of small pieces of variously coloured glass, and using enamel colours only for the necessary shading and details of drawing, was much in advance of the methods of most of the glass-painters of his generation, who continued to think of a window as a picture on glass. As F.M. Drake remarked, 'Impossible as it may seem to those acquainted with the works of the eighteenth century, things actually got worse and worse during the first quarter of the nineteenth.'[6] There is, if possible, even less sense of the quality of the glass itself in a window such as Joseph Backler's Ascension of 1821 in St Thomas's church, Dudley, than in Francis Eginton's Faith of 1795, after Guido Reni, in St Alkmund's, Shrewsbury (*4*). Though skilfully and not insensitively painted, Backler's work is simply a coloured painting in enamel colours, mostly on clear glass panes of regular rectangular shape. The slowness with which the advantages of the mediaeval mosaic system came to be recognized is well illustrated by a window of 1844, signed by G. Hoadley, at the west end of St James's, Fulmer, Buckinghamshire, which uses the design of one of Reynolds's Virtues, without the interruption of regular bar-lines, and with the minimum of lead-lines. The idea seems to have been widely held that both bar-lines and lead-lines were annoying interruptions of the painted representation, and if they could be eliminated entirely, so much the better. It was symptomatic that among the exhibits shown by the St Helen's Glass Company in the Great Exhibition of 1851 was a transparency of St Michael casting out the Great Red Dragon painted by Frank Howard on a single piece of glass nine feet high by five feet wide.[7] No doubt this was an astonishing technical achievement; but, since the painting must necessarily have been carried out entirely in enamels, it could have had none of the qualities of pure and luminous colour which only coloured pot-metal unclouded by enamel can give, and which were shortly to be so rapturously admired by Francis Oliphant.

A good deal more research is needed before a proper history of this period can be written; but it is clear that the work of a number of men gradually prepared the way for the high Victorian achievement. Examples of mediaeval glass were carefully studied from the points of view of technique, style and iconography. A paper by the German Dr M. A. Gessert, published in 1844, gave clear and precise accounts of the basic technical procedures of the mediaeval glaziers; and John Weale published descriptions and illustrations of mediaeval glass at York, Gouda, and Temple Church, London.[8] These and other publications of a similar kind[9] were followed only a few years later by the most influential writings of the century on stained glass, those by the lawyer Charles Winston (1814–64), who had devoted many years to the study of mediaeval, Renaissance and modern glass. His book, *An Inquiry into the Difference of Style observable in Ancient Glass Paintings, especially in England: with Hints on Glass Painting, by an Amateur*, the two volumes of which were published in Oxford in 1847, decisively marked the beginning of a new epoch.[10]

Winston's primary purpose was to provide for stained glass an historical and stylistic classification similar to that worked out by Thomas Rickman for Gothic architecture; and the main sections of his text examine in considerable detail the materials, processes, figures, foliage, borders, patterns, heraldry, lettering, canopies, etc., in the 'Early English', the 'Decorated', the 'Perpendicular', the 'Cinquecento' and the 'Intermediate' styles. The second volume provided a series of seventy-five plates, many in colour, illustrating carefully chosen examples. This was in itself an invaluable service which made easily available to the modern craftsman a comparative and historical corpus of material of which he had too often been ignorant. Even had he done no more than this, Winston's work must have contributed substantially to a new understanding of what constituted a good window. But in fact he went much further. In the second chapter of his book he discussed with intelligence the relationship between windows and the architectural interiors of which they formed part, the choice of suitable subjects, and what he regarded as the 'true principles of glass painting'. He continually emphasized the differences between what was appropriate in a window and what was better suited to painting in oil or watercolour. He understood very well the importance of lead-lines and saddle-bars as elements in the design; and he insisted on the importance of keeping the lights clear and bright, and consequently avoiding 'the heaviness occasioned by a disproportionate preponderance of shadow', which he found in 'most of the glass-paintings which were executed after the middle of the sixteenth century, including the production of the modern Munich school'.[11] These views certainly mark a decisive change of attitude from that of most glass-painters of the previous generation. Winston's general conclusions, which he conveniently summarized, were of the greatest importance and influence in the succeeding decades. 'I have thus endeavoured,' he wrote, 'however imperfectly, to point out the great principle adopted in the first half of the sixteenth century, of preserving the brilliancy and general transparency of the glass, and of promoting the distinctness of the design by the use of clear lights, transparent shadows, and strong contrasts of light and shade.'[12]

In general, Winston favoured the 'mosaic system' of glass-painting, according to which 'each colour of the design, except yellow, brown, and black, must be represented by a separate piece of glass',[13] yellow and brown being excepted because of the possibilities of staining. What he called the 'mosaic enamel method', employing both white and coloured glass and every known variety of stain and enamel colour, as practised in the first half of the sixteenth century in the Low Countries, represented for him the highest class of accomplishment. He especially admired the windows from the abbey of Herckenrode, installed in the Lady Chapel of Lichfield Cathedral.

Of course, the revival of this system had already taken place at the time Winston wrote, and he noted with commendation some examples of it, such as a window on the north side of the nave in Farningham church, Kent, in the style of the latter half of the fifteenth century, by Charles Clutterbuck.[14] He was emphatic, nevertheless, that mere imitation of the style or drawing of an earlier period should not be encouraged. He especially castigated 'the folly of admiring ancient art for the sake of its bad drawing, and of imitating its bad drawing',[15] of which Willement had been guilty at Wells Cathedral. The charm of mediaeval work was due, he asserted, not to its distortions, but to 'the real artistic feeling, and thorough conception of the subject, which are expressed' in it.[16] If such qualities were to be recovered, it was essential to the advancement of glass-painting as an art, that *artists* be encouraged to practise it, in distinction to 'those mere *artisans* who at present make it their trade'.[17]

Winston's remarkable book concluded with a series of appendixes almost as important as his main text. The first of these is a fully annotated translation of the second book of the *Schedula Diversarum Artium* by the monk Theophilus, on the making of glass and the methods of using it in pictorial windows, among other things.[18] This was, I believe, the first English edition of this important mediaeval craftsman's handbook.[19] Other appendixes deal with extracts from mediaeval account rolls relating to stained glass, lists of the subjects represented in the ancient windows of Canterbury Cathedral, extracts from *Piers Plowman* selected to show the practice of introducing armorial bearings and portraiture, and finally some examples of monumental inscriptions from late mediaeval windows.

The importance of Winston's achievement can hardly be exaggerated. The mosaic system now became the one almost universally used, supplanting within a few years the style of pictorial transparencies. Just how little we still know about the activities of Winston's generation, however, becomes clear when we extract a list of the recent and contemporary artists in stained glass whose works he mentions. The works of Miller, T. Ward, J. H. Nixon, Thomas Willement, Charles Clutterbuck, William Wailes, George Hedgeland and others all need to be thoroughly investigated before the situation at the end of the first half of the nineteenth century can be fully understood.[20]

The greatest difficulty which faced artists sympathetic to Winston's views was the poor quality of the glass that was available to them. The method of making 'flashed' ruby is said to have been rediscovered by Bontemps in 1826;[21] and pot-metals of various colours were again in use, but in their efforts to overcome the disadvantages of the thinness, smoothness and excessive transparency of the modern materials, artists such as Willement were in the habit of 'antiquating' glass by applying on the outside a coating of white enamel, which made it opaque and dull. Worse still, other artists such as William Warrington, described by a writer in *The Ecclesiologist* as 'a great practitioner in the "dirty" school,'[22] attempted to imitate the appearance of mediaeval windows by brushing on quantities of boot-black.

Winston pointed out at length the similarity in colour between modern and sixteenth-century glass, but the total dissimilarity in material. This he recognized as presenting a serious obstacle to the revival of any of the styles of mediaeval glass-painting. But colour was not the only consideration. As he wrote,

> The ancient *tints* have in many instances been reproduced, but not the *textures* of the more ancient material. Consequently there is a difference of effect between the modern and the ancient glass. The former is more homogeneous, and therefore clearer, and more perfectly transparent than the latter, especially than that belonging to the twelfth and the two following centuries: and I feel persuaded that it is to this

circumstance that we must refer the poor and *thin* appearance, which almost every modern glass painting . . . presents in comparison with an original specimen.[23]

Continually returning to these complaints, Winston supported his views by making, or having made, a series of physical and chemical investigations of ancient glass. He found that it was irregular in thickness, with many streaks and bubbles, and consequently exhibited varieties and shades of tone, and a sparkle not to be found in modern materials. By means of microscopic examination of sections, he demonstrated the significance of the variations in positions and thickness of the striations of colour within the body of flashed ruby of various mediaeval periods, which of course affected their translucency and depth of colour; and he recorded these observations in a series of beautiful drawings now in the British Museum.[24]

In all this, Winston was undoubtedly right, and it was largely due to his efforts that the materials available to the stained-glass trade were improved. In the autumn of 1849 Winston arranged with Dr Medlock of the Royal College of Chemistry to make a series of analyses of specimens of twelfth-century blue glass. When completed at Easter 1850, they showed that, contrary to the theory of Robert Hendrie and Mrs Merrifield, the colouring matter used was not lapis lazuli but cobalt.[25] Other colours also were analysed, and the next problem was that of synthesis. Winston offered the results of the analyses to Chance Brothers & Co. of Birmingham, the glass makers, if they would attempt to make glass based on these formulae; but the offer was refused. He then went to Powell and Sons of Whitefriars, London, where the firm's chemist, Edward Green, undertook the task. By 1856 Green had succeeded in making the blue, a streaky ruby, several kinds of green, yellow and white, and a few shades of purple.[26] Winston commemorated the triumph by having two windows of the new glass made at his own expense, for the north and south sides of the aisle of the round part of Temple Church, London. One contained Old Testament and the other New Testament subjects. They were made by Ward and Hughes of Frith Street, Soho.[27] Unfortunately, they do not survive; but they were a prelude to a widening sphere of activity on Winston's part.

Late in 1854, the Dean and chapter of Norwich Cathedral had invited him to superintend the production of a large window to be made of the new glass and painted by George Hedgeland. When it was completed, Winston proudly referred to this west window as 'the best window of modern times', which it may very well have been, if only for a few years.[28] The authorities of Lincoln Cathedral followed suit in 1856 with a commission for eight windows which, however, proved to be an unhappy experience for Winston. He complained bitterly that the glass-painters would not back him up, and he refused to accept the responsibility for this kind of supervision again. It is not completely clear from the references in his *Memoirs* which were the windows and the makers concerned; but according to an anonymous article criticizing Winston's opinions in the *Edinburgh Review* of January 1867, it was the firm of Clayton and Bell who 'refused to adopt the old blue'.[29]

What happened at Glasgow Cathedral in connection with the scheme of re-glazing undertaken between 1857 and 1865 was rather different. The actual superintendent of the work here was Charles Heath Wilson, aided (if, indeed, that is the appropriate word) by copious advice from Winston, who found himself in a real difficulty. The only British glass-painter whom Winston was really prepared to recommend was Hedgeland, who for some reason was not employed: perhaps he had already decided to emigrate to Australia, where he went in 1858. After many waverings and uncertainties, the whole project was eventually put into the hands of Max Ainmüller of the Royal Factory at Munich. Eminent artists were commissioned to produce cartoons, which were executed in a style which relied heavily upon painting in enamel colours. The results, surprisingly, were on the whole much to Winston's satisfaction, though they were regarded as disastrous by everyone else.[30]

Even this ill-fated Glasgow scheme, however, was not the end of Winston's activities. He was also a member of the committee concerned with the decoration of St Paul's Cathedral, London; and one of his last undertakings was a trip to Brussels to meet Ainmüller for a conference on the proposed windows. He was also an associate juror for the stained-glass section of the International Exhibition of 1862, when the Gold Medal was awarded to Michael O'Connor, and the exhibits of Morris, Marshall, Faulkner & Co. were awarded a minor medal.

The fact is that although Winston's elucidation of the basic principles of stained glass was sound — indeed it was a very considerable critical achievement — his eyes were too much turned towards the past to make him a sound critic of the work of his own time. In particular, he was out of sympathy with the majority of his contemporaries in preferring a Renaissance to a Gothic style, and in maintaining that the stained-glass artist should introduce as much relief as was consistent with the integrity of the design and a harmonious relationship with the architectural setting. The subtleties of Winston's thought were, of course, beyond the capacities of most of his critics. The Renaissance style which he advocated was too easily equated by more careless thinkers with the style of the old pictorial transparencies, which he abominated, and which had now come under general disapproval. Even Hedgeland, an ardent Renaissance stylist in most of his earlier works, became a Gothicist in many of his later ones, for instance the Rose memorial window at St Mary's, Great Brington, Northamptonshire. The future clearly lay with the Gothicists. But, for all the controversies which surrounded Winston's activities in his later years, there can be no doubt whatever of his central position in the nineteenth-century revival of the art. Both as critic and historian, and as prime mover in the recovery of mediaeval recipes for making coloured glass, he laid firm foundations for later achievements.

It must in fairness be added that in 1863 William Edward Chance, at his works at Oldbury, Birmingham, produced 'antique' glass which was probably the result of independent researches. So far as it is now possible to identify Chance's glass in surviving windows, such as those of Clayton and Bell, however, it had little of the pure colour or brilliant tone of the glass made by Powell's from Dr Medlock's analyses. The catalogue descriptions of the Chance firm's exhibits at the 1862 Exhibition mention 'coloured window glass, flashed colours, pot metals, and cathedral tints, in sheet, plain and antique, for leaded windows. Rolled plate, pot metals and cathedral tints are much liked for church windows; but Antique Sheet more nearly resembles old glass in appearance and effect'.[31] These varieties of glass, nevertheless, were distinguished from one another more by the method of manufacture, relative uniformity and surface texture than in the ingredients used for colouring. A similar worthy intention, which again did not penetrate to the root of the matter, is indicated by a note to the exhibits by Alexander Gibbs: 'To gain brilliancy, very thick glass has been used in these windows, and in consequence of which they have all been leaded with the ancient round lead.'[32] How very thick glass can produce brilliancy of effect, naturally, he does not explain.

In addition to the understanding of stylistic principles, and appropriate materials, what was needed were craftsmen with experience of the processes and techniques. The size of the trade, that is to say the number of firms involved, had been steadily expanding since the first quarter of the century, and the twenty-four firms which showed stained glass at the Great Exhibition of 1851, which represented only the best, indicated already a marked increase since pre-Victorian times. In the 1862 Exhibition the number of British exhibitors rose to twenty-eight, and indeed several of those which were to make the most impact in high Victorian times had been founded during the intervening years. It is certain that one of the most significant factors in this expansion was the fashion for memorial windows. In 1842 J. H. Markland published a paper addressed to the Oxford Architectural Society, with the title *Remarks on English Churches, and on the expediency of rendering Sepulchral Memorials subservient to pious and Christian uses*. In this, the author recommended the use of stained-glass windows as personal memorials; and one of the earliest Victorian memorial windows, made by William Wailes of Newcastle-upon-Tyne and placed in Chichester Cathedral, dates from the same year (*6*). It is a very pretty creation, and though no longer in the position for which it was intended, it survives in St Peter's sub-deanery church across the road from the Cathedral.[33] In 1847 Winston still found it necessary to argue against the objection 'that glass is too frail a material for a monument',[34] but in the 1862 Exhibition six of the windows shown were specifically described as memorial windows. The great tide of memorial glass, which by the end of the Victorian era had found its way into many hundreds of churches all over the kingdom, had begun to flow.

Clearly, Morris and the artists associated with him in the production of stained glass represented in some sense the culmination of a development which had been under way for a considerable time. He not only must have known and profited by the writings of Winston and others, but he was also able to employ in his stained-glass studio men who had already been trained in the trade, and who were familiar with the processes of cutting, staining, enamelling, etching, firing in the kiln, leading-up, and so on. In putting Morris's ideas about stained glass into practice, and in translating into glass the designs which he provided or commissioned, the practical experience of these men, particularly the studio foreman George Campfield, must have been invaluable. No doubt, in the first months of operation, they had as much to teach Morris in matters of craftsmanship as to learn from him about colour and design.

But if we are to judge correctly Morris's achievement, it is important not to underestimate the attainments of his predecessors in terms of materials, technique, design and composition. The early Victorian stained-glass men were, of course, ostensibly concerned in the first place with the imitation of historic styles. This necessitated the close study of grisaille patterns, pedestals and canopies, borders, diaper patterns, and many other aspects and details of design required in large windows; and much of their skill was a product of the intimate knowledge which they acquired during the course of restorations of ancient glass. It is significant that David Evans, for example, whose masterpiece is the east window of 1861 in St Julian's, Shrewsbury, was trained under Sir John Betton, with whom he 'restored' the windows of Winchester College Chapel in 1825–28. Though these 'restorations' were in fact complete copies of the original glass, they were carried out with considerable skill.[35] Similarly, George Hedgeland was presumably trained under his father John P. Hedgeland, notable for his restorations of the windows at St Neot's, Cornwall; and the younger man worked for three years on the restoration of the windows of King's College, Cambridge. Whatever may be thought of the procedures which they adopted as restorers, they obviously learnt a great deal from these undertakings. Restorations such as those carried out under the sharp eye of Winston himself, in St Mary's, Bushbury, Staffordshire, showed a scrupulous respect for whatever original glass remained, and the completion of the grisaille patterns and borders by Ward and Hughes is almost indistinguishable from the genuine early-fourteenth-century work (*8*).[36] So far as grisaille-work and borders go, indeed, the work of William Wailes in St Andrew's, Bradfield, Berkshire, carried out in the 1850s, has an exemplary refinement (*7*);[37] and that of William Miller at St Mary's, Frittenden, Kent, has a sparkle and inventiveness in no way inferior to genuine old work.[38] It would not be difficult to cite a score of instances of early Victorian windows with admirable canopy-work, etched diaper backgrounds and other ornamental parts which are as good as such work can be. In the case of Miller's east window of 1846 at Monkton Deverill church, Wiltshire, even the medallions with emblems of the Four Evangelists are such perfect imitations of mediaeval style as to be deceptive.[39]

But, while imitation was almost universally the declared aim of the stained-glass artists of the mid-century, as the catalogue descriptions of their works in the Great Exhibition of 1851 testify, many of them were unable to suppress qualities which speak unmistakably of their own time, their own sensibilities and imagination. David Evans's window at St Julian's, Shrewsbury, for instance, in spite of being old-fashioned enough to use an adaptation of Raphael's *Ascension of Christ* in its central light, is carried out in a strikingly bold and original scheme of colour, with the group of apostles draped in a variety of deep blues, mauves, purples, red and gold, which is entirely unlike anything to be found in sixteenth-century glass. George Hedgeland's masterpiece, the great east window of St John's, Halifax, made in 1855, has an extremely impressive clarity of organization, and a dramatic intensity in its six principal scenes, which are certainly not products of imitation;[40] and in other works, such as his Watson memorial window at St Leonard's, Rockingham, Northamptonshire, he introduced characteristic rustic canopies sprouting into flamboyant foliage in the heads of the lights, which are very personal, very Victorian, and utterly unmediaeval (*9*).[41] Francis Oliphant, who designed a large number of windows for John Hardman of Birmingham, and made a small number independently, of which the chancel east window at St Peter's, Seal, Kent is among the best, not only was a skilled draughtsman and accomplished executant, but possessed a highly personal colour sense, using pale turquoise and salmon pink draperies for figures placed against pale blue etched diaper backgrounds and under white canopies.[42] The distinctively individual character of Michael O'Connor's colour may be appreciated by comparing his windows from Pugin's designs in St Giles', Cheadle, Staffordshire, with Hardman's window, also after a Pugin design, at St Mary's, Whalley, Lancashire. O'Connor's dominant chord of scarlet and royal blue, with subordinate notes of acid green, astringent mauve, pale blue and gold, has a conviction and resonance lacking in Hardman's rather thin style of more brownish reds and greyer blues. Charles Gibbs, too, was capable of strikingly original colour schemes, as for instance in his signed window of about 1850 in the church at Aberffraw, Anglesey; and his borders of naturalistically treated white marguerites, and the rustic grisaille-work in the little chancel north window at Nannerch, Flintshire, have a charm which is purely of its own time.[43]

Where all these men except Hedgeland fell short was in creating major figure compositions with the expressive power of a great original work of art; and though Hedgeland at times perhaps achieved this, it was at the cost of a certain coarseness of grain, as apparent in the detail of his brushwork as in the insensitivity of his colour.

By the time that Morris, Marshall, Faulkner & Co. was founded in 1861, Winston's plea for a more creative approach had found some support. A writer in the *Art Journal*, reviewing the stained-glass contributions to the 1862 Exhibition, complained that 'it is the great error of our own best glass-painters that they have been content to aim at reproducing old work, or at any rate, that they consider it necessary to work in exact conformity with their early models. This copying — for it amounts to nothing more — must give way to originality'.[44] Though many exhibitors on this occasion still, indeed, described their work as 'in the style of the fourteenth century', or some other historic period, several firms featured work designed by young artists such as Alfred Bell, J. M. Allen and Edward Burne-Jones, and the Gold Medal was awarded to Michael O'Connor for parts of his great west window for St Mary's, Aylesbury, Buckinghamshire, very boldly designed in a modern style, with subjects from the Old Testament. Unfortunately, the designer's name does not appear to have been recorded.

Among the firms which, even before 1862, were attempting to respond to the call for designs of originality from real artists, credit must be given especially to two: Lavers and Barraud, and James Powell & Sons. Although it was apparently Powells who first placed commissions with Burne-Jones (as a result of the recommendation of D.G. Rossetti) and with Ford Madox Brown, it will be convenient to deal first with Lavers and Barraud since, so far as we know, Burne-Jones designed only one subject for them.

The partnership of F.P. Barraud and N.W. Lavers was formed in 1855, when their first recorded window, for St Paul's, Brighton, was made from designs by Alfred Bell (1832–95), a young architect trained in the office of Gilbert Scott. Bell was also a partner in the rival firm of Clayton and Bell, likewise established in 1855, and he ceased to design for Lavers and Barraud in 1857. In the following year, probably to replace Bell, the firm was joined by Nathaniel Hubert John Westlake (1833–1921), whose initiative probably led to the commissioning of designs from two other young architects, J.M. Allen and John Francis Bentley, as well as from Burne-Jones and Westlake himself. The eight main lights of the firm's west window for the parish church of St Peter and St Paul at Lavenham, Suffolk, from cartoons by J.M. Allen, very deservedly won a prize at the 1862 Exhibition. In the same exhibition, under the catalogue heading 'Specimens of glass for domestic buildings', they displayed, along with some scenes from the *Idylls of the King* designed by Allen, a single light, the Annunciation, from a cartoon by E.B. Jones, which was widely noticed in the press as 'of the Pre-Raphaelite School'.[45] The cartoon for this subject, in oils on canvas, was bequeathed to the Birmingham City Art Gallery in 1927 by J.R. Holliday, and listed in the 1930 *Catalogue of the Permanent Collection of Paintings* with the note 'early design for stained glass', but without any indication of where the glass might be found (*10*). The window, in St Columba's, Topcliffe, Yorkshire (*II*), was first drawn to my attention by Mr F.W. Challenger, and soon afterwards published by Sir Nikolaus Pevsner in his *Yorkshire: The North Riding* (1966).

The Annunciation forms the left-hand light in a three-light window, of which the other subjects are the Visitation and Nativity. All three lights are designed with a careful avoidance of three-dimensional modelling and receding spatial perspective, so as to preserve the integrity of the pictorial plane. That is to say, the figures are not set back as if existing in a pictorial space beyond the glass, but are brought forward so as to be identified with the actual plane of the glass. The long flowing outlines of the figures are accompanied by intricate patterning throughout the designs, and the backgrounds are filled with foliage, long inscribed scrolls held by the figures, and other details. The colouring, like all Lavers and Barraud windows of this date, is light and sweet, with a variety of pale reds and pinks, mauves, blues and greens, and gold; and, again typically, the glass is cut into very small pieces, producing a slightly fussy and restless effect. In the large naturalistic flowers in the foregrounds, and in the foliage at the heads of the panels, each leaf is cut separately; but the lead joints are handled with meticulous craftsmanship.

It was natural that Pevsner should assume that all three lights were designed by Burne-Jones, whose signature, *E. B. Jones inv.*, appears on the Annunciation panel. But in spite of their obviously close stylistic similarity, it seems that the other two panels were designed by Michael F. Halliday (1822–69), a pupil of William Holman Hunt and a member of the Pre-Raphaelite circle.[46] The Annunciation is undoubtedly the most original, not to say eccentric, composition, with the Virgin seated low in the panel, and not looking at all in the direction of the archangel who stands behind her; but it may well come as a surprise that a minor and hardly known artist was capable of producing designs of such quality as the Visitation and Nativity. A very close contact between the two artists must be presumed.

Turning from the Topcliffe window to the glass made from Burne-Jones's designs by Powells, we see that the differences of colour are extremely striking, and these must be due primarily to the artists in the glass-painting studios. Whereas Lavers and Barraud interpreted the cartoon freely, especially in the matter of tone, Powells tended to follow the designer's colour indications as closely as possible. Such distinction as Burne-Jones's early cartoons possessed, however, was not significantly due to their colour; in a sense he was never much of a colourist, and consequently the greatest limitations of the work which Powells did from his designs was due to their reliance on him at his weakest point.

The association between Burne-Jones and Powells began in 1857, when he was only twenty-four years of age, and in the process of learning his trade as a painter from Rossetti. The very first of his cartoons, according to Aymer Vallance, was the Good Shepherd, which now belongs to the Victoria and Albert Museum, and was translated into glass at King Street Congregational Church, Maidstone (*11*).[47] It has an attractive simplicity of conception, which delighted Rossetti and is supposed to have 'driven Ruskin wild with joy';[48] but in spite of the flowing wavelike rhythms of the landscape and sky background, and of the stream across the foreground, it suffers from a certain 'bittiness'. Exactly as in the Topcliffe Annunciation, every leaf of the large plants in the foreground consists of a separate piece of glass, and the cutting in the figure itself is markedly angular and awkward. Not surprisingly, it took a little time and experience for Burne-Jones to learn to adapt his cartoons to the special requirements of the medium, to design in simple masses and with long flowing contours. Even the remarkable windows for the dining hall of Bradfield College, Berkshire, illustrating Adam and Eve after the Fall, the Building of the Tower of Babel, and Solomon and the Queen of Sheba — also made in 1857 — though they show already a much better understanding of the need for simple drawing and clear outline, exhibit some odd disparities of scale between the three lights, which must be the result of inexperience (*13–17*).[49]

The intricacy of detail noticeable in the Topcliffe window was, nevertheless, so much a part of Burne-Jones's early style that he found it by no means easy to eliminate from his designs for stained glass. It is even more a weakness in the St Frideswide window in Christ Church Cathedral, Oxford, designed for Powells in 1859 (*19*).[50] From any distance away, indeed, this window is quite unintelligible. The sixteen scenes contained within the four main lights all include a considerable number of figures; and the fact that the boundaries between the subjects come at different levels in each light rules out any such simple overall pattern as was used, with excellent effect, in the Song of Solomon window at Darley Dale, made by Morris only a few years later. An early sketch-design connected with the Oxford project, which belongs to the Aberdeen Art Gallery, shows a smaller number of incidents arranged in five horizontal bands across a single broad lancet, which it is difficult to relate to the four lancets of the actual window (*20*). But at this early stage in the development of the design, Burne-Jones was evidently thinking of using the descending, meandering curve of the river Isis as a device for connecting the four lowest bands. This idea, however, was later abandoned, and no effective alternative to it was found. The only part of the window which reveals Burne-Jones's power as a designer of large-scale decorative pattern is the circle at the top of the tracery, St Ursula's Ship of Virgins, which already foreshadows the full Art Nouveau style of the end of the century (*22*). In colour, this Oxford window tends to be dark, with a great preponderance of browns and purples; however, it is a window of great charm and originality, especially when seen from close to, in individual scenes (*III*).

The high point of Burne-Jones's brief association with Powells is undoubtedly marked by the windows at Waltham Abbey. In the Tree of Jesse which occupies the three main lancets, he found the structural motif which had been lacking at Oxford (*23–25*). The twining branches of the tree, which encircle or support the figures, serve to unify and interconnect the whole area. But even here Burne-Jones could not restrain his early passion for intricate detail, and the designs are still somewhat overloaded with pictorial incident, such as the page in attendance upon King David, the cell behind the figure of Jeremiah, the crowd of adoring angels on either side of the Crucifix, and so on. Again it is in the tracery that he is most original and most effective. The seven lobes of the rose, with their abstractly treated scenes of the Days of Creation, have a breadth, scale and boldness quite astonishing at this date (*I*; *27*).[51]

Since his first design for stained glass, Burne-Jones had developed with phenomenal speed. In the Days of Creation at Waltham Abbey he revealed a capacity for large-scale decorative pattern which was quite unrivalled then and throughout his life. Before the foundation of the Morris firm, his work had advanced English stained glass from imitative mediaevalism to a modern creative art far ahead of anything being produced elsewhere. Compared with this achievement, the first windows made in Morris & Co.'s studio, those for G. F. Bodley's new church of All Saints, Selsley, Gloucestershire (*28–33*) were not specially remarkable, except in their relationship to the architecture; but, as we shall see, this architectural quality was due to Philip Webb rather than to Burne-Jones or Morris.

It is a curious fact that Winston nowhere mentioned Burne-Jones's early work for Powells or Lavers and Barraud; nor did he apparently realize the significance of the early productions of the Morris studio. These produced, indeed, very little impact at all. There was, however, some stir on the occasion of their exhibit in the Mediaeval Court of the International Exhibition of 1862 at South Kensington, when some other exhibitors complained that Rossetti's panels of the Parable of the Vineyard, subsequently incorporated into the east window at St Martin's-on-the-Hill, Scarborough, were actually mediaeval glass touched up (*64*). The attempts to have them disqualified of course failed; but the jury, in awarding two medals to the firm, commented of the furniture that 'the character of the details are [*sic*] satisfying to the archaeologist from the exactness of the imitation'.[52] They could not have known very much about mediaeval furniture, nor could the other exhibitors have been very familiar with mediaeval glass! It was curiously ironic that the very men who possessed that quality of genuine creative originality, and were to be the outstanding leaders of the transistion from the mainly imitative to the freshly creative phase of Victorian stained glass, should have been accused of producing too good an imitation. The accusers must have recognized some essential difference from their own works, and, their minds being completely attuned to seeking for quality by adopting the styles of long ago, no doubt felt in some way cheated, and jumped to totally wrong conclusions.

2

The Morris Firm: Early Years

It is unnecessary to recount here in detail the familiar tale of the foundation of 'the firm' in 1861, mainly in consequence of Morris's discovery that he could buy no furnishings of the kind he wanted for his new home, Red House, Bexley Heath, just built for him by Philip Webb.[1] The original partners were, besides Morris himself, Edward Burne-Jones, D.G. Rossetti, Ford Madox Brown, Philip Webb, C.J. Faulkner and P.P. Marshall. The firm began its activities at 8 Red Lion Square, Holborn, with a nominal capital of £7, consisting of single shares of £1 subscribed by each of the partners. This miniscule amount was supplemented, however, by an unsecured loan of £100 from Morris's mother, and on 15 January 1862 by a further call on the partners of £19 each, making a total capital of £240. The partners described themselves as 'Morris, Marshall, Faulkner & Co., Fine Art Workmen in Painting, Carving and the Metals', but from the beginning stained glass occupied an important place in their activities. Indeed, the first entries for the year 1861 in the account-books which two of the partners, Burne-Jones and Webb, kept of their transactions with the firm, were concerned with a series of designs for windows for All Saints church, Selsley, Gloucestershire, newly built by G.F. Bodley, who was then just beginning his independent career as an architect; and this department of the firm's production made a very successful beginning owing largely to his support.[2] Unfortunately, we do not know exactly how Bodley made contact with the newly established stained-glass department of the firm; the introduction may have been through William Burges, the architect for the alterations at Waltham Abbey, or possibly George Edmund Street, under whom Philip Webb and Morris had worked in Oxford. At all events, his first commission for the Selsley windows was followed very soon afterwards by further orders for his other new churches of St Martin's-on-the-Hill, Scarborough, St Michael's, Brighton, and All Saints, Cambridge.

Since most of the partners were beginners or mere amateurs in the applied arts and in matters of trade, it is perhaps surprising that the enterprise got off to such a good start. So far as the stained-glass work was concerned, both Burne-Jones and Madox Brown had some previous experience as designers, though Brown had only at this time designed one subject for Powells, a Transfiguration of which the cartoon has been reproduced (*12*), but of which the glass itself remains untraced.[3] How much or how little previous knowledge Morris and Webb may have had of stained glass is an unanswered question. They may very well have looked carefully at old stained glass in Oxford, and particularly at the fourteenth-century windows in Merton College Chapel, of which Webb made detailed water-colour copies in a sketch-book, and which he used as the basis for his canopy designs for the Selsley windows.[4] On the occasion of his commission for the designs for Waltham Abbey in 1859, Burne-Jones is reported to have received advice from Morris.[5] In view of Morris's total lack of experience in the medium at that date, this seems rather unlikely; and in the case of one of the windows for St Martin's, Scarborough, designed and made in 1862, it was Morris who needed the assistance of Burne-Jones in the preparation of his cartoon.[6] As the late John A. Knowles pointed out to me, some of the Scarborough windows, especially those from designs by Morris and Rossetti, contain shapes which are almost impossible to cut in glass, which shows how little either artist knew then about the technique of the medium.[7]

A very great deal of the translation of the cartoons into glass was left to the craftsmen of the studio, though Morris himself from the beginning seems to have assumed sole responsibility in the matter of colour.[8] Whereas Burne-Jones's cartoons for Lavers and Barraud and for Powells had been carried out in colours, his cartoons for the Morris firm are (with very few exceptions, and those of much later date) in black and white only, which implies an understanding between them on this point. In some of his early cartoons for the firm, the lead-lines seem to have been put in by Burne-Jones himself; but after 1862 such indications hardly ever appear, and the position of the lead-lines — inseparable, of course, from decisions about colouring — was left entirely to those who were to translate the designs into glass. Under these circumstances it was inevitable that eventually the special character and demands of the medium would be less and less considered by the designer. But it may be assumed that all the designers who supplied cartoons for windows would have watched the progress of work in the studio, and discussed many points of difficulty which arose in the course of the production, gaining in this way an insight into the limitations and possibilities of stained glass which would affect and influence their designs.

Morris, of course, never attempted to make his own glass. The glass was bought from Powells; but Morris was evidently slow to realize the advantages of the new glass which Powells were making according to the formulae provided by Winston. The windows of the firm's first years were generally executed in thin and excessively transparent glass which has exactly those deficiencies of which Winston had complained. The panels of the Story of Tristram and Isoude (*79*, *80*), made in 1862 and now in the Bradford City Art Gallery, for example, are not only rather thin and watery in substance, but show a preference for dull greens and reds which suggest that it took Morris a little while to acquire the courage of his convictions as a colourist. But the earliest of the firm's windows to show real distinction in colour, those at St Michael's, Brighton, were also produced in 1862; and although they still show Morris using very dull greens, it is in the contrasts between these tones and the small areas of brilliant gold, blue, and the luminous pale quarries above and below the subject panels, that his exceptional gifts become apparent.

The partners soon found themselves unable to cope with the demand for designs, and as early as 1862, in connection with the Tristram and Isoude panels ordered by Walter

Dunlop of Harden Grange near Bingley, Yorkshire, they obtained designs also from their friends Arthur Hughes (*78*) and Val Prinsep.[9] About two years later, Albert Moore was called upon for a cartoon (*196*) for the chancel south-east window at Bradford parish church (now the Cathedral), and in 1865 Simeon Solomon supplied cartoons for the procession of patriarchs in the east window at Middleton Cheney (*231*). With hardly more exceptions than these, however, all the cartoons were designed by the partners themselves. In a few years there accumulated a stock of designs which could be repeated with such modifications as were necessary, so that the proportion of windows requiring fresh designs was steadily reduced.

In June 1865, the premises in Red Lion Square having become inadequate, the firm moved to more commodious quarters at 26 Queen Square, Bloomsbury, which remained their workshops as well as showrooms and offices until the move to 449 Oxford Street in 1877, and the acquisition in 1881 of Merton Abbey, which became the workshops and studios. At Queen Square, 'the ground floor was turned into an office and showroom. A large ball-room which had been built at the end of the yard, and connected with the dwelling-house by a wooden gallery, was turned into a principal workshop. There was room for other workshops in the small court at the back, and further accommodation was found when needed in Ormond Yard close by.'[10] Morris now lived in the same house, in order to give as much time as possible to the firm's affairs. Rossetti had by this time ceased to take much part in its activities; P.P. Marshall, who had come into the circle as a friend of Madox Brown, and who was a surveyor and sanitary engineer at Tottenham, resumed his professional practice.[11] Charles Faulkner, a friend of Morris and Burne-Jones from Oxford days, who had taken part in the decoration of the Oxford Union in 1857 and had for a few years kept the firm's books, returned in 1864 to tutorial work at Oxford, and in his place George Warrington Taylor became business manager. The organization was settling down.

The employees and workmen must have been a very assorted group. The foreman of the stained-glass studio, George Campfield, 'had come under Morris's notice as a pupil at the evening classes of the Working Men's College in Great Ormond Street'; he had apparently been employed previously as a glass-painter, though unfortunately we do not know by whom.[12] He remained in the employment of the firm until 1898. About a dozen men and boys had been employed at Red Lion Square, and presumably this number was increased at Queen Square. Towards the end of 1861, Albert and Harry Goodwin joined the staff, together with a certain Weigand, who assisted Rossetti in the decoration of the famous cabinet made by the firm for the architect J.P. Seddon, which is now in the Victoria and Albert Museum; and, as the result of an advertisement in *The Builder* of 9 November 1861, for a first-rate fret-glazier, Charles Holloway, who later became a glass-painter, was engaged. Other workers in the early years included Charles Fairfax Murray, Charles Napier Hemy, James Egan, Fletcher and Wilday.[13] Several of these were to make their names in due course as independent artists. Faulkner and his two sisters Kate and

Lucy (later Mrs Orrinsmith) painted tiles, did gesso-work, and occasionally designed wallpapers. Mrs Morris and her sister embroidered, Mrs Campfield helped to make altar-cloths, and Mrs Burne-Jones painted tiles and embroidered. The boys could hardly have been chosen for possessing any special gifts: 'they were got', according to Mackail, 'from a Boys' Home in the Euston Road.'[14] That this miscellaneous assembly of ordinary workmen, young artists, and enthusiastic but amateur helpers could produce work of such importance and influence was due, no doubt, to the constant and scrupulous supervision by Morris himself, together with the quality of the original designs from which they worked.

We have a fairly detailed account of this supervision of the stained-glass work.

> When the cartoons for a window had been drawn . . . Morris personally 'coloured' the window; that is to say, he dictated in detail to Campfield, the foreman of the painters, what glass was to be used for each part. The various parts were then distributed to the painters, whose work he watched as it went on, though he usually reserved any comments till the painter had done all he could. Retouches were then made by his direction, and the glass was burned and leaded up. When this was done, there came the final review of the window, a work of great difficulty in any case, and to any ordinary eye impossible in the cramped premises in Queen Square, where some of his largest windows were made. But here his amazing eye and memory for colour enabled him to achieve the impossible: he could pass all the parts of a large window one by one before the light, and never lose sight of the general tone of the colour or of the relation of one part to another. If any part did not satisfy him, new glass was cut and that piece of the window done again.[15]

This description, however, does not begin at the beginning. Before the cartoons were drawn, someone had to decide in just what manner the various spaces of the window were to be filled: how many figures were to be included, the sort of background, borders, canopies and pattern-work, how much space was to be left for panels of quarries or for inscriptions, and so on. The subjects of the figure parts had then to be settled, and, if suitable designs were not already available, commissions for cartoons had to be placed with one or another of the designers. Templates of each of the window's lights had to be cut, the sizes of the component panels determined, and these measurements supplied to the artists. As soon as designs for all the parts had come in, a small 'sketch-design' of the whole window, usually on the scale of one inch to one foot, had to be made and sent off to the client for approval or comment. Until all this had been done, no cutting or painting could be commenced.

How important a role was played by the client's own ideas, in suggesting possible subjects and arrangements, in criticizing sketch-designs and proposing changes, remains largely a matter of conjecture. No doubt correspondence frequently passed between the firm and its customers, but no letters of this kind have been published, nor are they available in archives, so far as I know. It is likely that the important decisions were often reached in personal discussion, when the client called at the firm's premises, or a representative of the firm visited the building where the window was to be erected. Projects were generally discussed also at the monthly meetings of the partners, when commissions for new designs were allocated and fees settled. The firm's Minute Book, now in the collection of Mr Sanford Berger in California, records the outcome of many such discussions, but regrettably gives hardly an inkling of the processes through which decisions were reached. Always, of course, the client had the last word, and this fact alone is sufficient explanation of many inequalities of merit in both design and iconography. The most successful windows, such as the east window at Middleton Cheney, doubtless resulted from an intimate collaboration between client and artists, in which the contribution of the client, especially in regard to subject-matter, may well have been of vital importance.

The partners came to such discussions with certain ideas about style already in their minds, and it is important for us to know what these were. It is disappointing that Morris's many lectures on the lesser arts contain no statement of his views on the principles which should guide the worker in stained glass. On the occasion, however, of the Foreign Fair at Boston, Massachusetts, in 1883, the firm produced a pamphlet which describes its exhibits and contains a paragraph on stained glass which must certainly reflect Morris's own ideas, whether or not it was actually written by him.

> As regards the method of painting and the design, our glass differs so much from other kinds that we may be allowed a word in apology. Glass-painting differs from oil-painting and fresco, mostly in the translucency of the material and the strength, amounting to absolute blackness of the outlines. This blackness of outline is due to the use of lead frames, or settings, which are absolutely necessary for the support of the pieces of glass if various colours are used. It becomes therefore a condition and characteristic of glass-painting. Absolute blackness of outline and translucency of color are then the differentia between glass-painting and panel or wall-painting. They lead to treatment quite peculiar in its principles of light and shade and composition, and make glass-painting an art apart. In the first place, the drawing and composition have to be much more simple, and yet more carefully studied, than in paintings which have all the assistance of shadow and reflected lights to disguise the faults and assist the grouping. In the next place, the light and shade must be so managed that the strong outlines shall not appear crude, nor the work within it thin; this implies a certain conventionalism of treatment and makes the details of a figure much more an affair of drawing than of painting: because by drawing, — that is, by filling the outlines with other lines of proportionate strength, — the force of the predominant lines is less unnatural. These then, are the first conditions of good glass-painting as we perceive them — well-balanced and shapely figures, pure and simple drawing, and a minimum of light and shade. There is another reason for this last. Shading is a dulling of the glass: it is

> therefore inconsistent with the use of a material which was chosen for its brightness. After these we ask for beautiful color. There may be more of it, or less; but it is only rational and becoming that the light we stain should not be changed to dirt or ugliness. Color, pure and sweet, is the least you should ask for in a painted window.[16]

Obviously, these views owed a great deal to Winston's discussions of the basic principles of the art. Ford Madox Brown also had thought carefully about the special demands of the medium, as he made plain in some remarks on the subject in the descriptive catalogue of the exhibition of his works held in Piccadilly in 1865.

> With its heavy lead-lines surrounding every part (and no stained glass can be rational or good without strong lead-lines), stained glass does not admit of refined drawing, or else it is thrown away upon it. What it does admit of, and above all things imperatively requires, is fine colour: and what it *can* admit of, and does very much require also, is invention, expression, and good dramatic action. For this reason, work by the great historical artists is not thrown away upon stained-glass windows, because, though high finish of execution is superfluous and against the spirit of this beautiful decorative art, yet, as expression and action can be conveyed in a few strokes equally as in the most elaborate art, on this side therefore stained glass rises again to the epic height.[17]

These are interesting remarks, because it is precisely their vivid dramatic action — even occasionally somewhat overstated — which distinguishes Madox Brown's cartoons from those of his colleagues. Morris's emphasis is that of one who was primarily a colourist and decorator, whereas Madox Brown's stress upon invention, expression and action represents the views of the figure painter. We have no comparable statements from Rossetti and Burne-Jones; but very likely they would have inclined more to the views of Madox Brown. The outstanding fact about Morris's glass is that it was a product of the combination of these two attitudes: the designs not only easily surpassed in imaginative quality and originality almost everything which competitors could produce, but they were carried out in glass with a decorative craftsmanship and colouristic genius which was unique. This answered Winston's criticisms of the imaginative insufficiency of designs made by what he called 'mere glass-wrights', and his regret at the lack of real artists capable of designing for glass.

Many years ago, Herbert Read expressed some surprise that Morris's production method in his stained-glass studio did not meet the Arts and Crafts Movement ideal of the unification of the processes of design and execution in the person of one artist-craftsman.[18] Morris, in fact, realized that 'a good craftsman was not necessarily a great artist'.[19] What was required was, first, 'a design of imaginative worth, free from the cramping influence (and the mere imaginative insufficiency) of the craftsman, and (second), a technical execution of this design free from the craft amateurishness of the imaginative artist.'[20] So, it was vitally important that the craftsmen of the studio, from Morris down to the humblest cutter and glazier, should carry out their work with full professional efficiency and skill. Thus, after the initial phase of slightly uncertain experiment, represented by examples such as the 'King and Queen', and the panel of Jacob Patriarcha now in the Victoria and Albert Museum, there was nothing arty-crafty about the firm's windows.

In the early stages of planning it was necessary to take into account the desired general effect, and the relationship to be established with the architectural interior and with any windows already in place. The position which any particular window was to occupy would certainly affect its treatment in terms of colour, tone, and the amount of light which it would admit. The requirements for a window above the altar at the east end of the chancel would differ entirely from those for a window to be placed near the pulpit or in a baptistry, both in the choice of appropriate subject-matter and in the window's relationship to the light from outside. A window in a dark corner of a north aisle, shadowed almost always by the roof of the nave, would need a quite different treatment from one in full light at the end of a south transept, or in a south aisle. A design suitable for one position might be totally unsuitable for another, even in the same church, or might require to be executed in a quite different scheme of colour and tone. To whom did this vital work of initial planning fall?

Fortunately, it is possible to give an unequivocal answer to this question, at least for some of the most interesting early schemes. The first entry in Philip Webb's account-book with the firm is for 'Scale drawing of arrangement of Nave windows with scheme for whole church', for Selsley.[21] Similarly, Webb was responsible for the scale drawings of the general arrangements of the Scarborough east window and aisle windows, of the Southgate chancel aisle windows, of the scheme devised but not executed for Brasenose College, Oxford (*161*), of the east windows at Dedworth, Coity, and other churches. The evidence of the account-book is confirmed by W.R. Lethaby, who wrote positively that Webb 'planned the general layout of the windows, prepared small coloured sketches, arranged the disposition of the irons, insisting on thick bars from the first. "My dear fellow, they improve it!" He also designed any animals required, and at first the more ornamental parts.'[22] In a later chapter I shall examine Webb's designs for special parts of windows in some detail; here the intention is simply to emphasize the importance of his part in the planning.

The windows of the firm's first commission for stained glass, those at Selsley, are totally different from Burne-Jones's windows, made by Powells, at Bradfield College, in the Latin Chapel at Christ Church Cathedral, Oxford, or at Waltham Abbey. The same is true also of the Morris windows at Scarborough, Southgate, Brighton, Dedworth, and all the other commissions of the early years. The general character of these windows must have been due to Webb. It is worth while, therefore, to examine some of these early schemes in detail, in order to discover the chief characteristics of Webb's arrangements.

At All Saints, Selsley,[23] the windows of the nave and chancel apse are of different sizes and shapes: in the apse are five single trefoil-headed lights, with a circle above each;

there are two-light windows in the south wall of the chancel and at the west end; and in the south aisle are three triplet windows, two of which have the centre light taller than the side lights, one having the side lights taller (*28–30*, *33–35*, *40*, *43*, *46–48*, *53*). This varied scheme of fenestration is united by a band of richly coloured panels at a regular height throughout,[24] with uniform or similar borders, and quarries of identical pattern above and below them. The pattern-work of the tracery lights in the south aisle also is identical; and the borders of the subjects in tracery circles in both aisle and chancel are similar. Lastly, of course, the colour scheme throughout relates each panel to the whole. In spite of the depth and richness of the colour in the panels, the church is light because of the large area of nearly clear quarries. The only part of the scheme which at all resembles the earlier work of any of the partners in the firm is the rose-window at the west end (*48*), where the arrangement, with Christ in Majesty in the centre, and the Days of Creation in surrounding circles, obviously derives from Burne-Jones's window at Waltham Abbey (*27*). Any differences of style among the designs of the five artists responsible for the cartoons seem, in the totality, of very minor significance because of the firm control exercised by the general scheme of disposition.

St Michael's, Brighton, is a much bigger church,[25] and the stained glass inserted in 1862, since it did not fill all the windows, could hardly achieve the same degree of unity and interrelationship as at Selsley. In two of the windows — those of the Baptism of Christ and the Maries at the Sepulchre (*V*) — the subjects, as at Selsley, are contained within panels surrounded by borders, and with quarries above and below. Webb's controlling influence is still manifest here. In the little windows of the Flight into Egypt (*54*, *55*), however, Burne-Jones was solely responsible for the effect; the way in which the heads of two angels and of Joseph break into the narrow borders, to emphasize the movement and flow of line, is quite foreign to Webb's style of arrangement, and an early indication of the direction in which Burne-Jones's designs were to develop. At the west end, the four archangels completely fill the lights which they occupy, as do also the subjects in the sexfoils above them. If Webb shared any responsibility for these windows, it could only have been in suggesting the subjects. The rose-window high in the west gable is entirely from Burne-Jones's cartoons; but it is unlike his earlier rose-windows in that the seven angels striking bells in the surrounding circles are set in quarry grounds, so as to admit as much light as possible. Here again perhaps one may discern the effect of Webb's suggestions.

At Scarborough[26] not all the windows were put up in 1862–63, but it seems fairly certain that the later ones followed a general plan drawn up then. Again we find that the subjects in the east window are contained within panels surrounded by borders, leaving ample spaces above and below to be filled with quarries (*64*). The rose in the tracery above is also mostly quarries; and the Adam and Eve in the west lancets are surrounded by quarries (*67*, *68*). The St Martin window in the south-west corner of the church (*VII*) is very similar in its general disposition to the Maries window at Brighton. Horizontal lines of bordering, with quarries or bold geometrical pattern-work, are introduced in all the aisle windows. In all this, Webb's hand may be clearly detected. Only in the rose of the west gable (*69*) does a distinctly different style of design appear, and again this seems to be due to Burne-Jones, though the Annunciation which occupies this position was not specifically designed for it, but was adapted from a design originally intended for painted tiles. Unlike the rose at Brighton, this one has a dark background, throwing the white and gold figures into brilliant relief. In all three of these early schemes, but especially at Scarborough, it is noticeable that the wrought-iron tie-bars are of massive dimensions.

These brief descriptions should suffice to establish the character of Webb's ideas on the design of windows. At Dedworth, Cranborne, Ladock and elsewhere other windows follow the same principles. They are certainly among the finest of the firm's products. The pattern-work at Cranborne is of an unsurpassed virility (*97–99*); the quarries at Gatcombe, with their alternating circular pale blue and pale yellow flaming stars, are of an exquisite pearly delicacy (*253*). Without exaggeration, these windows are more Webb's creations than anyone else's. When his distinctive pattern-work and planning ceased to appear in the firm's windows, as it did by about 1874, something irretrievable was lost. So long as his directing intelligence was behind them, the windows were in no danger of becoming merely pictures in glass. Almost from the beginning, however, the pictorial tendency was implicit in Burne-Jones's designs, as we have seen already in the little Flight into Egypt window at Brighton.

We know from Webb's account-book that he personally designed quarries, borders, pattern-work and canopies. Some of the figure-and-canopy windows in which he participated present a rather different appearance from the windows we have so far considered; and we should glance briefly at these.

One of the great difficulties in designing for stained glass is, of course, to relate the subject to the entire area of the window opening, which is often of a shape that a painter would never encounter in any other medium. Lancets seven times as high as their width are by no means uncommon, not to mention the special problems presented by triangular, trefoil, quatrefoil, cinquefoil or sexfoil openings, rose-windows, and so on. Since an undistorted human figure shown in full-face view can seldom be much more than three times as high as its width, the placing of such a figure in a tall lancet necessitates the use of some additional device to occupy the space. The figure-and-canopy type of design was a well-tried historical expedient for dealing with this problem, much used by late mediaeval artists as well as by Pugin and others in the nineteenth century. It is therefore natural that the Morris firm should have used it, especially in situations where Webb's more favoured solution of quarry or pattern-work panels was unsuitable. Early examples of of the type occur in Morris windows at Banstead, Cheddleton, Camberwell, Haywards Heath, Southgate and elsewhere. In each instance the canopies were drawn by Webb, and it is clear that he aimed at relating the style of his canopy-work to that of the churches concerned. At Banstead, a village church mainly of the late twelfth or early thirteenth century, extensively restored in 1861, single figures under somewhat rustic canopies were placed above pedestals decorated with heraldic devices (*138*, *139*). At Southgate, a Gothic Revival church of 1863 by Gilbert Scott, single figures were provided with canopies containing upper storeys filled by half-length angels carrying shields, and pattern-work replaced pedestals at the bottom (*101–04*). The most elaborate and beautiful canopies were those at St Giles', Camberwell (unfortunately now destroyed),[27] an early Gilbert Scott church of 1844; the tall foliated gables again had angels in the upper storeys, but in place of pedestals the bottom sections of the lancets were occupied by small subject-panels containing a number of figures. This way of using two very different scales of figures in the same light was disapproved of by Winston, but it seems in many ways very satisfactory because the small figures at the bottom, being so much nearer to the viewer's eye-level, give the window an effectiveness from a close viewpoint but do not disturb the design of the light as a whole, which can be appreciated properly only from further off. This device evidently pleased Morris, and he continued to the end of his life to use predella panels of this type, and not only in conjunction with canopies.

In the baptistry window at St Wilfrid's, Haywards Heath, Sussex, made probably in 1867,[28] each light has two figures, one above the other, in tall canopies divided into two storeys by means of arches which become pedestals for the upper figures (*279*). The effect of this two-tiered arrangement is not altogether happy, and it was not repeated. In the chancel windows at Cheddleton,[29] there is no attempt to extend the canopies to fill the lights; the small canopies, indeed, seem hardly more than a rather elaborate type of panel-framing, and the rest of the lights are filled with pattern-work in grisaille and broad borders of creepers or fleurs-de-lys (*167*). Webb's inventiveness and resource are well illustrated by this variety of solution. In their own way the Cheddleton windows are very beautiful. When one looks at them, a certain regret that the figure-and-canopy window had a short history in the firm's output inevitably creeps into mind. Whatever the reason may have been — Webb's inability to find time to design them, or his gradual alienation from the Gothic, or Morris's preference for other solutions — canopies were to become rare after the 1860s. A few striking examples of later date, such as the windows at Coatbridge (1876) and the window of 1909 at Bolton Percy, were very probably due to the requests of clients or to the firm's desire to conform to a general pattern already established by other windows in these churches.

In the meantime Morris had been experimenting with other devices, and especially with ways of bringing unity of effect to large windows. Indeed, the more one studies the early windows made between 1862 and about 1868, the more one is impressed by the inventiveness shown in finding varied solutions to the complex problems involved. One of the earliest commissions which the firm received for a very large window was that for the east window of Bradford parish church, now the Cathedral (*174*). It was seven lights in width, divided into two tiers by stone transoms, and with three tiers of tracery panels; there were thus fourteen main openings, and something like three dozen tracery openings. How was such a complex arrangement to be designed, so as to obtain a unified effect? The lines of the tracery grouped together the three main lights on each side, thus isolating the central light and giving it a special importance; the principal subject had therefore to be placed here. The two tiers of this central light are each of a shape which could be filled by a single figure of about life-size. With two such large figures in the centre, however, it would have been almost impossible to do anything else in the side lights but fill them also with large figures, and this would have resulted in an excessively weighty appearance, impossible to relieve adequately in the tracery. Morris's solution was to use only one large figure, that of St Peter, in the lower tier of the centre, with Christ in Majesty seated and surrounded by angels in the upper tier; to reduce the scale in the lateral lights to one half of this, so as to accommodate two figures in each tier; and to reduce the scale again by a half for the angels in the tracery. The lateral lights all have wide borders, and quarry grounds crossed by diagonal bands of lettering; the central light has different, narrower borders, and distinctive backgrounds of positive colour. The result is not, perhaps, entirely satisfactory: the gigantic St Peter remains incompletely integrated with the rest, and the placing of the Christ in Majesty at a level below that of the top row of figures in the side lights gives it less prominence than it should properly have. But the scheme came very near to success, and Morris was not slow to learn from his mistakes.[30]

Somewhat similar problems arose in the east window at All Saints, Cambridge,[31] though this is a composition of only five very tall lights, with tracery above consisting of three small roses, two long curved triangles, and some smaller openings (*263*). The main lights increase in height towards the centre; thus, if the outside lights could accommodate four tiers of single figures, a single figure on the same scale in the top tier of the central light would have an excessively large blank space above it. The opportunity was realized, and a Christ in Majesty placed here so as to dominate the whole composition. The wide borders run round all five lights, and except for the panel of the Majesty, the backgrounds of quarries and diagonal bands of lettering run throughout. The window is more unified than the Bradford east window, and oddly enough the weakest part of it is Webb's work in the tracery, which is curiously lacking in his usual confidence.

At approximately the same time as the Cambridge window was being made, another five-light east window, for Christ Church, Sunderland,[32] was in progress (*219*). This is the largest window composed according to Webb's methods. Ten small subjects in rectangular panels are arranged in two horizontal bands across it, with splendid pattern-work above, between and below. Close integration of the five lights is thus achieved, and a fine decorative effect is combined with rich colour. But the scale of the figures is undeniably small for such an expanse of glass; and Morris must have felt that such a method of composition lost opportunities for a much more monumental effect. Although a similar plan was followed in the three-light west window of 1866 at St Oswald's, Durham (*209*),[33] it was never afterwards employed for a large composition.

The examples which mark most clearly the development of Morris's own ideas of composition in large windows are those at Lyndhurst, Middleton Cheney and Bloxham. The east window of 1862–63 at St Michael's, Lyndhurst,[34] is of a peculiar complexity: the three broad main lights alternate with four very narrow ones, while the tracery contains a rose, eight large trefoils, and a number of smaller openings (*116–18*). It must have presented a baffling problem, but the solution, in which doubtless Webb, Morris and Burne-Jones all collaborated, is a tour de force. The main lights are divided horizontally into two tiers, the lines of division running across all seven openings. The seraphim in the narrow ones punctuate, as it were, but do not disrupt the theme of the broader lights, with their groups of two, three or four figures, moving towards the centre, where stands the Virgin Mary, the only completely disclosed full-face figure among them. The interrelatedness of these broad lights is further emphasized by their identical borders, their colour, and the beautiful frieze of city walls, gates, towers and angels, along the top. The upward movement, implicit throughout these lower parts, carries the eye up from the figure of the Virgin towards the rose above, occupied by the symbol of the Trinity, probably designed by Webb. It seems likely that at one stage this rose was to have contained a figurative subject by Burne-Jones. An entry in his account-book dated 27 November 1862 specifically mentions the centre sexfoil but unfortunately does not indicate its subject; the most probable one would have been Christ in Majesty. It is not clear why such an idea was abandoned, but it is certain that in the window as executed the symbol which occupies this crucial position in the centre of the rose seems something of an anti-climax.

The basis of the success of the Lyndhurst east window lies primarily in the establishment of strong links horizontally connecting the subjects of the main lights with their neighbours. This was inherent in Webb's arrangements, as we have seen. In the Lyndhurst east window, however, each compartment is not independent, but forms rather a part of a larger theme complete only in the whole window, namely, the New Jerusalem. Morris, nevertheless, must have been seeking also for an alternative method of composition, because the Lyndhurst south transept window, of only a few months later, follows quite different principles (*131*, *136*). Horizontal lines are indeed drawn across all four main lights, near the top and near the bottom, to separate areas of pale quarries; and in this Webb's influence is apparent. But between these lines each of the four lights is treated by Burne-Jones quite independently of its neighbours, each with a many-figured subject rising in two or three unequal stages from bottom to top, and with different degrees of implied recession (*132–35*). Had the lights been more widely separated from one another, or had the disparities of scale among the figures been less pronounced, this vertical scheme of composition might have succeeded. As it is, however, the lack of a horizontal relationship proves disturbing. It is particularly surprising and regrettable that Burne-Jones should have made this mistake, since his Song of Solomon window at Darley Dale had struck such a happy balance between vertical and horizontal directions

(*107*), and since each of the Lyndhurst lights, considered independently, is composed with consummate mastery.

Again it is evident, however, that the mistake was recognized as such, for no other window by the firm errs in the same way. The east window of 1864–65 at Middleton Cheney,[35] a composition of four main lights and tracery (*230–35*), follows the general principle established in the first Lyndhurst window. The main lights are divided by horizontal lines into three tiers, and in each of these tiers the subject-matter is virtually continuous, and many devices are employed to reinforce their continuity: the bands of lettering running beneath them and crossing even the borders of the lights; their scheme of colour and tone; the postures of the figures, in pairs or groups, turning towards the centre of the window, and breaking here and there through the borders; above all the dramatic and brilliant array of the banners of the Tribes of Israel, designed by Webb, which occupy the heads of the lights, breaking into the borders here also, give a vivid effect of movement and jubilation. As against this horizontal emphasis, an adequate vertical movement is supplied by the shape of the main lights themselves, by the borders of alternating leaves and crowns, and by the arrangement of the tonal pattern, which lightens towards the top. The eye is thus led up to the climax and focal point of the whole composition, the big quatrefoil with the Worship of the Lamb, and its attendant censing angels. In spite of the difficulties inherent in a process of collaboration between five artists — Madox Brown, Burne-Jones, Morris, Simeon Solomon and Webb — this window is a triumphant success, a masterpiece, and one of the most splendid achievements in all English stained glass. Such an outcome must have been due above all to the clarity and firmness of the overall direction. But on this occasion it was most likely Morris himself who conceived the plan; the scale-drawing was done by Webb, but the relevant entries in his account-book significantly do not contain the phrase 'general arrangement'.

The east window at St Mary's, Bloxham,[36] though simpler in that it has only two tiers of main figures instead of three, and all the figures are arranged in pairs, follows the same general principles of composition (*296*). So far as large windows are concerned, Middleton Cheney and Bloxham mark the climax of achievement in the first period of Morris's production. By the time the Bloxham window was completed, at Christmas 1869, Webb's role in the preparation had been reduced to the provision of such accessories as the architectural background representing the walls of the Holy City, and conversely Morris's had expanded to include the overall arrangement and composition. Windows composed by Webb's method admit more light, whereas those directed by Morris give greater importance to the figures and attain a richness and expressiveness beyond Webb's range.

Although examination of these important windows reveals the development of the firm's large-scale compositional ideas, it would be misleading to omit all mention of the many smaller undertakings of the 1860s.[37] Not a few of these are, indeed, among the most charming and brilliant of all Morris's glass, and many of them are practically unknown.

A significant place in the work of these years is occupied by a number of panels intended for secular use. The Tristram and Isoude series commissioned by Walter Dunlop for Harden Grange in 1862, and now in the Bradford City Art Gallery, is the most extensive of these (*78–85*). The thirteen panels were designed by no fewer than six different artists, including Val Prinsep and Arthur Hughes, whose sole cartoons for the firm (so far as is known) belong to this set. Records of their original arrangement unluckily do not survive, so it is possible to consider them only as separate panels related in theme and treatment. As a secular narrative sequence this is unique in the firm's output; but the series of seven panels illustrating the Parable of the Vineyard, in the east window at Scarborough (*64–66*), and the set of six panels of the Story of St George, in the Victoria and Albert Museum (*91–96*), both entirely from Rossetti's designs, belong to the same phase of thought. It may be doubted whether stained glass lends itself very readily to narrative treatment; the restrictions imposed by the medium render it much more suitable to relatively static and monumental effects. Nevertheless, Rossetti's cartoons are brilliant and dramatic designs. Their limitations become apparent only when one struggles to make out what is happening in the Scarborough panels, which are unhappily almost entirely unintelligible in the lofty position in which they are fixed. Burne-Jones's series of 1864 illustrating Chaucer's Dream of Good Women, at Peterhouse, Cambridge (*325*, *326*), and the three related panels in the Victoria and Albert Museum (*197–99*), attempt no narrative. As the Peterhouse ones are still in the positions for which they were made, it is possible to appreciate their considerable decorative charm; but their most outstanding quality is the extraordinary delicacy and precision of the grisaille-work in the flowers of the foregrounds and the architecture of the backgrounds. The glass itself is thin, and the panels are kept as free from lead-lines as possible, in order, presumably, to keep the effect as light as possible. The same approach is found in the set of six panels in the windows of the Green Dining Room in the South Kensington Museum (now the Victoria and Albert Museum; *267–70*). The fate of these when the packing-case in which they were stored was battered by bomb-blast during the Second World War shows only too well that it might have been better, even at the cost of some darkening of effect, to use more leads and smaller pieces of glass, or else glass of heavier substance; for the borders, where the cutting was smaller, hardly suffered at all when much of the panels themselves was shattered. However this may be, these early secular windows seem preferable to nearly all the firm's later domestic glass, which became less transparent and heavier in tone.[38]

Returning to church windows, it may be noted that the majority of the less important ones of the years 1861 to 1869 have either rectangular panels with pattern-work and quarries, as at Bishop's Tachbrook (*143*), Bournemouth (St Peter's; *168*), Cheddleton (south aisle, west window), Dedworth (Annunciation window), Oxford (St Edmund Hall; *225*, *229*), or Rodbourne (*106*); or else figures set against quarry grounds, usually with borders following the outlines of the openings, as at Coity (*148*), Furneaux Pelham,

Henley-in-Arden (*217*, *218*), Langton Green and Llandaff Cathedral (*265*, *284*, *305*). Simple quarry grounds provide, indeed, a type of window which is particularly pleasing and well adapted to situations where it is desirable to admit as much light as possible; and this method continued to be used by Morris long afterwards. But the quarries themselves, generally very pale and of white or nearly white glass at this early period, acquired later on, especially after the middle 1880s, a positive greenish tone which is by no means so pleasant.

There are windows of another type, however, which are more interesting, namely those in which Morris began to experiment with patterned backgrounds. A number of the very early windows have coloured grounds, usually without pattern, except such as may be supplied by lead-lines; the three-light window now at Doddington, and originally (most probably) at Langton Green, is a case in point (*216*). The grounds, blue in the lateral lights and red in the centre, have no pattern other than the 'crazy-paving' arrangement of the lead-lines. This is characteristic of the earliest phase, about 1862. As early as 1864, in the three-light east window at Amington[39] — the upper parts of which represent the same subject as the little central panel at Doddington, namely Christ on the Cross between the Virgin and St John — Morris made a decisive and typical departure from this simple treatment (*169*). The subject is spread out over the three lights, so that the compartments become much more closely interdependent and the composition more monumental; the backgrounds are filled with a pattern of tall, straight, pale green palm leaves. This background device was used again at St Michael Penkevil two years later,[40] and at Catton in Yorkshire with slightly greater complexity. Both of these are three-light windows, with Christ on the Cross in the centre, but with groups of three figures in each of the side lights, and trios of weeping angels above them, all designed by Burne-Jones. They are both windows of outstanding quality, and a comparison between them is particularly instructive. The Penkevil window has, below the main subjects, three small subjects under canopies designed by Webb; the horizontal line dividing these from the upper parts runs continuously across all three lights, and there are wide borders round each light (*261*). This results in a certain emphasis on the independence of these lower panels, an effect rather in contradiction to the treatment of the upper parts as a single composition. At Catton,[41] on the other hand, where the centre light is considerably taller than the others, the opportunity was taken to move the crucified Christ up to a more dominating position, and although the Cross itself is much taller and two angels clasping its base are added, the bottom edge of this subject still comes at a level appreciably higher than the tops of the lower subjects in the side lights (*262*). In this way the horizontal line of division between the main subject and the small panels below is broken. There are no canopies and the borders are much narrower. The consequence is an immeasurably greater dramatic effect, expressiveness, and overall unity. The patterned background does not, maybe, play a role of crucial significance here, but it is possible to regard it as in some degree an alternative to the canopy conceived as a space-filler —

a device linking adjoining compartments rather than separating them. It is therefore surprising to find that in the five-light east window of 1868 in St John the Baptist, Tuebrook, Liverpool,[42] Morris reverted to the canopy system, not only for the subsidiary lower subjects but also for the main upper subjects (*275–78*). The Tuebrook window thus remains a sum of its parts, or little more, and is in no way a match for the masterpiece at Catton. This demonstrates, perhaps, that even a highly intelligent and sensitive artist like Morris did not always at once fully understand the implications of his own methods of design.

Foliage backgrounds, it has been assumed on the authority of Mackail, were always supplied by Morris himself.[43] It is worth a pause, therefore, to point out that three cartoons by Burne-Jones in the Fitzwilliam Museum, Cambridge, have foliage backgrounds fully indicated, and clearly in Burne-Jones's hand; two of these are for compartments in the Lyndhurst east window, and were drawn in December 1862 (*121*, *122*), while the third, drawn in 1865, is for a section of the east window at St John the Evangelist, Torquay (*223*). The gradual development of richer textural effects, as well as of greater pictorialism and interdependence of parts, seems then to be rooted in Burne-Jones's conceptions. It is an interesting question whether the scrolled 'treework' background of the cartoon for the figure of Faith, in the William Morris Gallery at Walthamstow (BLA 407), which refers to a window of 1866–67 in the North Church at Greenock, was put in by Burne-Jones, who certainly designed the figure, or by Morris. What is clear is that as Webb's influence declined, Morris was more and more carried along by the tendencies implicit in Burne-Jones's style.

In the narrow spaces between and around the figures in the Middleton Cheney east window (1866) there is a foliage background of a more elaborate kind, consisting of oak, rose, pomegranate and apple leaves, with fruits; but the tone is limited to a pale blue-green, and the effect tends to be flat and abstract rather than naturalistic. At the same time Morris was using a still more abstract and flat diaper and scroll pattern in the backgrounds of the Faith, Hope and Charity windows at Sculthorpe (ca. 1865; *241–43*) and Bicester (1866; *240*). At Farnham Royal (1868; *285*) and Cardiff (1869) backgrounds of this type appear above curtains hung on rails behind the figures at about shoulder-height — a device which was continued in use to the end of the firm's activity, though in later windows the spaces above the curtains were more commonly filled with scrolled, naturalistic or dense foliage, as in the case of the north transept window of 1876 in Jesus College Chapel, Cambridge, with figures of Patience, Obedience and Docility (*443*). More interesting than these, however, are the backgrounds of formalized shell, wave or cloud patterns combined with scrolls as in the chancel south window at St John the Baptist, Tuebrook (ca. 1868; *276*), or with stars as in the very beautiful east window at St Michael's, Tilehurst near Reading (1869; *303*, *304*), and in the east window at St John's, Dalton near Thirsk (1868). At Tilehurst the full potentialities of this background, in bringing the window together as a whole, are realized. No horizontal divisions separate the six figures in two tiers which occupy the three main lights. There are, indeed, still borders running round the edges, but they are not emphatic enough to disturb the continuity of the vibrating background.

Another window which must certainly be mentioned as one of the culminating points in this phase of rather flat abstract backgrounds is the superb Archangels window at St Mary's, King's Walden (ca. 1869; *IX*). This window is entirely Morris's creation, for all the figures are from his designs, and there can be no doubt that he also designed the wonderful variety of diaper patterns in gold, red, green and blue which make this so rich and jewel-like a treasure.

The conception of Morris's interest in pattern for its own sake which emerges from this analysis should be related to the chronology of his wallpaper and fabric designs established by the researches of Peter Floud.[44] Of the three early wallpaper designs produced by Morris in 1864, one, the Trellis pattern, has no parallel in stained glass; but the other two, the Daisy and Pomegranate papers, though naturalistic in their basis, are relatively very simple in structure, relying on the repetition in rows of alternating units. Floud was inclined to dismiss them as unsophisticated, immature and untypical. Certainly, when compared with even the earliest designs of the seventies, such as the Jasmine and the Scroll papers, they noticeably lack the long flowing curves which were to become a leading feature of his patterns. The reason for this, without any doubt, must be that Morris's thought, in the field of pattern design, was at this time dominated by consideration of the special demands of the media with which he was most occupied, namely diaper-patterns for stained glass and simple unit patterns for stained-glass quarries and for tiles. The wallpaper designs fit well into the context of his other pattern designs of the sixties.

One other important window of these early years remains to be discussed, namely the west window of 1864–65 in St Stephen's, Guernsey (*204–06*). Its exceptional character necessitates its consideration out of chronological sequence. It represents the Tree of Jesse and is the only known example of this subject among the firm's windows, apart from the small lancet at St Margaret's, Rottingdean, designed by Burne-Jones in 1896, and the much later large window of 1923 at All Saints, Leek. After Burne-Jones's considerable success with his Jesse window at Waltham Abbey, it might have been expected that Morris would have relied on his friend and partner for the greater part of the design, perhaps reserving for himself the design of a foliage background, which he could have done so well. In fact, however, Burne-Jones seems to have had no share in the work at all, though several figures by him, and others by Ford Madox Brown, originally designed for the Bradford east window, were incorporated in it. The paucity of documentation relating to the window unfortunately leaves some doubt about the responsibility for the general design and layout, but it was probably mainly Morris's own work.[45] Since, as we have seen, by 1864 Morris was already developing the use of foliage backgrounds, and since such backgrounds traditionally belonged to the Jesse Tree subject,[46] it is a little surprising that the foliage in the Guernsey window is decidedly sparse, and the tree motif confined to the minimum indications, with trunk and branches of pale purple, and leaves of very pale green. The explanation of these features is, I think, that in relation to the size of the church, which is yet another of Bodley's buildings, the three main lights of the west window are very narrow and are separated by considerable expanses of wall. Had they been filled with dark green foliage, they would not have admitted enough light. Morris had perhaps been warned by his experience at St Martin's-on-the-Hill, Scarborough, of the dangers of too dark a general tone. At Guernsey he obviously aimed, as in the east window at All Saints, Cambridge, at keeping the tone as light as was consistent with an effect of richness. The background had therefore to contain as much clear glass as possible, and even in the tree itself dark tones had to be studiously avoided. The result is remarkably successful, and an eloquent tribute to the sensibility Morris nearly always showed, especially in the early decades, to the demands of the particular situation of his windows, and their relationship to the architecture and the lighting of the interior. If one thinks, in this connection, of such later works as the great windows at St Philip's, Birmingham (1885–97), it is clear that, whatever qualities may have been gained by later stylistic developments, a great deal was also lost.

3
The Morris Firm: 1869-1875

The story of the first seven years or so of stained-glass windows produced in Morris's studio is one of the gradual substitution of pictorial for architectural principles of composition. By 1869 the general direction of design and arrangement in this department of the firm's activities had left the hands of Philip Webb, and Morris himself had established a sure grasp of all the problems involved, as the King's Walden window amply proves. In the next phase of his stained-glass work, from 1869 to about 1874 or 1875, he continued to use his own cartoons and those by several other artists, including Ford Madox Brown and Webb; but no further designs were commissioned from Arthur Hughes, Val Prinsep, Albert Moore or Simeon Solomon. Burne-Jones's share of the responsibility tended steadily to increase, and it was in connection with his cartoons that Morris's colouristic imagination was stimulated to its highest flights. It was a prolific period, and it is possible here to discuss only briefly a few typical or outstanding examples, selected to illustrate the character and direction of development which was taking place.

A fairly considerable proportion of the new windows embodied no fresh principles of design or composition, but continued to utilize already tested formulae, either with repetitions of figures originally designed in the first period, or with newly drawn figures. Thus we find figures placed against quarry grounds in windows at Furneaux Pelham (1874), Haywards Heath (ca. 1870, 1871), Leeds, Mill Hill Unitarian Chapel (1875; *494, 495*), Llandaff Cathedral (1869, 1874; *306, 468*), Ruskington (1874; *476*), and Tamworth (1874), all of which have wide borders; while simple quarry grounds without borders appear in windows at Eaton Hastings, Flockton (*372*), King's Bromley, Kirkbampton (*358*), Knaresborough (*450*), Leeds (St Saviour's; *348*), Lewknor, Llantrisant, Margam, Monkton (*474*), Over Stowey (*398*), Ponsonby (*492*), St Florence, Ventnor (*379*), Waterford (*374, 375*), Westerfield (*488*), and elsewhere. Backgrounds of 'round glass' occur at Burnley (Habergham Eaves) and Haltwhistle; pattern-work grounds are to be found at Liverpool (Edge Hill; *406*), Speldhurst (east window of the north aisle), and Winteringham; while in the Dorcas and Good Samaritan window at Southgate (*517*), the quarries are treated in such a way as to connect with one another in larger flowing patterns. One or two rather isolated instances of Gothic canopies exist, as at Stratton, Cornwall; and in a few cases subject-panels continued to be arranged in horizontal bands according to Webb's manner, as at St Martin's, Brighouse. At St James's, Brighouse, and at Bromham (*319*) there are windows of high quality following fairly closely the principles of design used at St Michael Penkevil, Catton, or Torquay (St John the Evangelist). All this, however, is naturally of less interest than designs which depart from established practice. Only by examining these can we realize how prolific in new ideas Morris and his associates were. Certainly no other stained-glass artists of the Victorian period could compete with them in this respect.

In spite of the extensive use which he still made of quarry grounds, it is evident that Morris, on occasion, wished for a type of background treatment richer in colour and texture, and capable also of relating the figures placed before it to a wider pictorial field. As we have seen, the drapery and scroll-work grounds used at Farnham Royal and Cardiff, and the cloud-pattern ground at Tilehurst, must have been devised for this purpose. But Morris had not yet succeeded in producing such a foliage background, and he was particularly interested in foliage as material for decorative design. The problem was to find just the right manner in which to treat it. Five quite different treatments were evolved and tried out between 1870 and 1873, two of them being more or less discontinued after a few trials, the other three becoming characteristic of a great many later Morris windows, in which the styles, evolved no doubt by Morris himself, were imitated and adapted by other members of the studio. These five types of foliage backgrounds may be called: open foliage with winding stems; rose-hedge; Gothic tree; scrolled foliage; and dense foliage with fruit or flowers.

The idea for the open foliage backgrounds with winding stems probably first arose in connection with the bay window of the hall at Peterhouse, Cambridge, made in 1870–71 (*329*, *332*). In addition to the figures of seven great scholars, designed by Madox Brown, this window contains many shields of arms and mottoes on scrolls. There are no fewer than twenty-one main lights, arranged in three tiers, with the figures occupying the middle tier, and panel tracery above. In order to link together this complex scheme, Morris employed the device of a tree, whose trunk appears in the centre bottom light and whose branches and leaves extend throughout the window, even into the tracery. No doubt he got the idea from mediaeval Jesse Tree windows. Considering the difficulty of the problem, this window attains a quite remarkable unity of effect, though it is not among Morris's best works.

Not long afterwards, in 1872, Morris received a commission for a window with the figures of Absalom, Samuel and Timothy, for the church of St John the Evangelist, Knotty Ash, near Liverpool (*350*).[1] The subject of Absalom, who was caught in an oak tree during the battle with the forces of King David his father, and killed there by Joab,[2] seemed specifically to call for a treatment similar to that of the Peterhouse bay window. The branches and foliage of the Absalom light actually spread out to form a background to the subjects in the two lateral lights, and bind the whole triptych together.[3]

In these examples the foliage is open, that is to say that interstices of clear white glass show between the leaves and branches. A somewhat similar effect appears in the Adam and Eve window of 1873 at Frankby in the Wirral, where apple trees, one growing in each of the twin lights, provide rich backgrounds for the nude figures and at the same time cover their private parts (*XIV*). The cartoons of Absalom and the Frankby Adam and Eve were provided by Burne-Jones, and it is very possible that he designed the foliage backgrounds in these cases; but the possibilities of the extension of the idea were quickly seized upon by Morris. It was very likely the Frankby window which gave him the idea for the dense foliage and fruit backgrounds evolved soon afterwards in the windows of Jesus College Chapel. Unfortunately, the Absalom and Adam and Eve cartoons seem at present to be untraced, so that we cannot be sure whether Burne-Jones did in fact put in the foliage. Indeed, even when we have a cartoon with foliage background fully indicated, it is by no means easy to decide which artist was responsible. A cartoon for the figure of Faith, with a foreground of wild flowers, and a background of vines in fruit supported by a trellis, and above it trees with apples and pomegranates, is in the William Morris Gallery at Walthamstow.[4] There is some doubt as to the authorship of the figure itself, which was certainly designed in the first place by Burne-Jones, probably for a window at Sculthorpe, but which in this version looks more like a copy by Charles Fairfax Murray. The background, however, was almost certainly drawn by Morris; and, since the cartoon is for a window made for the Old West Kirk, Greenock (and now in the North Church) in 1866–67, this must be the earliest example of the backgrounds with dense foliage and fruits. More open foliage grounds with long winding stems, usually of willow, were used at Nun Monkton (1873), Paisley Abbey (1874 and later), Bramley near Leeds (1875; *505–07*) and Madeley (1873; *403*); the most attractive of these are perhaps the north transept windows at Bramley, where the subjects are enclosed within small roundels, framed by the foliage. Where large figures were placed against such a ground, their outlines were inevitably a little obscured, and it became necessary to employ rather dark colours in the draperies in order to obtain an adequate relief effect. This resulted in the background appearing more emphatic than the figures, whereas if the background were kept more solid and deeper in tone, as was done in the case of the 1873 window at Madeley, it became possible to use light colours for the figures and thus to give them predominance. This must undoubtedly have been the process of development which led to the backgrounds of dense foliage and fruit, as employed at Jesus College Chapel. We shall discuss these further below.

The problems which Morris had to face were not merely those of choosing between open and dense forms of foliage, but also of determining the proper degree of conventionalization in the treatment of the foliage. The Peterhouse, Knotty Ash and Frankby windows had been relatively naturalistic, whereas those at Nun Monkton, Bramley and Madeley were rather more formalized. A similar contrast may be found between two groups of windows employing on the one hand the rather naturalistic rose-hedge background, and on the other the much more conventionalized Gothic tree background. The rose-hedge background first appeared, with two trees rising from it, in the Annunciation window at St John's, Dalton near Thirsk, Yorkshire, about 1868. This background is certainly from Morris's own design, and his cartoon for an example of it, used in a window representing the Virgin Mary and St Elizabeth at St Martin's, Marple, Cheshire

(1873), is in the Victoria and Albert Museum (*396*).[5] Another Marple window representing the Annunciation, also of 1873, repeated the Dalton design; and yet another version, with only trifling changes, was made for St Michael's, Waterford, Hertfordshire, in 1874–76.[6] When the same figures were repeated, however, in 1880 for Holy Trinity, Ashford-in-the-Water, Derbyshire, the trees were omitted.

Similar backgrounds of flowering hedges up to the shoulder-height of the figures were used in the windows representing Faith, Hope and Charity at St Chad's, Rochdale (1873; *397*) and St Mary's, Bishopsbourne (1875). The differences in the treatment of colour in these last two windows are instructive. At Rochdale, the robes of two of the main figures are predominantly dark in tone, and their outlines against the dense hedge are therefore not very clear. The figure of Hope, however, is draped in brilliant tones, and consequently every fold and loop of her flowing Botticellian gown and ribbons tells with great effect. It is hardly surprising, then, to find that at Bishopsbourne all three figures have been given white robes. In this case, however, clear quarries were obviously no longer appropriate for the upper parts of the background. The idea of figures in light tones placed in front of a generally dark background was leading Morris towards the all-over dark foliage backgrounds which were to become typical of so many later windows. At all events, the rose-hedge background had a comparatively short life, and examples later than 1880 are rare.

The Gothic tree background, again probably designed by Morris himself, was first used in two pairs of tall lancets, each with three tiers of minstrel angels from Morris's own cartoons, at St Nicholas, Whiston (*399*), and St Mary's, Speldhurst, both made in or about 1873. The trees are severely conventionalized, rather on the lines of those in Giotto's frescoes of the Arena Chapel at Padua; their tones are dark, and the spaces between and around them are filled with blue glass covered with formal diaper patterns. The effect is somewhat mediaeval, and very beautiful, with the white and gold robes, wings and hair of the angels standing out with a glowing brilliance. When one looks at such windows, it is a little hard to sympathize with the tendencies which led Morris and Burne-Jones away from this purity and simplicity of style in the direction of greater pictorialism and naturalism. A comparison between these lancets, at the east end of the south aisle at Whiston, and the nave west windows in the same church (filled in 1896 with rather similar minstrel angels, but no longer in three distinct tiers, and with much more naturalistic landscape backgrounds), must surely lead to a judgement wholly favourable to the earlier and more conventional style. All the same, Morris must have felt less than completely satisfied with the Gothic tree background; perhaps his taste rejected such a high degree of conventionalization, or perhaps he felt the motif was too open to charges of deliberate and imitative mediaevalism. Whatever his reasons, when he came to use four of these same minstrel angels in the chancel east window at Waterford in 1874–76, he made the trees more naturalistic, and extended their foliage so as to fill the upper parts of the lights with a dense mass of green. Like the rose-hedge, the Gothic tree backgrounds make only rare appearances after the 1870s.

One form of conventionalism which apparently did satisfy Morris was the scrolled foliage background, first used at Brown Edge, Staffordshire (*471*), and at St Philip's, Alderley Edge, Cheshire, in 1874 (*472*). The treatment is open, with innumerable small interstices of clear glass, as in the Nun Monkton, Bramley and Madeley windows, but the stems are thicker and form regular scrolls in alternating directions, instead of trailing in loose flowing curves. It is a stronger pattern, with a more obvious and powerful rhythm in its structure. It was used again in the east windows of the Gordon Chapel at Fochabers in 1877, and on many subsequent occasions, not least successfully in the great west window of 1883 at St Stephen's, Gateacre near Liverpool (*567*).

In all these developments Morris was inclining steadily towards richer effects of texture, tone and colour, even at the cost of reducing, sometimes drastically, the amount of light which a window would admit. The windows in which he employed backgrounds of dense foliage with fruit and flowers had to rely very largely for their luminosity on the brilliant tones of their figures. Something has already been said about the origins of this style of background, of which the developed form first appeared in the upper parts of the Vyner memorial window at Christ Church, Oxford, made in 1872–73 (*353*). The four main figures are all robed in white patterned with yellow-stain, and the background up to shoulder-height is of deep blue curtains; above these, a long scroll runs right across the window, and above this again is the dense foliage, which extends also throughout the tracery. The effect is certainly beautiful, and Morris was encouraged to use similar backgrounds in most of the great series of windows made for Jesus College Chapel from 1873 onwards, in the east window at Troutbeck (1873), at Marlborough College Chapel (1875), and in many other places. It had the great advantage of giving dramatic emphasis to the figures, and of enhancing by means of the deep surrounding tones the brilliant yellows, blues, reds and greens of their robes. It was in windows of this type that Morris was most eminently a colourist and ventured with an unmatched boldness, as for instance in the Marlborough window, where the two principal figures are draped entirely in very pale yellow, or in the window of Moses, Samuel, David and Solomon at Jesus College, with its rich harmony of crimson and green, grey-blue and brown, and pale blue. The Marlborough window, indeed, is so bold and effective a piece of colour that it makes all its neighbours look like faded posters.

This somewhat lengthy analysis of foliage backgrounds, however, must not overshadow entirely the other interesting developments taking place in Morris's windows at this time. A special problem arose in connection with a commission of 1872 for windows for the chapel at Castle Howard, which was being newly decorated and rearranged. The windows form part of the façade of the north wing, and their rectangular shape could consequently not be interfered with. With one exception Morris had not previously been required to furnish windows for a building of late Baroque or Palladian style,[7] and something fresh was obviously called for. In this situation it was Philip Webb who was again asked to design the general layout. His solution took the form of enclosing the main subject of each window in a square panel, framed in an elaborate feigned architectural setting which consisted of niches flanked by columns carrying imitation bronze putti, and a pedestal bearing an inscribed tablet and topped by a tiled floor seen in receding perspective. Above the main panels are a carved frieze and an attic storey with broken pediment and a circular opening containing an imitation bronze emblem of one of the evangelists. The style of this concoction, intended presumably to harmonize with Vanbrugh's architecture, is of course totally unlike Webb's own architecture, and more like the Lyons Corner House style of a generation later. The cartoons for all the main subjects, the Emblems of the Evangelists, and the 'bronze boys' (as he called them), were supplied by Burne-Jones. They are a great deal more sympathetic to a modern eye than their settings, especially the scene of the Adoration of the Magi, and the very fine emblems of which the cartoons, powerfully executed in body-colour, are in the Victoria and Albert Museum (*364–67*). They prompt the interesting speculation that, had he interested himself in sculpture, Burne-Jones might well have created fine works in that medium. At one stage it was evidently intended that the fifth window be filled with a similar composition showing the Resurrection, but for some reason this plan was not carried out, and the window was eventually filled with quarries of a rather unpleasant yellowish-green tint.

Gothic canopies and pedestals being generally out of favour, the firm found it occasionally necessary to devise alternative methods of framing the small subjects often placed below large figures in tall lights, as for instance at Speldhurst and Christ Church, Oxford. For Speldhurst in 1874 Webb designed a very simple and elegant little frame of running foliage pattern in grisaille, with an ogee-arched top (*447*). For the similar scenes at the base of the Vyner and St Cecilia windows at Christ Church, simple architectural frames with attached columns at the sides were used, but the designs in this case were not Webb's (*353*, *497–500*).

If we turn from these mere accessories to the new figure cartoons supplied by Burne-Jones during the years 1869–75, developments of great interest become apparent. In 1869, 1870 and 1874 he designed for Cheddleton, Middleton Cheney and Lytham respectively, compositions in the form of triptychs in which the pictorial tendencies we have already indicated gained new momentum. The three angels blowing long trumpets at Cheddleton are more dynamic than any of his earlier designs: the figures in the outer lights turn towards the centre, their long robes sway and flutter, and even the foliage which fills the trefoil heads of the lights seems to shoot energetically upwards (*X*). This vigour is matched by the extraordinary boldness of Morris's colour, for the figures are carried out entirely in silver-stain on white glass, varying from the palest yellow to deep orange-gold, while their wings, which almost completely fill the backgrounds, are a rich red.[8] The effect is both striking and exhilarating.

A year later Burne-Jones drew the cartoons for the Three Holy Children window at the west end of All Saints, Middleton Cheney (*322*). The figures of Shadrach, Meshach and Abednego in the three main lights are robed in green, blue and greenish-blue, and surrounded by the curling flames of the fiery furnace.[9] This again is a design of striking individuality, and Morris's colour scheme, which contrasts the cool tones of the figures with the orange-yellow of the flames, matches the linear energy of the drawing. To all intents and purposes this is one subject extending over three lights; borders and framing are eliminated in order to achieve complete integration of the parts in the overall design.

A further step in this direction was taken in 1874, when Burne-Jones designed the Transfiguration window for St Cuthbert's, Lytham (*XII*). Each of the three lights here contains a principal standing figure and a crouching apostle below, so that the whole composition comprises six figures; but it is a single scene without horizontal lines of demarcation between the sleeping figures and the standing ones, and although the figures are separated by the vertical stone mullions, the luminous pictorial space behind them seems to be continuous. In addition to the dramatic unity of the theme, the treatment of background motifs contributes to this effect. Moses, Christ and Elias stand on top of a rocky mound which extends to the full width of the window, and which provides the background behind the sleeping apostles; and above, the sky is filled with stars.[10] Unfortunately, this masterpiece is in unsatisfactory condition, some of the colour, especially in the flesh tints of the main figures, having partially peeled off;[11] but in spite of this the window is one of those rarest of phenomena in stained glass, a work of real imaginative intensity.

The Lytham Transfiguration, however, by no means represented the climax of Burne-Jones's pictorial tendency. A month or two before he entered the charge for the Transfiguration in his account-book, he had made a similar entry for the 'pen and ink design of Last Judgement' for the east window of the church of St Michael and St Mary Magdalene, Easthampstead, Berkshire (*510*), and only a month or two later, another for the design of the Rivers of Paradise window for the chancel of All Hallows, Allerton, Liverpool (*508*). The cartoons for both of these major works appear in the account-book in the month of April 1875. They are windows of very considerable size: the Easthampstead one consists of three wide, trefoil-headed main lights, with a rose above, while the Allerton window has five main lights with complicated tracery; but in each a single composition fills the entire expanse. At Easthampstead, Christ seated in judgement, robed in white and with a red halo, occupies the centre of the rose against a grey star-spangled sky. The smaller surrounding circles have half-length angels all robed in red. In the centre light stands St Michael in silver armour, with golden wings; and the angels to left and right have red wings and white robes. The souls of the dead arising from their tombs at the bottom are mostly draped in white or in pale tints of brown and yellow; and the Blessed, seated in rows at the top, are all in white, with red, gold or white haloes. This scheme of colouring, with its dominant chord of red and white against the blue sky, has a powerful simplicity which contributes magnificently to the effect of grandeur produced by the window. Indeed, translated into colour by Morris, Burne-Jones's designs achieve a monumental splendour which eluded him in his own largest paintings. This window, resulting from their intimate collaboration, surpasses by far anything which either artist could do separately, and equally surpasses what any other stained-glass artists in the nineteenth century could produce.

The Easthampstead Last Judgement stands also at a crucial point in the development of Burne-Jones's treatment of pictorial space. The composition is by no means without implications of spatial recession, produced by the contrast between the figures and the background of the sky, and by the arrangement of the row of Blessed in a receding semi-circle. But the figures in each of the three principal levels in the main lights seem to come forward so as to lie in the same pictorial plane, closely related to the actual plane of the glass. There is enough relief to avoid any undue effect of flatness, yet the relationship with the architectural setting remains secure. We have already noted that Burne-Jones possessed an unusual facility for handling complex compositions with the minimum of perspective recession, for example in his cartoons for the south transept window at Lyndhurst (*132–35*); and other instances, such as the Cleansing of Naaman and Baptism of Christ windows of 1865 at Cheddleton, show how skilled he was in the use of the raised horizon, bringing further planes into positions above instead of behind nearer ones.

Yet, for all this skill, the transition from the Easthampstead Last Judgement to the Allerton Rivers of Paradise window seems to involve a subtle shift in the wrong direction (*508*). At the top of the centre main light the Lamb of God stands on a rocky mound, from which flow four rivers like silver ribbons, spreading outwards to the lower corners of the composition. On either side, at the tops of the inner left and right lights, are the Emblems of the Four Evangelists; along the bottom of all five lights stand angels and the Blessed, looking towards the Lamb, and consequently seen from behind or in profile. There is thus a flow of movement from these foreground figures upwards and inwards to the Lamb, and a complementary downwards and outwards flow along the lines of the rivers. These rhythms possess a certain validity in terms of two-dimensional pattern, but they imply also a considerable degree of three-dimensional spatial recession, which tends to receive further emphasis from the fact that the three angels in each of the two outer lights, instead of being arranged in three distinct tiers in equal relationship to the picture plane, overlap to a certain extent. Moreover, some of the figures overlap from one light into another. In this way the architectural interrelationship of the parts is overridden by pictorial considerations, and the delicate balance between architectural setting and pictured opening is upset. If Webb's first arrangements may be criticized for having gone too far in the direction of architectural methods, Burne-Jones now reverses the position. Certainly the Allerton window marks the end of one phase and the opening of another.

Such a rather extreme instance of pictorial tendencies was still exceptional, however, and most of the windows made between 1869 and 1875 retain more sense of architectural form. This is especially true of the fine series at Holy Trinity, Meole Brace, Shropshire (1870–72), where the apse windows are divided horizontally into three tiers, with the exception of the two-tiered centre light of the middle window, containing Christ on the Cross (*317*). The Jesus College Chapel windows (1872–78) also, certainly among the best products of the period, show an admirable respect for the limitations of their architectural frames, though the attitudes and gestures of the figures, introducing strong diagonals which are particularly effective in the famous and somewhat Michelangelesque evangelists, serve to link the parts with one another. The same is true of the windows at Tavistock and Youlgreave, which incorporate repetitions of the Jesus College evangelists.

These immensely productive years, full of experiment and rich in creative enterprise, may thus be regarded in some sense as the firm's best period, Morris's own participation in the work of the studio, especially as colourist and as designer of backgrounds, was still active and intimate; Burne-Jones's powers as designer had reached maturity, and he had replaced the slightly rigid early style of composition, established under Webb's influence, with a new pictorialism which was yet restrained, with very few exceptions, by a sense of the limitations of the window as an architectural member. And the contributions of cartoons by Ford Madox Brown, as in three of the Jesus College windows, at Troutbeck, Meole Brace and elsewhere, addded an intensity and an occasional note of drama which no other designer could achieve.[12]

4
The Morris Firm: 1875-1898

In March 1875 the original partnership of Morris, Marshall, Faulkner & Co. was dissolved, and Morris bought out the others to become sole proprietor.[1] Three of the partners, Ford Madox Brown, D.G. Rossetti and P.P. Marshall, stood upon their legal rights to an equal share in the value of the business which Morris had built up, and a breach between them and Morris ensued. Madox Brown was eventually reconciled, but one result of this disagreement was that he contributed no further designs for stained glass to the firm.[2] Rossetti and Marshall had in any case long ceased to take any real part in the firm's affairs, as also had Charles Faulkner. Edward Burne-Jones and Philip Webb, on the other hand, refused to accept any payment in respect of their claims as partners, and in a circular issued by the firm on 31 March stated that they would continue to help as before with designs for stained glass and furniture.[3] In fact, however, Webb made no further contributions towards the firm's windows, though he continued for another three years to design and advise on furniture and interior decoration.[4] The task of designing for stained glass therefore devolved entirely upon Burne-Jones and Morris. Burne-Jones became in effect sole designer, for it is impossible to identify with confidence any figure designs for glass by Morris himself dating from after 1875, with the exception only of two minstrel angels of 1876 or 1877 for the tracery of the window at St Martin's, Birmingham.[5] In these years Morris was absorbed in experiments in dyeing and other matters concerning textiles, and he was also composing his epic poem *Sigurd the Volsung*, so it is unlikely that he would have been able to give more than occasional attention to the work that was going on in the stained-glass studio.[6]

On the other hand, a very substantial body of cartoons had by now accumulated, most of which could be used again, with whatever modifications and adaptations might be required;[7] and a number of valuable precedents for general arrangements and types of composition had been established, by which the studio might be guided. For the most part it continued to run on the lines already laid down. The most creative and exciting period was over. Whatever further developments of style took place depended mainly upon Burne-Jones's ideas. The pressure of work upon him was very heavy, and it is hardly surprising that the quality of his cartoons began to vary widely, as he himself was quite well aware. If we take the list of stained-glass cartoons given by Malcolm Bell as a rough guide,[8] the quantity of designs which Burne-Jones produced during the 1870s is quite astonishing, especially when it is remembered that these were also some of his most productive years as a painter — years in which he was occupied for many months with *The Mirror of Venus*, *Laus Veneris*, *Cupid and Psyche*, the *Briar Rose* cycle, the

Angels of Creation, *The Beguiling of Merlin* and other major works. Between 1872 and 1878 he made over 270 cartoons, an average of 39 per year, or one approximately every eight and a half days. Such an output would be remarkable for an artist occupied solely with designing for stained glass. In the case of Burne-Jones it implies not only fierce and sustained application, but also a well-organized studio system.

Considering how comparatively recent the period is, it is unfortunate and disappointing that the organization of Burne-Jones's studio remains an obscure subject. In her memoirs of her husband,[9] Lady Georgiana Burne-Jones scarcely referred to the matter; but various scraps of evidence from the account-books and elsewhere can be brought to bear upon it. It seems clear that from the autumn of 1874 Burne-Jones began to use photographic enlargements of his small sketch-designs as a basis for the full-size cartoons. Thus, in his account-book there is an entry on the debit side dated 30 October 1874, for 'Hollyer photo Christ in Judgement £2.2.0.' In June 1875 further entries make it plain that the same procedure was adopted with the Dorcas and Good Samaritan designs for a window at Christ Church, Southgate, the Fortitude and Prudence designs for one of the Jesus College Chapel windows, and other designs, the photographs being touched up or 'doctored' by Burne-Jones himself. Similarly with the Temperance design in 1876, again for Jesus College Chapel, and in June of the same year there is a charge of £1 for redrawing the head in a large photograph of St Helena for 'Newman's window'. A number of other charges for 'touching-up' very likely refer also to work on photographic enlargements.[10] There must, however, remain some element of doubt in this, and the many entries for 'touching-up' which are of dates earlier than the first specific mention of photographs in 1874 more probably refer to work on enlargements from his sketch-designs produced by assistants in the firm's studio.[11] If such were the procedure, one would expect to find a debit entry in Burne-Jones's account-book; but in fact such debits are very hard to identify. Quite a number of debit entries for payments in cash to various people occur during the period between 1862 and the middle seventies; some of these people, however, were insurance agents, like Edward Butler of the Reliance Assurance Company, and probably E. G. Priestley. Certainly from about 1869 onwards, a considerable proportion of Burne-Jones's net earnings from his work for the firm was paid directly in the form of premiums to various insurance companies. But Bowman and Stennett, whose names occur with some frequency in the account-book as recipients of cash, were employees of the firm, engaged on work of various kinds for Burne-Jones. In October 1865, for instance, Bowman was paid for one week and one day's work at Burne-Jones's charge; and in January 1866 Stennett was similarly paid £2.14.2 for 'work at your house'. Again in March 1866, Burne-Jones was charged 12s.3d. for 'work by Stennett', another 7s.6d. in April, when there was also an entry for £3.5.0 paid to Bowman. This was presumably the same Bowman whose name is recorded in the firm's records on innumerable occasions from 1879 to 1909 as one of the chief glass-painters in the studio, and as an occasional designer of foliage backgrounds, scrolls and other accessories for windows. Stennett's name, on the other hand, does not occur among those of the recorded glass-painters, and he was probably either a decorator or a joiner and cabinet-maker. So, the exact meaning of such references in the account-book remains doubtful: the payments to Bowman may have been for assistance with the preparation of cartoons; on the other hand, all such mentions could equally well refer to decorations in progress at Burne-Jones's house.

Not until 1879 is it possible to find any more positive evidence, and even then it is tantalizingly vague. The entry of 20 January 1879: 'Cash for C.F. Murray £5', and another dated 28 April 1879: 'Transfer from T.M. Rooke, Esq. £46.2.5', almost certainly refer to assistance given in Burne-Jones's studio, and therefore charged to his account. Charles Fairfax Murray, the most brilliant glass-painter in the firm's service, had been responsible for the painting of the Vyner memorial window at Christ Church, Oxford, in 1872–73.[12] Thomas Matthews Rooke had been an assistant to Burne-Jones before being taken on as an employee of the firm in 1869.[13] With Walter Crane, he had assisted Burne-Jones in the execution of the *Cupid and Psyche* panels for the dining-room of No. 1 Palace Green, Kensington, for the Hon. George Howard, between 1872 and 1881;[14] and in 1871–72 he was working with Frank Lathrop and others on *The Story of Troy*. According to a note by Rooke himself, 'an early cherished idea of his [Burne-Jones's] was to get much done by means of a "school" of artists and assistants he should train'.[15]

It is often tempting, in view of the wide variations in quality of actual execution from one cartoon to another, to attribute some of the inferior ones to assistants. Four cartoons which belong to the Whitworth Art Gallery, University of Manchester, provide excellent examples. The two large full-length figures of St Barnabas (or Bernard) and St David, drawn in 1873 for a window at Margam Abbey, are of superb quality, full of confidence, and stated with striking economy (*404–05*); whereas the two cartoons for scenes in small panels, representing St Paul Preaching and the Calling of Sts Peter and Andrew, done in 1875 for Coatbridge, Lanarkshire, seem so hesitant, tired and unsure that it could well be argued that they must be the work of some assistant (*501–02*). All four, however, are fully documented in the account-book, with long comments by the artist which make it quite clear that he was personally responsible, and was well aware of the differences. He admitted that the Coatbridge cartoons 'are the worst things I ever did in my whole life', while proudly describing the Margam ones as 'of colossal size and excellence — entirely priceless.' Here is an object-lesson to the art-historian who is too ready to draw conclusions from the variations of quality which he observes among works attributed to an artist! Quality alone is not a safe criterion of authorship.

Certain cartoons of the 1870s, all the same, reveal characteristics of handling which do not appear to belong to Burne-Jones himself. The outstanding examples are the set of Angels of the Hierarchy in the Birmingham City Art Gallery, designed in 1873 for the south transept window of Jesus College Chapel (*413–23*).[16] The handling of these cartoons shows a crisper and more incisive touch than is usual in Burne-Jones's works, suggesting an executant accustomed to the strict economy of means required of a glass-painter; and I suspect that the whole series of cartoons may have been carried out by Fairfax Murray, presumably from small drawings by Burne-Jones. The account-book entry neither confirms nor disproves this hypothesis: it reads simply: '10 Angels of Hierarchy. £12 ea. £120.' The same hand may be recognized in the cartoon of St James as Bishop of Jerusalem, at the Victoria and Albert Museum;[17] this was originally designed by Burne-Jones in 1862–63 for a window at Christ Church, Southgate, and redrawn with some modifications in 1870 for a window in the Chapel Royal, Savoy Hill, which no longer exists (*105*). It would be particularly interesting if we could compare the cartoon at the Victoria and Albert Museum, presumably drawn in 1870 by Fairfax Murray, with Burne-Jones's original, but this is unfortunately at present untraced. Another example by the same hand is the cartoon of Mary of Bethany, in the William Morris Gallery at Walthamstow,[18] which is an enlarged version of a figure originally designed by Morris in 1862 for the window of the Three Maries at the Sepulchre in St Michael's, Brighton, and used separately in the Bradford Cathedral east window, 1864, and at St Mary's, Edge Hill, Liverpool, in 1873 (*408*). The Walthamstow cartoon is apparently the one prepared for use at Edge Hill. It is possible that a closer study of the very considerable mass of Burne-Jones's cartoons for stained glass may yet enable the distinctive characteristics of T.M. Rooke's handling also to be recognized; but the task will be a delicate as well as a speculative one.[19]

It is not my intention to suggest that there was as yet any positive decline in the quality of Burne-Jones's figure designs. A number of factors, however, tended to bring about some loss of quality in the firm's windows: Morris's own interests were by now centred elsewhere, and his personal share in the work declined; many windows merely repeated stock designs; new designs came only from Burne-Jones, who was overworked and who employed assistants and photographic devices in the preparation of cartoons; and the dense foliage backgrounds, deeper colour, and greener quarries which had come into use produced a lowering of the general level of luminosity.

The general character of the foliage or 'treework' backgrounds, of course, followed precedents established no doubt by Morris himself; but from about 1877 onwards these details, especially in tracery lights, were often drawn by the glass-painters rather than by the artist-designers. The first mention of a glass-painter's name in this connection occurs with reference to the tracery lights of the big window in St Martin's, Birmingham, completed in March 1877, when the so-called Catalogue of Designs (see p. 103) records the name of Mr Pozzi against 'Treework, 10 Pieces in Tracery'. This may mean merely that he painted these lights, and other similar ones such as the treework and the angels' wings in the window at St Leonard's, Ribbesford, Worcestershire, also completed in March 1877, when his name is repeated. But it is difficult to imagine that Morris or Burne-Jones could have been personally involved in designing and drawing every detail of this kind that was needed, and it seems at least probable that not only Pozzi, but also other glass-painters, including Campfield, Dearle and Bowman, may have drawn the cartoons for many minor accessories from as early as about 1880. The first specific documentation of Pozzi as designer refers to the treework background of the great west window of St Stephen's, Gateacre, completed in December 1883; and in November 1884, the Catalogue of Designs records that the treework background of the apse windows for St Stephen's, Broughty Ferry (no longer there), was drawn by Bowman and Dearle, and painted by Stokes. Whenever one of the earlier figure cartoons had to be enlarged or reduced in order to fit a new destination, the redrawn copies inevitably tended to lose a little of their original quality; and seraphim for tracery lights, frequently extracted from Burne-Jones's cartoons and adapted for other uses by Bowman, Dearle or others, were especially subject to this gradual attrition. But the work of the glass-painters is a subject to which we shall return in the last chapter.

All this must not be taken to mean, nevertheless, that the firm did not continue to produce many very beautiful windows — to mention only a few, the Whatton south aisle window of 1878, with its three main figures in white and gold, against a rich foliage background, and the three specially designed small panels below (*535*); the Tadcaster east window of 1879, with its foliage grounds, white scrolls, and brilliant golden rays separating the three tiers of figures (*Frontispiece*); the Staveley east window of 1881, with its marvellous background of deep and pale blue spattered with gold, silver and red stars (*558*); the east window of 1882 at St Margaret's, Hopton-on-Sea near Yarmouth, with its intense colour and its fine Resurrection panel in the centre (*559*); the south transept window of 1877 at St Martin's, Birmingham (already mentioned), with its four tiers of minstrel angels in the tracery (*519*); the St Cecilia window of 1880 at St Catherine's, Baglan, which has some of the most beautiful colour and the most accomplished silver-stain work ever produced in English glass; and the St Catherine window of 1877–78 at Christ Church, Oxford, which has colour of a range and subtlety altogether new in the medium (*529–32*). But it would be difficult to find, even among these beautiful productions, much evidence that fresh thought was given to the fundamental principles of composition and design.

The most original windows, but not necessarily the best, of the decade following the dissolution of the original partnership, are those in which Burne-Jones's pictorial imagination was stimulated by a new subject and a fresh opportunity for grand pictorial treatment. A few examples will illustrate this phase of development. The St Mary Magdalene window of 1877 at Easthampstead occupies two lights with two closely related scenes (*523*). The figures are very large in relation to the total area of the window; and their strong movements and rather massive forms seem to impinge forcibly upon the architectural framing. Indeed, a substantial portion of the saint's figure in the left light is cut off by the edge of the window, with the result that her form seems to pass behind the mullion, giving the sensation that the pictorial space of the two scenes joins together behind this interruption. That is to say, the picture asserts its independence from the plane and setting of the architecture. It is a disturbing and rather unsatisfactory effect.

Such an error of judgement as regards spatial implications was, however, rather exceptional; and, as we shall see in due course, Burne-Jones later returned to a style of composition which respected and preserved the essential integrity of the two-dimensional surface of his windows. On the other hand, in many of his designs from the 1870s he introduced a much greater degree of movement in his figures than he generally used earlier or later. This tendency towards mobility was accompanied by a noticeable increase in the mass and bulk of his figures.

Perhaps the first cartoons to show these characteristics clearly were the three trumpet-blowing angels of 1869 for Cheddleton, with their fluttering draperies (*X*). The Hope of 1871, and the young Samuel of 1872, both for windows at Christ Church, Oxford, are other examples which show a striking degree of movement and flow of curving line (*351*). As yet, however, the forms of the figures themselves remain slender, and the movement involves principally the draperies. The effect achieved in the Four Evangelists, designed in 1873–74 for Jesus College Chapel, Cambridge, is quite different (*424 425*, *432–37*). The Botticellian linear arabesques have given place to a much more powerful, Michelangelesque manner, which is especially evident in the St Matthew: his right foot is raised on a stool, the great book is open on his knee, his whole trunk swings to the left, and his head turns over his left shoulder as he listens to the inspiration of the angel behind him. The Enoch, originally designed for Frankby in 1872, but of which the most imposing version is the one in Jesus College Chapel made in 1873–74, is in a sense a transitional work, from this point of view: the movement is still stated mainly in terms of the draperies, which wind themselves, as it were, almost in knots around the body of the prophet, yet cling so closely to the forms beneath that the final effect is almost as much one of mass as of line (*400*, *402*).

Burne-Jones's art was a highly subjective one, and his style never remained static. Even within short periods of time one finds considerable variations of method and mood. The window at Jesus College Chapel with the four Virtues of Temperance, Justice, Fortitude and Prudence, designed in 1875, seems indeed to imply a good deal of movement, especially in the swirling draperies of Temperance, but the figures themselves are passive rather than active. The four prophets Isaiah, Jeremiah, Ezekiel and Daniel, originally designed in 1875 for a window at St Eustachius, Tavistock, and repeated two years later at Jesus College, lack altogether the power of the Jesus College evangelists, their forms being almost smothered in the voluminous folds of their draperies, and their excessively small hands gesticulating rather weakly (*509*). Yet this stylistic uncertainty is splendidly resolved in the St Catherine window at Christ Church, Oxford, designed in 1876 (*529–32*). The calm and massive figure of the saint in the central light is brilliantly contrasted with the agitated activity of the flame-bearing angel on the left, and the tender passivity of the cloth-bearing angel on the right. The three tracery angel musicians, their bodies following three graceful curves, introduce a subtle and delightful variation of mood, their jubilation forming a commentary and climax to the scenes below. Perhaps the most static and massive of all Burne-Jones's figures in stained glass is the Fra Angelico at St Saviour's, Leeds, designed in 1870 (*349*);[20] but the figures of Constantine, St Helena, Queen Bertha and King Ethelbert at St Helen's, Welton, Yorkshire, designed in 1879, have something of the same calm power and immobility (*541–43*). Only a year later he designed for the east window at St Martin's, Brampton, Cumberland, the series of scroll-bearing angels which seem full of movement when one looks at each figure separately; yet they counterbalance one another so exactly that the effect of the window as a whole is one of timeless stillness (*XIII*). Such wide fluctuations of style make one wary of generalizations based only on selected and not wholly typical examples such as the Easthampstead Magdalene window (*523*).

There is another window from these years, nevertheless, which also seems unsatisfactory, though in a different way, in the relationship between the figures and the architectural setting: namely the four angels in a south choir aisle window at Salisbury Cathedral, designed in 1878. These 'colossal and sublime figures', as Burne-Jones himself called them,[21] swathed in enormous and bulky draperies, are set against a background of scrolled foliage which covers a far greater area of the lights than the figures themselves, which occupy only about one third of the great height of the window. The consequence of this arrangement is that the foliage background establishes itself in a plane only just beyond the actual surface of the glass, and the figures seem to advance forward from it in an uncomfortable and unstable relationship with the architecture, restrained only by the heavy iron tie-bars running horizontally across the window.[22] The disharmonious effect was conceivably a factor in Burne-Jones's increasing use, during the ensuing years, of designs in which he controlled the setting or backgrounds of his figures, instead of leaving them to Morris or to the glass-painters of the studio. This practice was an aspect of the growing pictorialism which came eventually to dominate a great many of Burne-Jones's later windows.

This growing pictorialism can be illustrated very well, during its early stages, in the small panels below the main figures in three windows at Christ Church Cathedral, Oxford. The four predella subjects in the Vyner window, designed in March 1872, are firmly contained within painted architectural frames; the two outer ones (Eli and Samuel, Timothy and Eunice) are very calm and static, and there is very little spatial recession in any of them, even the violent activity of David killing Goliath being ingeniously arranged so that all the principal forms lie in the immediate foreground, which is further emphasized by scrolls carrying inscriptions (*354–57*). In the St Cecilia window, designed in August 1874, the three predella scenes have painted architectural frames, though slightly more complex ones; but the inscribed scrolls have been dropped, and two of the scenes have a considerable amount of perspective recession, though this is firmly controlled and related to the picture plane (*498–500*). In the scene of the saint's martyrdom, all the chief forms again lie in a plane parallel to and not far beyond the painted surface.

A great change has come about in the three scenes of the St Catherine window, designed in 1878 (*529–32*). The architectural framing has gone; the figures occupy a much smaller proportion of the surface; space and depth of recession are developed to such an extent that the sense of the continuity of the actual glass surface no longer seems significant. These are still brilliant designs, and effective illustrations of the saintly legend, but they are paintings that happen to be executed on glass, rather than works of an artist whose conceptions are dominated by consideration for the medium in which they are to be expressed.

When carried to its logical conclusion, this pictorial tendency was to result in multi-light windows containing what is to all intents and purposes a single picture, with a unified pictorial space overriding the boundaries between the lights. So long as the studio continued to use abstract and space-denying backgrounds, whether of quarries, foliage or other types of pattern-work, Burne-Jones's pictorialism was held within strict limits. In a number of windows dating from the 1880s, this limitation and control was removed. The clearest examples are the series of three-light windows at All Hallows, Allerton, Liverpool. The first of these, the Ascension window of 1882, utilized the angels with scrolls and the figure of Christ Ascending originally designed in 1874 for All Saints, Ruskington, Lincolnshire, where they were placed against backgrounds of quarries (*473*). At Allerton, however, they have a background of landscape, and the tracery lights, with the Holy Trinity at the top, continue the sky and cloud motif of this landscape, so that the entire window has become virtually one scene (*577*). The three figures of the main lights, in this case, still retain a certain independence in the sense that there is no dramatic relationship between them. In the next window of the series, the Annunciation to the Shepherds, designed in 1883, Burne-Jones went further: the two shepherds standing in the side lights look up diagonally at the angel in the top of the centre light, while the angels in the tops of the side lights look downwards across the scene (*578*). The absence of any figure in the lower part of the centre light reinforces this effect of diagonal links from corner to corner of the composition. It is an adventurous and perhaps somewhat experimental scheme, and the artist noted in his account-book that he had 'certain qualms about' it.[23] In two of the three windows added to the series in 1885, the Resurrection and Crucifixion, he returned to the use of a central figure. The Crucifixion is the more formal and abstract design of the two, with the three principal figures all placed at roughly the same distance beyond the picture plane and a band of lettering running right across, above a 'crazy-paving' system of plain colour (*581*). In the Resurrection window, the perspective of the sepulchre which runs across all three lights, the over-arching rocky cavern, and the placement of the figure of Christ appreciably further back in space than the two soldiers in the lateral lights, give the effect a more pictorial character (*579*). The third window of this year, representing the Feast in the House of Simon, again omits any central figure: St Mary Magdalene stands in the foreground of the left light, looking towards Christ, who is seated further back in the right light; the centre light has only two incomplete minor figures seated beyond the table which runs across the entire scene (*580*). The stone mullions dividing the window into three panels are virtually ignored — the pictorial space is continuous behind them.

The three windows of 1886 do not repeat this rather extreme method, but each uses a centrally placed principal figure, allowing the side lights a degree of compositional self-sufficiency. It is clear, too, that Burne-Jones was well aware of the dangers of excessive pictorialism: for example, the landscape setting of the Baptism of Christ is treated with a highly abstract pattern of flowing lines, so as to eliminate any steep recession in the surface of the water (*583*). Similarly, in the windows of the Nativity and Christ among the Doctors in the Temple, the spatial recession is controlled and reduced by the use of architectural background or abstract pattern (*582*, *584*). But the general principle of pictorialism had been established.

It is possible that this stylistic development was to some extent associated with several important commissions for windows in what may be called, in a rather loose sense, Palladian churches. Such windows, being without Gothic mullions and tracery, offered large continuous expanses of glass, for which a highly pictorial style would be appropriate. One of the first orders of this kind, for the east window of St Peter's, Vere Street, Marylebone — or Saints Marshall and Snelgrove, as Burne-Jones irreverently dubbed it[24] — did not produce a very interesting solution (*557*). This design of 1880 has a rectangular panel in each of the three lights, surrounded by wide areas of rather fussy quarries. The next opportunity was seized with more imagination. This was the south chapel east window for Trinity Church, Boston, Massachusetts — a famous and remarkable building by Henry Hobson Richardson, in neo-Romanesque style,[25] but providing a large, almost square opening similar in character to those in Palladian churches. Burne-Jones's design of 1882 fills this opening with a single composition on the theme of David instructing Solomon in the Building of the Temple (*563*). The glass is without any architectural framing, even without any kind of border. The artist himself noted in his account-book: 'This work may be said to represent the culmination of my power'[26] and indeed this complex subject, containing scores of figures, is handled with masterly skill, ingenuity and respect for the special requirements of the medium. The figures of Solomon and David, on a raised dais or throne of octagonal plan, occupy two of the nine squares into which the whole composition is divided by the iron saddle- and tie-bars. The perspective of the throne is tipped up, as it were, so as to bring these figures into the forward plane; and they are on the same scale as the scribes, secretaries or architects who occupy the centre foreground below them. At the sides, the rows of old men, women and warriors rise up steeply one above the other, without perspective diminution, and without indication of intervening space; the angels in the top corners, who are logically understood to be in a distant plane behind the entire structure of the throne, appear as if immediately above the heads of the foreground figures. This is the sort of compositional system used in the fifteenth century by such artists as Fra Angelico and Filippo Lippi, but not fully understood by critics or intellectually analysed until recent times. It seems likely that Burne-Jones's scheme was derived in fact from his studies of Florentine quattrocento art, and in particular from compositions of the Coronation of the Virgin.[27]

In 1883, when he designed the south aisle window of St Peter's, Vere Street, he used a different sort of scheme altogether (*572*). The long procession of Christ's Entry into Jerusalem approaches from the distance in the top right corner; Christ himself is near the foreground, moving towards the left where a crowd awaits him, up to the gate of the city, guarded by Roman soldiers, in the top left corner. Perspective depth is not entirely denied but is reduced to a minimum, and the most distant figures are still about half the size of the nearest ones in the foreground. It is a remarkable composition, in which this amount of spatial depth seems acceptable and does not appreciably disrupt the sense of the planar continuity of the glass, probably because the height of the panel would in any case involve some unavoidable diminution in the apparent size of the upper figures. But the border of vines which surrounds this subject is surely a mistake: it would have been better either to make the subject fill the entire space of the opening, or to surround it with an architectural framework. When Burne-Jones, in his half-jocular way, described his cartoon as 'another masterpiece',[28] he was in a sense justified, but it is a masterpiece of ingenuity and the adaptation of art-historical learning, rather than one of design for stained glass. His source was most probably Benozzo Gozzoli's Journey of the Magi in the chapel of the Palazzo Medici-Riccardi, Florence; but he was perhaps forgetting that what is appropriate in a large fresco painted upon a wall is not necessarily suitable in a stained-glass window. It is certainly possible to prefer the simpler, earlier schemes of composition, based more upon mediaeval models — for instance, that of the Song of Solomon window at Darley Dale (*107*).

The climax of Burne-Jones's pictorialism was reached in the four great windows made for the cathedral (then St Philip's church) at Birmingham. The earliest was the chancel east window, representing the Ascension of Christ, designed in 1884 and completed in the following year (*XV*). According to Burne-Jones's note in his account-book, it was on a visit to the church in 1885 that he was 'so struck with admiration at [his] own work' that 'in a moment of enthusiasm' he undertook to fill the windows on either side also.[29] These, however, representing the Nativity and Crucifixion, were not actually designed until 1887 and were completed in June 1888 (*599*, *600*). The fourth window, of the Last Judgement at the west end, was designed in sketch form in 1889 and completed in 1897. These windows, especially the three in the chancel apse, were considered by both Morris and Burne-Jones as their greatest achievement in stained glass, and most writers on the subject have been content to follow this opinion.[30] It is not a view, however, which I feel able to accept; and consequently it is necessary to argue for a quite different estimate of their quality.

The windows' most obvious fault is their lack of luminosity and transparency. The whole effect of Thomas Archer's masterpiece of English ecclesiastical Baroque, with which J.A. Chatwin's enlarged eastern apse of 1883–84 blends sympathetically, depends on the clarity and even diffusion of light within it; otherwise, the logic and elegance of its proportions, and the simple geometry of its volumes of enclosed space, can hardly be realized. But at St Philip's, the chancel is plunged into darkness, which makes an unpleasantly sharp contrast with the brightly lit nave. This darkness is due partly to the colour scheme — red and deep blue being the predominant hues, with smaller areas of white and pink. There is very little gold, used only as diaper patterns on the white robes of the figures. The flesh tints are very dark, and there is no clear glass, no borders or quarries, and hardly any appreciable portion of sky even left clear of detail. In spite of what Sir Nikolaus Pevsner has appreciatively called the 'taut and dramatic' quality of the designs, and the 'vibrant and exciting' colour,[31] the windows destroy the architectural unity of the interior. Morris's probable view that the architecture was a monstrosity and not worth consideration in no way lessens the offence.

Another flaw in the relationship between the windows and the architecture is more elusive of definition. The style of the building demands not only that the windows should admit a generous amount of light, but also that they should appear as spaces in contrast to the solid forms of the arches which frame them. This demand is certainly not met. The large figures filling the windows, even to the tops, lead to a sense of top-heaviness, of crowding, and of overactivity; and the placing of all these figures within a single plane, without any appreciable degree of recession, converts the windows, in their architectural function, from spaces into solids. The weight and density of the glass even makes the white interior of the building look flimsy and insubstantial.

One further objection should be raised: namely, that the effect of the windows is somewhat restless. This applies less to the Ascension than to the other subjects, but Pevsner describes the effect graphically when he writes that the apse windows 'shout triumphantly from behind the altar'.[32] There could hardly be an effect less appropriate to the lucid calm of Archer's architectural style. The very considerable amount of internal movement, and the energetic flow of line within each subject, prove disturbing despite the breadth of the treatment and the massing of the forms into basically simple and almost geometrical outlines.

The conclusion to which all these considerations lead is that Morris and Burne-Jones lacked the sympathy for the essential requirements of windows for Baroque and Palladian buildings, which they so surely possessed for the Gothic. It was, indeed, paradoxical that Morris should accept commissions for windows in churches whose style he detested, while at the same time feeling obliged to refuse commissions for windows in mediaeval churches, which he loved. This crisis of conscience arose from his participation in the newly founded Society for the Protection of Ancient Buildings (1877), or 'Anti-scrape' as it was familiarly known.[33] His bitter opposition to the current practice of so-called restoration of ancient churches, which only too often involved an almost complete rebuilding or resurfacing of the structure, obliged him to reconsider his whole position when there was any question of supplying windows for old churches. Very delicate problems were involved. Commissions for windows had frequently arisen out of restorations drastically carried out by Street, Scott and other architects. Acceptance of such commissions might be seen to imply his approval of the restorations. Even when complete restorations had not been undertaken, a commission for a new window in a mediaeval church would often necessitate the renewal of stone mullions and tracery. After giving the matter very careful thought, Morris issued a circular in which he explained that 'we are prepared as heretofore to give estimates for windows in churches and other buildings, *except in the case of such as can be considered monuments of Ancient Art*, the glazing of which we cannot conscientiously undertake, as our doing so would seem to sanction the disastrous practice of so-called Restoration.'[34] The point was that Morris would never consent to make an imitation mediaeval window; on the other hand, the insertion of a window of modern style in a mediaeval church would inevitably compromise and falsify to some extent the precious integrity of the art of the past. As he wrote in connection with a proposal to erect a new reredos in the church at Stratford-on-Avon, 'Will not every fresh piece of modern work make "the old place" . . . look less old and more like a nineteenth century mediaeval furniture-dealer's warehouse?'[35]

Fortunately, in time the decision not to supply windows to mediaeval churches was somewhat relaxed. Not only did Morris make a few exceptions, apparently, in the case of churches to which he had already supplied windows, such as Middleton Cheney, but he appears to have been ready to work in old churches, provided they did not qualify as 'monuments of Ancient Art'. Thus, while he turned down a commission for windows in Westminster Abbey, he was willing to supply windows for St Mary's, Dundee, and for such parish churches as those of Whalley, Cromer and Ilkley. Eighteenth-century churches such as St Peter's, Vere Street, and St Philip's, Birmingham, he did not consider to be 'monuments of Ancient Art'. The decision must have been a bitter one for Morris, since it meant that he felt himself free to accept commissions only for modern buildings or inferior old ones, but never for those he loved best. Undoubtedly, his conscientious gesture deprived him of a great many of the most challenging and lucrative commissions; yet his attitude can have had little effect on the general situation, except that commissions went instead to designers less sensitive than he would have been to the requirements of mediaeval buildings. The consequences of his decision included the abrupt termination of the great series of windows which he had been making for Jesus College Chapel; they were resumed only about 1920, when the designs used were mere repetitions of Burne-Jones's cartoons originally prepared for Allerton thirty-five years earlier. That the firm's stained-glass studio was deprived of the challenge offered by the architectural masterpieces of mediaeval times may well have contributed to the decline which seems to have overtaken many of its productions in the last years of Morris's and Burne-Jones's lives.

Nevertheless, a number of important and extensive schemes of glazing date from the 1890s, and Burne-Jones continued to produce many new cartoons right up to 1898, the year of his death. The great majority of these, however, were for single figures; and with comparatively few exceptions — among which the most important are the already-discussed Last Judgement for St Philip's, Birmingham, and the Nativity for the west window of St Deiniol's, Hawarden, Flintshire, designed in 1898 (*636*, *637*) — the windows of this last period tended to be assemblages of individual figures rather than large-scale pictorial designs. The most striking and extreme instance of this reversal of the earlier tendency occurs in the enormous east window of J. D. Sedding's great church of the Holy Trinity, Sloane Street, Chelsea, built in 1889–90. This window, it must be admitted, posed a problem that was perhaps incapable of real solution (*628*). The twelve main lights, grouped in three sets of four, would have permitted a design comprising three large main subjects, each extending over four lights, or alternatively, had the lights also been divided horizontally, comprising six principal subjects. Similarly, the complex decorated tracery, with well over one hundred openings, readily groups itself into six major areas. Had it been designed in this way, the window might have assumed the primary importance in the interior effect which the architect doubtless expected. This remarkable opportunity was lost. The main lights are occupied by a monotonous array of forty-eight single figures in four tiers, while the tracery contains seven principal subjects and a multiplicity of small angels and seraph heads which are practically impossible to distinguish when seen from the floor of the church. One cannot resist the feeling that had Morris himself been as interested and as active in the work of his stained-glass studio in the 1890s as he was in the 1860s, the result at Sloane Street would have been very different.[36]

The three large windows in Albion Congregational church, Ashton-under-Lyne, are in some ways much better. For one thing, their scale is not so preposterous. The earliest is the chancel east window of 1893, consisting of fourteen main lights arranged in two tiers separated by stone transoms, and a large expanse of beautiful decorated tracery which does credit to the architect, John Brooke (*624*). None of the figures was specially designed — all, in fact, are from old Burne-Jones cartoons — but unity is effectively established, chiefly by two devices: firstly, the use of broad borders of formalized creeper round all the main lights, and secondly, the employment of a background of sky with clouds, moon and stars throughout the tracery. The way in which the main figures in many places overlap the borders imparts life and activity to the whole.

The north and south transept windows, designed respectively in 1892 and 1895, and made in 1895 and 1896, are smaller, with only ten main lights each, similarly arranged in two tiers (*625*). For both, Burne-Jones designed all the main figures and the series of angels in the tracery; but the result is decidedly less vigorous than the east window. There are no borders, and all the main figures stand immobile against backgrounds of draped curtains, producing a curious aquarium-like stillness.

The style of Burne-Jones's last figure designs for windows, exemplified by the twenty main figures for Albion church, and others for Rottingdean church, Whitelands College, and elsewhere, is distinctly different from that of his best period. The figures are very tall, with small heads and hands, and they stand in calm, relaxed and dreamy attitudes. Their draperies fall in long straight folds, with rather angular ridges. The St Mary Virgin and the Archangel Raphael at Rottingdean (*618*, *620*), the St Lucia and St Barbara at Whitelands College (*607*, *608*), and the Ruth, Samuel, David and Isaiah at Ashton-under-Lyne, which typify this style, lack altogether the energy of such earlier figures as the Jesus College evangelists; they look tired, anaemic and occasionally sexless.

One of the most successful series of windows made from Burne-Jones's designs in the 1890s is at Manchester College Chapel, Oxford, where inscribed scrolls and foliage backgrounds help to unify the scheme (*629*). Few of these figures are new designs, however, and the most interesting of them, the series of six Days of Creation, had been designed originally in 1870 for a window at Middleton Cheney,[37] and subsequently enlarged and elaborated in the splendid series of paintings now in the Fogg Art Museum, Harvard.[38] These paintings of 1876 are among the artist's best works, and perhaps his most personal and original contribution to the iconography of Christian art.

If the view here offered of Burne-Jones's late works in stained glass is correct, the decline in vitality may perhaps reflect the shifting of his interests away from this medium, into which he had poured a copious stream of creative energy for more than thirty years. It should be recollected that his five immense designs for the mosaics in the apse of the American church in Rome were prepared in 1883–87, and the tapestries of the Adoration of the Magi, the Quest of the San Grael (comprising seven subjects), and the Passing of Venus were all designed between 1887 and 1898. In addition, the great increase in his reputation and international renown which resulted from his exhibitions at the Grosvenor Gallery, the New Gallery and elsewhere, and from the gold medals and other honours conferred upon him by foreign academies,[39] led him to concentrate his efforts to a great extent on his paintings. With the exception of the Nativity for Hawarden, his last design for stained glass, which concerned him so much that he went several times to Merton Abbey while it was being made,[40] his work for stained glass in his last years no longer occupied a principal position in his creative output.

5
Designers of Stained Glass for the Morris Firm

The previous three chapters have dealt at some length with Edward Burne-Jones's designs for stained glass at various periods of his career; and the principles of design and arrangement employed by Philip Webb in some of the firm's early windows have been explained. But so far little comment has been devoted to the contributions of other designers to the firm's windows. These will now be briefly reviewed.

WILLIAM MORRIS

Morris's own share in the work of designing for windows has generally been much misunderstood and underestimated. The misconception is primarily due to a passage in Mackail's *Life:*

> He seldom at any time, and never in more recent years, made complete designs for windows himself. From the first, the figure-subjects were mainly supplied by those of his colleagues who were professional painters. As time went on, they came almost exclusively from the studio of Burne-Jones, who supplied no cartoons for glass except to the firm. But backgrounds and foliage were, as a rule, of Morris's designing, the animals and certain kinds of ornament being often drawn by Webb.[1]

As a highly condensed summary of the practices of the stained-glass studio through a period of some thirty-five years, this is fair enough. The trouble is that the degree and nature of Morris's participation in the work of the studio changed a great deal from one period to another. It is especially the single word 'seldom' to which too much force has been allowed. Mackail's statement would hardly lead one to expect what other evidence conclusively demonstrates; and it is therefore not surprising that for a long time the impression prevailed that Morris's work as a figure designer was confined to his contributions to the Oxford Union 'frescoes', the angels on the ceiling of Jesus College Chapel, one or two cartoons for embroidery, a few painted panels on furniture, and one oil-painting.

The evidence which points to quite a different conclusion consists, in the first place, of a body of surviving cartoons, drawings and sketch-books, and in the second, of documents. This evidence is adduced in detail at the appropriate points in the catalogue of windows which will form the second volume of this work; all that is possible here is a general indication of its nature. Regarding cartoons, a number of museums possess examples attributed to Morris on the basis of information deriving from excellent sources at the time of their acquisition. For instance, the cartoon for the Ascension, drawn about 1861, for the window in All Saints, Selsley, was presented to the Birmingham City Art Gallery in 1904 by Charles Fairfax Murray (*51*);[2] others were acquired from Morris & Co. at the time of its closure in 1940, by the William Morris Gallery, Walthamstow, the Victoria and Albert Museum, and other institutions. These attributions are, with one or two exceptions only, borne out by the style of the designs themselves, which is recognizably different from the work of D. G. Rossetti, Burne-Jones, Ford Madox Brown and the other artists who designed glass for the firm during Morris's lifetime. Two of Morris's sketch-books, now in the British Museum, contain a number of studies connected with stained glass, among them some relating to the Selsley Ascension, and to the Marriage Feast at Cana, in St Peter's, Cranborne, Berkshire. Also, a substantial body of drapery studies for figures in stained glass exists in the collection belonging to Mr Sanford Berger in California, and previously in the possession of J. Henry Dearle, Morris's pupil and later manager of the stained-glass department of the firm.

Even this body of evidence, however, hardly prepares one for the surprise that must result from the study of the documents. The firm's Minute-Book, containing the records of the partners' meetings from 1861 to 1875, provides details of a few early subjects assigned to Morris; but the most comprehensive of the surviving documents, the so-called Catalogue of Designs in Mr Sanford Berger's collection, is disappointing in its lack of detail about the authorship of designs. The most fruitful documents from this point of view are the manuscript volumes of notes and indexes compiled by H. C. Marillier, the last managing director of the firm, which now belong to the Birmingham City Art Gallery, together with the Window-Books, which seem to have been the albums of photographs of windows and cartoons kept in the firm's London showrooms to be shown to prospective customers, now also at Birmingham.[3] Marillier's attempt at an alphabetical index of stained-glass cartoons arranged by subject gives the clearest indication of the situation.[4] It attributes to Morris himself no fewer than 129 cartoons, not counting a few which were in fact by Webb, as can be shown from the latter's account-book with the firm covering the years 1861 to 1878, now in the possession of Mr John Brandon-Jones.[5] A large proportion of this number consists, it is true, of small minstrel angels for tracery lights, but there is also a considerable number of designs for large figures, as well as compositions of several figures. Single figure subjects include St Catherine, St Cecilia, Jacob, St James the Greater, Joseph, St Luke, Martha, several St Mary Magdalenes, two Ruths, St Thomas, Zacharias and others.

Compositions include the Annunciation, the Ascension, the Marriage Feast at Cana, the Last Supper, St Paul Preaching, the Presentation in the Temple, and several scenes from the set of designs illustrating the Story of Tristram and Isoude, made for Walter Dunlop of Harden Grange near Bingley, Yorkshire, and now in the Bradford City Art Gallery. On the basis of these attributions, which provide a secure basis for an understanding of Morris's style as a designer of figures and draperies, further designs may be assigned to him with some confidence, bringing the total number of his cartoons for stained glass to about 150. This certainly throws a totally new light on Morris's activity as a figure artist. There is, moreover, every reason to attribute to him most of the designs for quarries used as surrounds or backgrounds in windows,[6] as well as almost all of the foliage and other patterns often used in backgrounds in windows, down at least to the later 1870s. Even when all due allowance has been made for Webb's contributions of pattern-work, borders, canopies and pedestals, heraldic designs, Emblems of the Evangelists, Banners of the Tribes of Israel, and so forth, it seems that Morris in the early years must also have designed large numbers of scrolls, borders and inscriptions. Most important of all, of course, was his responsibility for the colouring and interpretation of the designs, which, as all the evidence emphatically indicates, came under his personal direction.[7] This amounts, it must be said, to a well-nigh incredible addition to the activities of a man whose life, quite apart from this field of work, was filled with more creative production than most busy artists could achieve in a dozen lifetimes; but with Morris normal measures of what is credible simply seem inapplicable.

The vast majority of Morris's designs of figures and figure compositions for windows belongs to the early years of the firm, from 1861 to about 1868, and they ceased altogether by about 1873 at the latest, though repetitions of some of them continued to be produced long afterwards. The earliest cartoons reveal clearly both the quality of his pictorial imagination and his lack of experience and facility in drawing the human figure. The Selsley Ascension cartoon at Birmingham (*51*), or the St Paul Preaching, for the same church, at Walthamstow (*37*),[8] both of which were done in 1861, are characteristic. The Ascension is, indeed, particularly interesting as an example of the way in which Morris's designs are so often based upon his studies of historic material. The kneeling figures in the lower part of the subject are based upon miniatures in the fourteenth-century illuminated manuscript, Queen Mary's Psalter; and these are combined with the conventional representation of the ascending Christ by his feet only, the rest of his figure, as it were, having already passed out of the picture at the top, which he took from some other source.[9] The scene has a certain gawky expressiveness, but the forms beneath the robes are not well realized, the draperies themselves are awkward, and there is a lack of spatial clarity. It is interesting to compare this with another rather similar cartoon of the same subject, drawn in 1865–66 for a window at St Olave's, Gatcombe, Isle of Wight (*256*).[10] The progress which Morris had made is very evident: the introduction of the hill in the background, in spite of its conventionalism, brings a more spatial effect to the composition, which is clarified also by the separation of the rays surrounding the ascending Christ from the haloes of the kneeling figures. These figures, too, are much more elegantly draped, without losing their expressiveness.

Morris improved rapidly in his ability to design draperies; and by the middle 1860s his figures had acquired more relaxed and easy postures. But always, in his early figure designs, he tended to use draperies as a means of avoiding the drawing of the figure itself. It is significant that whereas Burne-Jones nearly always made nude studies for his figures before draping them, no nude studies by Morris are known.[11] The most elaborate and ambitious of his figure compositions is perhaps the Presentation in the Temple, in two separate panels, designed about 1863 for a window in St Chad's, Bishop's Tachbrook, and repeated on a smaller scale later elsewhere (*144*, *145*).[12] One cannot help noticing that although there are altogether nine figures, only eight hands are actually revealed, the rest being concealed under draperies or behind the nearer figures.

One of the best of Morris's multifigure designs is the Three Maries at the Sepulchre, designed in 1862 for a window at St Michael's, Brighton (*V*).[13] There is some awkwardness in the placing of the lead-lines, and in the uncertain relationship of the angel's figure to the tomb on which he is supposedly sitting; but the draperies are certainly more graceful than those of the Presentation scene. Moreover, the grouping of the three Maries in the right-hand panel, leaving plenty of space around the angel in the left light, makes this the most dramatically effective of his compositions. The colour scheme of this window is characteristic of Morris at his best and most personal; the deep blues, greens and rubies of which he was so fond gain most of their effect by contrast with the broad areas of white and pale gold.

Though Morris, of course, had an exceptional gift for two-dimensional design, he never attained real ease in spatial compositions. His style always maintained a strong sense of the continuity of the actual pictorial plane; for instance, his Annunciation window of 1862 at St Michael's, Brighton, insists even emphatically upon the principle of flatness, but without subjecting this to any strain he developed a rich surface patterning which is highly decorative as well as entirely personal (*62*). Below this Annunciation, Morris used a similar rich patterning in the four archangels, of which two are from his cartoons, and two from designs by Ford Madox Brown. Morris's cartoon for the Archangel Gabriel, in the Tate Gallery, looks in black and white rather too densely covered with diaper and other patterns; but as carried out in yellow-stain on white glass, with small contrasting areas of deep ruby and green, these diapers are largely responsible for the brilliant luminosity which makes this window memorable (*59*).

Morris's early designs for single figures on a large scale are often decidedly awkward. In the St John the Baptist of 1863 at All Saints, Banstead, for instance, he seems to have been aiming at an expressive attitude; but the drawing is coarse, and the quality of line harsh. The imperfections of the drawing have resulted in the saint's looking uncomfortably flat-footed (*139*). At about this time, Morris must have set himself to make some systematic studies of drapery, and as early as the St Barnabas which he designed for the Bradford Cathedral east window about 1863, the fruits of these studies begin to be apparent (*193*). The figure is wrapped in a voluminous cloak, which passes loosely round his shoulder and left arm, and creates a number of small folds before falling in a great sweep to the ground. The silhouette of the figure against the background, however, is still a little stiff.[14]

All traces of this stiffness have disappeared in what must be regarded as the finest of all Morris's male figures, the St Paul which he designed in 1864 for a window, no longer existing, at St Giles, Camberwell. Fortunately, the splendid cartoon is preserved at the William Morris Gallery, Walthamstow (*165*).[15] Clearly, Morris had been studying French Gothic sculpture, well known to him from his visits to Rouen, Mantes, and elsewhere. His St Paul is not a literal copy, I think, of any mediaeval original; but a comparison with the famous Beau Dieu in the North Porch at Reims leaves no doubt of the source of his inspiration. This St Paul is a really superb piece of drapery design, with a broad, eloquent rhythm, and an admirable variety of folds cleverly used to aid the effect of recession around the sides of the figure.

Something of this sculptural character is present also in St Paul's companion figure for Camberwell, the St John the Baptist, the cartoon for which is likewise at Walthamstow (*166*).[16] His cloak, falling in a great loop between his two raised hands, again probably derives from French Gothic sculpture, perhaps from the St Laumer(?) in the south porch at Chartres, or some similar figure. Another particularly fine figure was probably drawn also about 1864, when Morris's feeling for this sculptural style was at its height: the design of which the cartoon is also in the William Morris Gallery, where it is called mistakenly King Arthur (*162*).[17] This was probably designed originally as Josiah for an undated window in St Stephen's, Guernsey, and later used as King Alfred in a window of 1868 at St Mary's, Bloxham.

Morris never achieved an equivalent success in his female figures. The early Mary of Bethany, designed for a window at Scarborough, has a charming simplicity and modesty, but the outline suffers from that stiffness which we have already noticed. In the cartoon of Eve and the Virgin, drawn in 1864 for a panel in the east window at Middleton Cheney, Morris was perhaps attempting to produce something of the sculpturesque effect of his St Paul; the figures have dignity, and the draperies fall with a pleasing rhythm, but the figure of the Virgin especially is a little too much like a bas-relief, and one is not altogether convinced that she has a further side (*234*, *238*).[18] The most satisfying of his female figures are the Seasons, of which there is an attractive set in glass in the Birmingham City Art Gallery, and others at Oakwood Hall, Bingley, and in the dining-room of Lord Armstrong's house at Cragside, Rothbury, Northumberland (*271–74*, *459*, *460*). Winter, in her heavy fur-lined gown, is especially good. Again, the inspiration seems to have come from French — probably Burgundian — sculpture, but of a later period, about 1400.[19]

None of Morris's figures ever proved so popular with the firm's clients as certain of Burne-Jones's, which were used almost forty times.[20] Probably the most popular was the series of six minstrel angels drawn originally about 1867 or 1868, probably for the chancel south window at St John the Baptist, Tuebrook, Liverpool, and repeated many times elsewhere in various colours, against different backgrounds, and on varying scales, sometimes with wings, sometimes without (*276*). In these figures Morris managed to suggest enough movement to make them seem alive, without producing a disturbing degree of activity, and just the right amount of sculptural relief to liberate them from their backgrounds, without endangering the unity of the whole composition.

Next to small angels and minstrel figures, the most frequently repeated of Morris's single figures was the St Peter designed in the first place for Middleton Cheney in 1865 and used over a dozen times elsewhere (*233*). This may be significant, for all his figures have a certain strength, weight and stiff dignity appropriate in this particular subject, which distinguishes them from Madox Brown's more dramatic, and Burne-Jones's more elegant designs. Had Morris continued to design figures for stained glass, he very likely would have steadily acquired a more easy and graceful style. As it was, however, the best of his figures hold their own when placed beside Burne-Jones's and Madox Brown's, as can be seen, for instance, in the very interesting series of windows in All Saints, Coddington, Nottinghamshire (*220*). Nevertheless, it would be impossible for the most ardent of Morris's admirers to claim that he brought to the designing of figures any gifts which his colleagues and friends did not possess more abundantly, and it was presumably his realization of this fact, as much as the pressure of other interests, which induced him to give up designing figures for windows. His familiarity with the processes of the workshop, however, as well as his genius for exploiting the technical possibilities of whatever medium he worked in, opened up for him new potentialities in pattern-work which could be applied to the enrichment of figures, whether his own or those of others.

Possibly the most interesting, and certainly the most distinctive, of all Morris's own contributions as designer to the work of the stained-glass workshop were the various kinds of pattern-work and backgrounds. These, indeed, influenced in a fundamental way the whole style and appearance of the windows made at certain periods. We have already described and analysed the different kinds of foliage backgrounds, of which he probably provided the prototypes; but there are still further types of backgrounds and pattern-work which were very likely due to his designs. The background of ripe corn and trees behind his figures of Ruth and Boaz, probably designed for use at Scarborough about 1863, and repeated a few years later at Cheddleton, must surely be from Morris's own design (*288*). The cloud, wave and shell patterns, sometimes interspersed with stars or scrolls, which can be seen at St John's, Dalton near Thirsk, Yorkshire (ca. 1868), in the chancel south window at St John the Baptist, Tuebrook, Liverpool (ca. 1868), and at St Michael's, Tilehurst, Berkshire (1869; *303*, *304*), can confidently be attributed to him, since the early examples are found in windows for which he supplied all the figure cartoons. A number of designs for quarries, and perhaps also for borders, as well as the abstract scroll-work of which one of the most beautiful examples is the background of the archangels window of about 1869 at King's Walden, Hertfordshire, were also most probably his responsibility (*IX*).

In chapter 3 it was suggested that Burne-Jones may have been the one who first devised the kind of open foliage design so widely used from the early 1870s onwards, in his cartoons of Absalom for Knotty Ash, and Adam for Frankby. Indeed, Burne-Jones had introduced foliage backgrounds of a rather simpler kind, consisting of tall palm leaves, in designs for windows at Lyndhurst (1862) and for St John the Evangelist, Torquay (1865). But Morris too saw the possibilities of developing foliage backgrounds on a more extensive principle, and apparently began himself to design foliage backgrounds early in the 1870s, at the same time that he was working on his early wallpaper patterns, the Jasmine, Scroll, Vine, Tulip and Willow, and Rose patterns. The scrolled and intertwined vines of the window at Brown Edge, and the strange, rather Celtic-looking scrolled foliage of the backgrounds and borders of the window at St Philip's, Alderley Edge, both of 1874, belong to this period (*471*, *472*). The willow-foliage background at Bramley (1875; *505–07*), and the more densely packed rich foliage grounds at Tadcaster (1879; *Frontispiece*) are closely related to the wallpaper designs which Morris designed in the years 1872–77. Stained-glass windows, however, do not provide examples of backgrounds of a character similar to that of Morris's later designs for textiles and wallpapers.[21] The formalism which was typical of his chintzes in the years 1876–83 was not very suitable for the large surfaces of stained-glass windows; and the only example where something of this kind was attempted is the window at All Saints, Harrow Weald (1883), with its tufts of daisies growing in the clefts of a wall (*568*). The diagonal structure of Morris's later wallpaper and chintz designs of 1883–90, and the swaying vertical lines of his last wallpapers of 1890–96, are not reflected in backgrounds for windows, which continued to use the types established in the 1870s. These naturalistic foliage grounds provide, indeed, one of the most easily recognizable features of later Morris windows; and in general the paler, more open types with prominent stems running in long continuous curves tended to give way, especially after about 1883, to the denser type, though there are exceptions. Thus, while the comparison between the backgrounds to windows and Morris's designs for wallpapers and textiles does not reveal any close or exact correspondence either of types or of development, it tends on the whole to confirm the idea that all the principal types of foliage backgrounds used in windows were established in the first place by designs from Morris's own hand.

Almost every example of these backgrounds for windows — and there are hundreds of them — must, of course, have been individually and separately drawn. If Morris had undertaken all this work personally, he could have had no time for anything else. The many variations, adaptations and repetitions must have been produced by assistants in the studio, and we have ample documentary evidence of this from 1881 onwards, which will be more fully discussed later. In the same way, when one finds an exceptional background like the draperies unevenly hung from rods over the heads of the figures in the St Nicholas window at St Helen's, Welton, Yorkshire, made in 1882, it is reasonable to assume that it was either actually designed or at least suggested by Morris himself (*561*).

In a number of the firm's later windows we find an increasing use of architectural and landscape backgrounds, the early examples of which occur in cartoons by Burne-Jones;

but these types of background also were often drawn by members of the glass-painting studio, especially by J.H. Dearle and W.H. Knight. In repetitions of many of Burne-Jones's figures, the original backgrounds were replaced by landscapes; but this development dated mostly from the period after Morris's death, and the introduction of such a degree of spatial recession as a landscape background implies was, in general, contrary to his conception of style appropriate to the medium of stained glass.

In the words of Lewis F. Day, who knew Morris well, and who knew as much about ornament as anyone in his generation, Morris 'preferred pattern which did not hide its structure; much ingenuity, he thought, was wasted in masking the constructional lines of design, they gave largeness and nobility to it; and "the obvious presence of geometric order" prevented the effect of restlessness.'[22] This comment seems very relevant when we look at a typical product of the early 1880s, such as the west window at Gateacre, even though we now know that in fact this was designed by Pozzi (*567*); but in the dense foliage backgrounds of the kind used at Jesus College, Cambridge, the structural lines are much less apparent, as they are also in his later designs for woven and printed textiles (*442*). It is difficult to be sure whether this resulted from changing views on Morris's part, or whether it may have been due to influences other than his in this period when his personal participation in the work of the stained-glass studio declined.

D. G. ROSSETTI

Of the group of artists upon whom Morris called for designs when he set up his stained-glass studio in 1861, Dante Gabriel Rossetti was perhaps the most distinguished, certainly the best established in reputation. But his contribution of cartoons, though highly personal and interesting, was not very large. As against the one hundred and fifty cartoons (or thereabouts) supplied by Morris, and a comparable number by Ford Madox Brown, not to mention the many hundreds by Burne-Jones, Rossetti's cartoons for glass number fewer than three dozen.[23] These were all drawn, I believe, in the short period from 1861 to 1864, after which date he apparently ceased to take any interest in the medium.

Rossetti's understanding of the special requirements of design for stained glass was highly praised by H.C. Marillier, the author of what is still the standard monograph on his work as an artist. 'It is characteristic of his original mind', he wrote, 'that he went right back to the fundamental principles of *vitraux*, paying no attention whatever to the elaborations which had grown around them, and recognizing that a picture which was transparent, that is, seen by transmitted light, must be conceived in flat tones and not made to give the illusion of shading, as can be done in the case of a surface from which light is reflected.'[24] This statement, however, may well be questioned, and Madox Brown was probably nearer to the truth when he referred to Rossetti's maxim, 'Anything will do for stained glass'.[25] It is only necessary to look at his panels of the Parable of the Vineyard in the east window at Scarborough to realize that Rossetti failed to consider the importance of clarity and simplicity of line, with the result that, from any distance, the effect is confused and the subjects practically impossible to decipher. And although, in the cartoons for this series,[26] it is evident that he deliberately stressed certain lines with the idea of lead-lines in mind, he had no conception of what sort of lines could or could not be cut in glass. In innumerable passages his outlines meander in and out, and sharp concave edges follow immediately upon sharp convex ones in a way that must have been the despair of any cutter. The most extreme instance occurs in the vines in the foreground of the first scene, which were quite impossible to make in the way indicated on the cartoon (*64–66*). The same tendency to complication and confusion is apparent in the panels of the Story of St George and the Princess Sabra (1862), now in the Victoria and Albert Museum;[27] and it would be even more obvious were these set all together in a window at any appreciable height above eye-level (*91–96*). In comparison with these, the cartoon for the panel of King René's Honeymoon: Music[28] has the advantage of containing only two figures; but even here the problems which Rossetti set the cutter, especially in the costume of the queen and in the conjunction of the two heads, proved insoluble, and the cutting and leading of the stained-glass panel in the Victoria and Albert Museum are consequently very clumsy and awkward (*IV*).[29]

Rossetti's own note scribbled on the first version of his cartoon for the central panel of the Sermon on the Mount, for Selsley (1861), makes it clear that he could hardly bother even to work within the strict and necessary limits of size determined by the window opening for which the subject was intended (*36*). As a result, the firm's studio had to produce a copy-cartoon to the correct size in pencil, which Rossetti then worked over in ink.[30]

The most effective of Rossetti's compositions of several figures is the Christ in Majesty, with angels, designed for the east window of Bradford Cathedral in 1862 and repeated on a smaller scale at St Paul's, Manningham, Bradford (*175*);[31] though the Christ on the Cross between the Virgin and St John, originally designed in 1862 for a window at All Saints, Langton Green, Kent, and repeated with variations at Dedworth and Gatcombe, has a moving intensity of feeling (*216*, *149*, *251*).[32]

Generally speaking, Rossetti's designs for individual figures were more successful, especially the Martha and the St Mary Magdalene for the Bradford Cathedral east window, and the two censing angels designed in 1861 for tracery circles at Selsley, and later repeated at Lyndhurst and at St James's, Brighouse. Martha, with her burly, bustling figure, her saucepan, jug and ladle, and her sleeves rolled up above the elbow, is an exceptionally vigorous conception, though evidently too realistic and unsaintly to prove popular (*179*).[33] Indeed, Rossetti's figures for stained glass sometimes have a character rather different from that of his other works, to which the term 'realistic' could be properly applied only, perhaps, in the case of his unfinished painting *Found*. It was probably the influence of Ford Madox Brown which was responsible, in the instance of the Martha, very much to the advantage of the figure. That of St Mary Magdalene (*180*), on the other hand, provides another example of Rossetti's carelessness, for a resolution of the partners' meeting on 22 April 1863 asked him to 'alter the costume of his Mary Magdalene for Bradford East window on account of its inappropriateness for its destination'.[34] Presumably, she was exposing too much flesh. Even in its modified form, the design fits rather uncomfortably into the ensemble because of a slight disparity of scale with all its neighbours. On the other hand, the censing angels, of which the finest versions are those at Lyndhurst, are brilliant solutions of the difficult problem of designing within a circle (*116*). The vigour of their action is most effectively set off, in the Lyndhurst tracery, with the softer rhythm of a third censing angel designed by Burne-Jones within a rhombus, and with Philip Webb's Agnus Dei, also set inside a rhombus.

It must be regretted that Rossetti's power as a designer, apparent in these subjects, and almost equally in his Annunciation at Holy Rood, Rodbourne (*106*),[35] and his Abraham's Sacrifice, and Joseph lifted from the Pit, in Peterborough Cathedral (*90*), was not more frequently applied to stained glass. Perhaps his unwillingness to consider the special demands of the medium made his cartoons so difficult to translate into glass that Morris preferred to give the commissions to others, especially Burne-Jones.

FORD MADOX BROWN

Like Burne-Jones, Ford Madox Brown had had some experience in designing for stained glass before the foundation of the Morris firm in 1861. But the commission from Powells in 1857 for the vesica-shaped Transfiguration, already mentioned, was an isolated occasion (*12*).[36] Consequently, when the Morris firm began to call on him for stained-glass cartoons in 1862, he was considerably less experienced in the medium than Burne-Jones. Nevertheless, during the thirteen years between 1862 and 1874 he produced, according to Hueffer's estimate, some one hundred and fifty stained-glass cartoons.[37] That figure may conceivably be correct, but I have not succeeded in identifying so many. Even so, the total comes to almost one hundred and thirty items.[38]

At the time when Madox Brown began designing windows for Morris, he was already a mature artist of forty years of age. It is not surprising, therefore, that although his cartoons extend over more than a decade, no striking developments are apparent in their style. From the first, however, his designs express a very distinctive personality, in their vivid and dramatic action, in the characterization of the heads, and in the emphasis on unusual details of costume.

His own statement, in the preface to the catalogue of his Piccadilly exhibition in 1865, shows the importance which he attached, above all, to 'invention, expression and good dramatic action.'[39] These are undoubtedly the keynotes of his style. The figure of Adam in the west windows at St Martin's, Scarborough (1862), who hooks one arm over the branch of a tree while he tickles a bear with his toes, is nothing if not an original invention

(*67*); and even the Christ on the Cross between the Virgin and St John in the east window of the same church (1861–62), one of his most static and almost conventional designs, is enlivened by the sympathetic gesture of the apostle as he clasps the Virgin's outstretched hands (*64*). The least characteristic of all his early designs is the Gideon in one of the aisle windows at Scarborough; the only way of accounting for this very formal, frontal pose — if indeed it is by Madox Brown — is to assume that he was attempting to achieve an hieratic effect, without complete success (*73*, *75*).[40] His only other efforts in this direction are the two Archangels Michael and Uriel in the west windows at St Michael's, Brighton (1862), where Morris's own Raphael and Gabriel possibly determined to some extent the nature of the treatment.[41] Far more typical of Madox Brown's approach are the strikingly asymmetrical designs of the two panels illustrating the story of St Martin at Scarborough (*VII*),[42] and the Nativity at Selsley (1862; *29*), with their realistic details, such as the lame beggar's crutch and leg-sling in the former, and the basket of eggs, the ox and sheep with their legs hobbled, in the latter. Details of this sort, had they not been accompanied by strength of characterization in the heads and vigour of action in the postures, might easily have produced what we should now term a 'gimmicky' effect. How completely Madox Brown avoided such dangers is seen in the St Mark at Christ Church, Southgate (1862), who examines the point of his quill, which he has just cut, while his papers lie on a one-legged table resting against his knees, and a basketful of rolled papers stands at his feet (*101*). The whole figure has a concentration which lifts it to a level entirely above such oddities, and which makes its neighbour, Morris's St Matthew, look by comparison rather weak and formless (*102*).

Madox Brown's fondness for the dramatic, however, was occasionally carried to an excess which makes his figures look so frenzied as to be slightly absurd, as in the case of Isoude in the Death of Tristram (1862; *84*);[43] but this happened only rarely. That Morris appreciated Brown's special gifts for heightened emotional expression is attested by his assigning to him such subjects as Christ carrying the Cross, the Entombment of Christ, the Scourging at the Pillar, and the Agony in the Garden.[44] Nevertheless, it is possible to feel that Burne-Jones's calmer and more restrained temperament could sometimes lead him to a result that is more moving by reason of its simplicity. For instance, a comparison of Madox Brown's Entombment of Christ, in the east window at Gatcombe (1865–66),[45] with Burne-Jones's treatment of the same subject at St Martin's, Birmingham (1876), reveals that the limp nude body of Burne-Jones's Christ is surely more expressive than Brown's hurrying figures and masses of agitated drapery (*252*, *521*, *522*).

One place where the distinctive styles of the two designers are brought into most revealing juxtaposition is in the beautiful east window at Troutbeck, made in 1873, where two small panels by each are placed under the main figures of the side lights: the Baptism of Christ and Christ blessing Children by Burne-Jones on the left, Christ's Charge to St Peter and the Supper at Emmaus by Madox Brown on the right (*384–87*). Even on this scale and with such subjects, Burne-Jones's scenes are calm and Madox

Brown's agitated. Whereas there is little recession in Burne-Jones's, and all the forms lie parallel to the surface within simple outlines, in Brown's there are deep recessions, Christ's and St Peter's draperies are described with massive but fluttering folds, and in the Supper at Emmaus, Christ's arms jut startlingly forward in sharp foreshortening, hands are thrown up, and a stool is knocked over.

It is not that Madox Brown's small scenes contain anything inappropriate to the medium of stained glass; it is rather that his personality was so distinctive that it became very difficult to incorporate such scenes in a large window, with parts by other artists, without risking the integrity of the whole. This almost impossible feat is brought off in the apse left window at Holy Trinity, Meole Brace (1870), where two of Burne-Jones's panels accompany seven by Madox Brown (*309*). It is true that the collaboration of Morris himself with Burne-Jones in the corresponding window on the right of the apse is more harmonious (*318*); yet, without doubt, it is the left one in which the force of imagination makes the deeper and more lasting impression. The total effect of these windows is, perhaps, a little overwhelming — the series of intense and dramatic subjects separated from one another only by the simplest possible lines of inscription have almost too much richness and compression. Madox Brown's energetic style benefits greatly from more breathing space around the scenes, as in the chancel east windows at Holy Cross, Haltwhistle, Northumberland (1872), where his small scenes of Abraham's Sacrifice, the Worship of the Brazen Serpent, and Christ carrying the Cross, are separated by panels of round glass from Burne-Jones's figures of Christ on the Cross, the Virgin and St John, in the principal spaces above (*XI*, *377*, *378*). A similar device was successfully employed in the north aisle west window at St Edward the Confessor, Cheddleton (1866; *249*), and elsewhere. It is interesting, therefore, to notice that when Morris came to plan the windows for Jesus College Chapel in 1873 and 1874, with the experience of these compositional problems behind him, he avoided mixing small panels by his two collaborators, and Madox Brown's contributions, in the St Luke window, the window with Moses, Samuel, David and Solomon, and the St Mark window, occupy the whole of the lower parts (*424*, *435*).

The series of six scenes from the Life of St. Oswald which Madox Brown designed in 1864 and 1865 for the church of that dedication in Durham, are as usual vivid and dramatic, but the decorative effect of the window as a whole is due more to the strength of Philip Webb's system of composition than to the narrative sequence (*209–15*).[46] Indeed, the small scale of these panels, and the considerable height at which some of them are set, make them more or less unintelligible when seen from the nave. This defect must have been recognized by Brown, however, for in the other narrative sequence which he designed, the Legend of St Editha, for St Editha's, Tamworth (1873), he adopted a totally different method (*455*). Here, of course, the problem was exaggerated by the fact that the windows in question are high up in the chancel clerestory. His solution was to place a single large-scale figure (or occasionally two) in each light, and to link them together in scenes which run across two or more lights. Perhaps this method is not altogether satisfactory either — the hands passing behind the mullions, as Sigtrig puts the ring on St Editha's finger, and Bishop Ella gives his blessing, involve some awkwardness.[47] But these are problems to which, possibly, there could never be any totally satisfactory answer.

At least from 1863, when he designed a series of patriarchs and saints for the east window of Bradford Cathedral, Madox Brown's distinctive personality is as apparent in his single-figure cartoons as in his narrative scenes. The Blakean head of Abraham, the hollow-eyed and long-bearded Isaac, the lean, withdrawn, visionary head of St John the Evangelist, are all characterizations showing a power beyond what Burne-Jones or Morris, perhaps Rossetti also, were capable of (*185*, *186*). Typical also are the two little bare-legged boys, the young Isaac clinging to his father's belt, and the boy John wrapped in the protecting arms of his mother St Elizabeth (*177*). Already, too, we notice Madox Brown's fondness for slightly eccentric costumes, especially the jerkin and puffed sleeves of St John, the fur-trimmed robe of Isaac, and the prominently displayed boots or sandals worn by all the men.[48]

That the eight figures designed for the chancel windows at Cheddleton in 1864 have less power is largely due to their small scale; but this is an interesting series, with the figures set under canopies of fourteenth-century style by Philip Webb, who also provided the grisaille patterns above and below, and the strong borders of fleurs-de-lys and creeper, all of which are probably reconstructions based upon fragmentary remains of the ancient glass (*167*)[49]. Figures with any less vigorous effect of inner life would have been annihilated by this setting, but Madox Brown's survive it.

The other series of small figures, the poets and philosophers in the Combination Room at Peterhouse, Cambridge (1871–74), which Madox Brown shared with Burne-Jones, are less personal, except maybe the Hugo de Balsham, Bishop of Ely, wrapped in his voluminous cope, his face tense and worn (*326*, *328*).[50] Generally speaking, it seems that Madox Brown's figures needed the larger scale. On the other hand, the extensive series of figures by him in the Peterhouse Hall windows are of very uneven merit. The best are those in the bay window, especially Homer, Aristotle and Cicero, whose draperies fall with a rare simplicity (*330*, *331*).[51] The later ones, and in particular the trio of Thomas Gray, the Duke of Grafton and Henry Cavendish, seem almost Baroque in the exuberance of their forms and the irregularity of their outlines (*337*). Something of this same rather discordant quality is apparent in the Good Shepherd at St James the Greater, Flockton (ca. 1872), who strides energetically forward and almost thrusts his crook, as it were, out of the window towards us (*372*, *373*); and also in the St Philip at Waterford, Hertfordshire (1872; *374*). In this latter instance, however, Brown created an image of such intensity that the disruption of the picture plane by the foreshortened right arm is very readily forgiven.

The most frequently repeated of all Madox Brown's stained-glass cartoons, Noah holding a model of the Ark in the folds of his cloak, originally designed in 1864 for a window at Middleton Cheney, and existing in at least nine other versions, threatens no such disturbance of the picture plane, but possesses a striking concentration and intentness (*232*). Of all his large figures, this one is the nearest to Burne-Jones in style. But possibly the finest windows with single figures by Madox Brown are to be found at Llandaff Cathedral and at St John the Baptist, Knaresborough. The Sts Simon and Jude at Llandaff (*463–65*)[52] and Hannah at Knaresborough are among the most convincing and memorable figures in all nineteenth-century stained glass. The Anna Prophesying and Simeon, on either side of Burne-Jones's Virgin and Child, also at Knaresborough, have a quality of humble devotion which is hardly less moving (*450–52*).

It must therefore be a matter of the greatest regret that, through unfortunate financial squabbles which ought to have been beneath him, a designer of such power was deprived of the opportunity of making further contributions to an art so well suited to his gifts, after the break-up of the firm's original partnership. However much one may respect the abilities of Burne-Jones, and however much one may dislike Madox Brown's occasional eccentricities, it has to be admitted that no one else could have produced figures with the special qualities which his have at his best.

PHILIP WEBB

Philip Webb's share in the designing of stained-glass windows was, as we have already shown, considerably more important than would appear from Mackail's brief statement that 'the animals and certain kinds of ornament' were often drawn by him.[53] In addition to his responsibility for such details, and for the general planning and layout of a number of the firm's early windows, he also designed at least five sets of Emblems of the Evangelists, including the very fine large ones for the chancel clerestory windows at St Martin's, Scarborough (1871), the cartoons for which now belong to the Ashmolean Museum, Oxford (*344–47*); he shared with Morris the designs for the eight circles of the Creation in the western rose window at All Saints, Selsley, including the subject of Adam naming the Beasts (*48*, *49*);[54] and he drew at least two full-length censing angels, several versions of the Agnus Dei, and a great many other emblems, heraldic shields, borders, canopies and pedestals, and quarries. The censing angels form part of the east window at Middleton Cheney (1865), which contains some of his best work. As well as these two figures, which occupy the tall quatrefoils in the tracery, and the Emblems of the Evangelists in the four trefoils above the main lights, he was responsible also for the twelve Banners of the Tribes of Israel, in the heads of the main lights themselves, which, more than any other components of the window, create the effect of jubilation which is the dominant note of its expression, the rose and crown borders of the main lights, and possibly the ornamental bands and inscriptions which divide the three tiers of figures from one another (*230*, *231*, *237*).[55] Similarly, the towers and gates of the Holy City in the main lights of the east windows at Lyndhurst (1862–63) and Bloxham (1869), which Webb designed, are hardly less significant contributions towards the total effects than the figures of the principal subjects (*117, 297*).

There is a crispness and decision in Webb's designs, apparent in the rather tense, sharp curves of his scrolls and banners, and most especially in his abstract pattern-work, which made him an exceptionally good heraldic artist. His contributions invariably add something to the effectiveness of the windows of which they form parts. In relation to the total impact of the west window in St Stephen's, Guernsey (1864–65), it is almost impossible to overestimate the significance of the 'cloud-wave' patterns which separate the main subject of the Tree of Jesse from the Annunciation and the Virgin and Child in the heads of the main lights (*VI*). This motif, the fore-runner of similar patterns in the Bloxham window, with its emphatic linear animation and its pure strong colour, is already pure Art Nouveau, thirty years before the full international establishment of this style; and there can be no doubt that it was Webb's invention, attested by entries in his account-book.[56]

When Webb ceased to participate actively in designing for Morris's windows, after about 1875, a certain irreplaceable quality was lost. His pattern-work and borders have a distinction unmatched elsewhere in nineteenth-century stained glass.

OTHER DESIGNERS

Apart from these major contributors, no single artist provided designs in considerable numbers. Of the other original partners in the firm, Peter Paul Marshall drew at least ten or eleven cartoons, of widely varying quality, during the years 1862–63. His artistic personality, however, remains elusive, and the attributions in some cases open to doubt. He was a sanitary engineer by profession, and had no artistic training, so far as we know; nevertheless, the best of his cartoons testify to a high degree of natural talent. What was possibly his first design, St Michael and the Dragon, drawn in 1862 for a tracery opening at St Michael's, Brighton, has tremendous dramatic energy (*61*).[57] The dominant influence in it is certainly that of Rossetti, and it may be suspected that Marshall had been a student at some of Rossetti's classes at Great Ormond Street. His Joshua for a north aisle window at Scarborough is also like Rossetti (*73, 74*), but on the other hand his Moses and Solomon in the east window at Bradford Cathedral are more akin respectively to the styles of Morris and Burne-Jones (*174,189*).[58] The cartoon of Daniel, possibly designed for the same window but discarded in favour of another design by Rossetti, shows the signs of amateurism and inexperience which might have been expected in all Marshall's work, but which otherwise he seems to have overcome.[59] At least two of Marshall's designs seem to be lost, namely Gideon with lamp and trumpet attacking the Midianites, for a window at Cranborne, the design of which was allotted to him by a meeting of the partners on 10 December 1862, but of which neither window nor cartoon is known; and Henry V and his Queen Crowned, one of a series of historical subjects for a large domestic window ordered by Hastings & Co. in 1863, which has eluded identification.[60] Marshall's most delightful achievement, however, is the chancel east window in the little church of St Mary, Coity near Bridgend, Glamorganshire, made in 1863 (*148*).[61] For this, he designed three subjects: Christ rescuing St Peter from the Water, Christ and the Woman with an Issue of Blood, and the Incredulity of St Thomas, which are set against light quarry grounds, with borders and pattern-work by Philip Webb. The designs have a certain naïveté, but also considerable charm.

But Marshall's most surprising success is the figure of St Peter centrally placed in the Bradford Cathedral east window, below Rossetti's Christ in Majesty (*174*). If there had been no documentary evidence, the attribution of this figure would have presented a very tricky problem, as the gesture with which the saint holds his chin with his right hand, while his left hand grasps the right wrist, has an inventive and surprising expressiveness which suggests that Rossetti could have been its originator, yet the draughtsmanship of the cartoon, in the William Morris Gallery at Walthamstow, is plainly not Rossetti's (*176*). Luckily the firm's Minute Book provides clear authority for assigning the figure to Marshall, and it is interesting that the partners must have had sufficient confidence in his abilities to entrust him with such an important commission.

Still more uncertainty surrounds designs by George Campfield, the foreman of the glass-painters from the beginning of the firm's activity. Marillier attributed to him the figures of Isaiah, Moses, Abraham's Sacrifice and Enoch, in the west windows at Selsley (*46, 47*). Of the figures in the aisle windows at Scarborough, which Marillier mentioned as possibly by Campfield and Marshall,[62] those most likely to be Campfield's are the St Michael in the centre of the Gideon window (*73*), and the two kings on either side of the King David window (*77*). All these date from 1862, after which he seems not to have been entrusted with further commissions for figures. The Selsley designs are tolerably capable, but the Scarborough ones lack any distinction either of character or of attitude. Much later, Campfield, along with other members of the glass-painting studio, participated in designing foliage backgrounds, and other subordinate parts of windows; this aspect of his work is discussed in the section on the glass-painters at the end of this chapter.

Albert Moore (1841–93), whose name is not usually associated with the Morris circle, was responsible for one cartoon of outstanding quality, the Christ as Salvator Mundi in the centre of the chancel south window at Bradford Cathedral, now unfortunately inaccessible in store (*190*). The cartoon for this figure was presented to Birmingham City Art Gallery in 1900 by Charles Fairfax Murray, and presumably the attribution carried his authority (*196*).[63] Its rather static and classical effect is, indeed, fully in accordance with the tendencies of Moore's style, and the details of the sword pommel, the keys, and the ornamentation of the costume are all consistent with his manner. This figure is certainly worthy of the prominence which Morris gave it, and it is consequently surprising that it remained an isolated contribution to Morris stained glass.

Figures designed by Simeon Solomon (1840–1905) are confined to two windows only: in the east window at Middleton Cheney, the second tier includes his David and Isaiah (*232*), and the bottom tier his Abraham and Moses (*234*), and all four were repeated in similar positions in the west window of the Old West Kirk, Greenock, now transferred to the North Church. But there is some doubt over the attribution to him of the Procession of Saints and Martyrs, otherwise known as the Twelve Tribes of Israel, which occupy the top tier of the Middleton Cheney window (*231*).[64] Marillier's notes give no attribution, but a framed diagram and key to the window which belongs to the church, and which is based upon a manuscript 'log-book' apparently kept by the Rev. W.E. Buckley, rector from 1853 to 1892, attributes the whole of this tier to Simeon Solomon.[65] This is quite possibly correct, in spite of the fact that the figures lack the characteristic swaying posture evident particularly in the King David below; but then, so also do the figures of Isaiah, Abraham and Moses.

Arthur Hughes (1832–1915), so far as documentation reveals, seems to have been called upon for only one unimportant design, the Birth of Tristram, for the series of panels supplied to Walter Dunlop of Harden Grange, Bingley, and now in the Bradford City Art Gallery (*78*).[66] Dr. W.E. Fredeman of the University of British Columbia, Vancouver, however, considers that two panels in his possession, representing The Well of Love and Goblin Market, illustrations of Christina Rossetti's poems, may be by Hughes; in my opinion they are more probably by D. G. Rossetti.

Another member of the Morris circle, Val Prinsep (1836–1904),[67] contributed one design to the Tristram and Isoude series, representing Tristram leaving the King of Ireland with La Belle Isoude his daughter (*80*). This can hardly be said to claim any special interest, and Prinsep's rather puppet-like king is very much inferior to the figure of Tristram's reclining mother in Arthur Hughes's design.

It is possible that other designers, such as Charles Faulkner, Henry Holiday, and Frederic Shields, for example, may have been employed occasionally, but I have not discovered any documentation to connect them with Morris stained glass, except for the puzzling occurrence, in the Morris & Co. Window-Book now in the Birmingham City Art Gallery, of photographs of designs by Holiday for a window representing Christ as the Good Shepherd in St Mary's, Binsted near Arundel, Sussex, made by Powells in 1869.[68] It is clear from Walter Crane's autobiography that some windows designed by him were made by Morris & Co.,[69] but the only examples that I have been able to identify are two undocumented minstrel figures at Adcote near Shrewsbury.[70] It is likely that in such cases the orders came from Crane and not from the firm.

It is curious that Morris appears never to have invited the other Pre-Raphaelite Brethren to design figures for his windows. William Holman Hunt, so far as I am aware, never made any designs specifically for stained glass, but his painting *The Light of the World* was certainly translated into stained glass on a number of occasions, and once indeed by Morris & Co., in a window for Unley Park church, Adelaide, Australia, though as late as 1930–31.[71] Sir John Everett Millais, on the other hand, did actually make one design for stained glass. In 1864 he accepted a commission for six designs for windows in Worcester College Chapel, Oxford, but resigned the task after completing only one cartoon, the Adoration of the Magi, which was exhibited the same year. He asked for twelve months in which to complete his undertaking, and as this request was unacceptable to the College, the order was cancelled and the series completed by Henry Holiday and N. H. J. Westlake, the glass being executed by Messrs. Lavers and Barraud.[72]

THE GLASS-PAINTERS

We know from the documentation provided by the so-called Catalogue of Designs now in the collection of Mr Sanford Berger that in later years various members of the glass-painting studio contributed a considerable number of designs for the minor and ornamental parts of windows. The first reference of this kind occurs in November 1876, when the name of Pozzi is mentioned in connection with the treework background of a window for Norfolk Island. Such mentions in the records are only occasional down to July 1881, but from then onwards the names of the glass-painters responsible for the various parts of windows are normally given until the firm closed down in 1940. With figures, of course, the glass-painters would have been responsible only for the translation of the cartoon into glass; but in the case of minor parts such as scrolls, treework, landscape or architectural backgrounds, ornamental bases, bands, pattern-work and inscriptions, they were very often left to make the designs as well. The records are quite specific in some instances, supplying the names of the artists who did the drawings, as well as those of the glass-painters who carried them out. In the years 1876–78, 1881–83, and 1886–88, Pozzi is mentioned on several occasions as the painter of treework, angels' wings, scrolls, etc.; and in June 1881 we find the first unambiguous references to designs as distinct from their execution on the glass, when the treework background and tracery for a window at Forest School, Walthamstow, were designed by Campfield and painted by Stokes, and the treework for the apse windows at Boughton, Chester, was designed by Pozzi and painted by Stokes. By this date, the style of such foliage backgrounds had been established, almost certainly by designs from Morris's own hand, and what Pozzi and Campfield did was to adapt and make variations upon Morris's themes.

Pozzi's employment in the glass-painters' studio appears to have been intermittent, and in one of the intermissions we come across the first reference to designs from the hand of John Henry Dearle. This was in November 1884, when he and Bowman are recorded as having drawn the treework for the apse windows at Broughty Ferry, carried out by Stokes. Either jointly or separately, Pozzi, Bowman and Dearle designed many examples of foliage backgrounds, for instance in the St Matthew window at Frome, the St Cecilia window at Fochabers, and windows at Heckfield, Kirkcaldy, Whitelands Training College, Bordighera, Irton, Weybridge, Leek, Boughton, Berlin, Latchingdon,

Didsbury, Stanmore, etc. On certain occasions, as in the window with Enoch, St Paul and Elijah at Blackburn Cathedral, the figures of angels holding scrolls in the base panels were also designed by Bowman and Dearle. In 1892 another glass-painter, Brown, began to share in the designing of scrolls borders and other accessories. By about 1891 Dearle, who at this time was taking a good share in the painting of figures, was responsible also for the design of many foregrounds, backgrounds, and more important details such as the minstrel angels in the window at Ilford Hospital Chapel, tracery seraphim at Brushford, and the extension in width of Burne-Jones's cartoon of the Miraculous Draught of Fishes for the window at Maxwell church, Glasgow. He generally drew the landscape backgrounds which became frequent in the firm's windows in the 1890s, characteristic examples being those in the Good Shepherd window at Buscot (1892), the windows at Loddington and Whalley (1893), and the St Stephen window at Elton (1895); though some landscape backgrounds were drawn by Campfield, for example those at Malvern Wells and in the Angels of Paradise window at Buscot (1897). Dearle's development as a designer of figures and major subjects will be discussed in the following chapter.

Campfield's name ceases to appear in the records after 5 October 1898, the last window on which he worked being the circular angels window at Brampton. W.H. Knight, whose name first appears in January 1899, perhaps joined the studio as a replacement for Campfield; at any rate, he immediately took a share of the work of designing treework, tracery ornament and landscape backgrounds, and in August of the same year it was he who arranged and adapted Burne-Jones's tapestry designs for the Holy Grael window at Haslemere. When, after Morris's and Burne-Jones's deaths, Dearle assumed overall responsibility for the stained-glass department, his name appeared less frequently as designer, except of important new figure subjects, and Knight became the chief designer of foliage, treework, landscape and architectural backgrounds. From 1901 onwards Knight occasionally designed minor figures, such as the tracery seraphim in the south transept rose window at Meole Brace, and he eventually graduated to major figure designs, but only after an apparent absence from the studio; except for a single mention in 1930, he seems to have taken no part in the work of the studio between 1924 and 1932. In this last year Dearle died, and Knight then became the principal designer. His most important figure subjects are the St Augustine window at Stoke St Gregory (1932), the five-light window with St Sebastian and other saints for Ingatestone (1934–35), the Joseph and Naomi window at Brecon (1935), a window with the Holy Family outside the Temple, for St Alban's, Streatham Park (1937), the Virgin Mary at St George's, Norwich (1937), the Calling of St John for St Saviour's, Llandudno (1939), and Christ among the Doctors in the Temple, for Nelson (1940).

Designs by Dearle and Knight belonging to the period after 1898 will be discussed more fully in the next chapter; and an abstract of information relating to the glass-painters employed in the studio is given in the appendix at the end of this volume.

6
The Morris Firm after 1898

The stained-glass work of the Morris firm suffered the severest blows possible by the deaths of Morris in 1896 and of Burne-Jones two years later. Although the prestige of the firm remained very high and its volume of business showed little decline, no further radical developments of style followed, and the general tendency was to repeat with little modification earlier designs, mostly by Burne-Jones. The position of chief designer of cartoons for glass passed to John Henry Dearle, who had worked for many years with Morris, and, according to the testimony of Lewis Day, had 'learnt to work so like him that the design of the pupil may well be mistaken, even by the experienced in design, for that of the master'.[1] A great deal of the floral and other detail in the Merton Abbey tapestries was designed by him, and as we have seen he had already taken responsibility for much similar work in stained glass. Indeed as early as 1893 he had been entrusted with designing cartoons for figures of Shakespeare and Milton for a series of poets for the central west window of Bute Hall at Glasgow University, the rest of which were enlarged versions of earlier Burne-Jones designs (*615*). Dearle's are competent imitations of Burne-Jones's manner, without revealing any distinctive artistic personality. By 1900, however, when he designed a further twelve figures for the east windows of the same building, some signs of individuality have become apparent, at least in the heads. These rather pale, broad-faced early churchmen, with deep-set eyes and concerned expressions, are drawn with great sensitivity and conscientiousness, though without any of Burne-Jones's economy (*614*). The same qualities were already evident, in fact, in the figure of Christ Preaching (usually inscribed 'Consider the Lilies') which he had designed for a window at St John the Baptist, Wolverley, Worcestershire, in 1899 (*638*). As always with Dearle, the attitude of the figure is uninteresting; but this Wolverley window has two features which remained typical of many of Dearle's designs, the background of rather bare hilly landscape,[2] and the foreground filled with a profusion of wild flowers.

The Paradise or Last Judgement window in Rugby School Chapel, made in 1902, was Dearle's first really large-scale composition, running across seven main lights of considerable height, and including some scores of figures arranged in concentric circles around the central figure of the Archangel Michael, with Christ Seated in Glory at the top, surrounded by angels (*640*). It is a little diffuse and utterly undramatic, defects of which Dearle himself was possibly aware, since another design of the same year, the Calling of St Peter, for St Peter's, Swinton, clearly attempts a much more dramatic style (*XVI*). The figure of Christ is placed over on the right, and the central figure of Peter is surrounded by five other fishermen engaged in the vigorous activities of their trade. There is more movement here than Dearle could successfully control with a unifying rhythm, and in all his other important designs he seems to have recognized his own limitations, and avoided any attempt at unusual compositional arrangements.

Dearle's figures nearly always lack any real feeling for mass or three-dimensional bulk, but occasionally this deficiency turned to his advantage. One of his most successful windows is the Ascension of Christ in the Troon old parish church, Ayrshire, made in 1903 (*644*). Although strictly symmetrical in arrangement, it has indeed a rather dramatic effect, as the figure of Christ seems to rise weightlessly in the air above a group of the apostles gathered below, all looking upwards. Undoubtedly much of the dynamic upward movement, however, is due to the structure of the window tracery; and it is significant that none of the dozen repetitions and variations of the design in other churches produces a comparable effect. But Dearle at least realized the considerable potentialities of this setting, and created in this instance not only a moving representation of his subject in a pictorial sense, but also a window admirably related to its architectural position.

None of Dearle's later designs, indeed, attains quite the same level of quality. His window of 1905 at All Saints, Elton, Huntingdonshire, with Christ in Glory at the top, is a singularly uninspired piece of iconography (*645*); the series of single figures of eminent Puritans at Emmanuel Church, Cambridge, thoroughly competent though they are, produces a rather boring and even pedantic effect; while the Last Supper window of 1906 at Dundonald parish church, Ayrshire, where this subject is enclosed within a rectangle cutting across the five lights, with disconnected angels and the Agnus Dei poised, as it were, above the roof of the chamber in which the main scene is set, simply fails to relate the main theme to the overall form of the window (*646*). It might have been expected that Dearle, with his many years of practical experience as a glass-painter, would have had an exceptional appreciation of what was appropriate to the medium of stained glass. But this example reveals the essentially pictorial nature of his thinking, and his lack of any clear understanding of the differences between stained glass and painting. The composition is, of course, derived from Andrea del Castagno's fresco in the refectory of Sant'Apollonia in Florence; but its division into five sections by the strong vertical lines of the stone mullions results in the destruction of its unity and power. The design of Christ blessing Children, designed in 1907 for a window at Brechin Cathedral, Angus, and repeated two years later at Swinton, is among Dearle's most attractive achievements, with its beautifully drawn and gracefully characterized women in the side lights; but even here Dearle's limitations are obvious, for the figure of Christ is weak and characterless, and the babes are singularly without charm (*649*).

The church of St Stephen, Tonbridge, Kent, possesses one of the most interesting series of windows from Dearle's designs. The earliest of them, the Maries at the Sepulchre, made in 1910, employs again the asymmetrical principle which Dearle never fully mastered, so that the right-hand light here seems insufficiently linked with the other two, looking like an afterthought (*652*). A glance, for comparison, at Burne-Jones's Mary

Magdalene at the Sepulchre, designed for Easthampstead in 1877 (*523*), is enough to show up the weakness of Dearle's conception, with its static, expressionless angel and its lack of any embracing rhythm. The Road to Emmaus, of 1911, is also without any sense of the drama of the event, but is nevertheless more satisfactory as a window, because of the very simplicity of its presentation (*653*). The three-light Resurrection, also made in 1911, follows the general arrangement of Burne-Jones's Allerton window of 1885, so far as the central figure and the position of the tomb are concerned; but the two angels at the sides and the sleeping guards in the foreground characteristically replace Burne-Jones's dramatically conceived guards recoiling and shielding their eyes from the divine radiance (*654*). For once, in the Agony in the Garden, Dearle makes effective use of asymmetry: the raising of the Angel of Martyrdom in the right light above the level of the kneeling Christ's head begins, at least, to convey some feeling of spiritual elevation (*655*). But how little this window has of the intensity and expressiveness of Ford Madox Brown's treatment of the same subject in a window at Jesus College Chapel, Cambridge, is sadly obvious.

Dearle's window of Christ among the Doctors, at St Silas, Blackburn, made in 1911, and another design of the same subject made in 1915 at St Mary's, Newent, Gloucestershire, are essentially essays in the later manner of Burne-Jones, with elaborated architectural backgrounds and a self-conscious scrupulousness with the draperies which tend to distract attention from the essential theme.

The last phase of Dearle's work as a designer for stained glass is typically represented by the three war memorial windows of 1920 at St Bartholomew's, Wilmslow, Cheshire, with the themes of War, Peace and Victory (*658*, *659*). The style is obviously, even slightly ridiculously, retrospective: the soldiers are all conceived as knights in mediaeval armour. An unconvincing sentimentality precludes any attempt to come to grips with the horrifying realities of modern war. There is no genuine emotion or imagination here at all. No doubt this is indicative of the reasons for the firm's eventual failure; instead of keeping abreast of the developments of twentieth-century art, it contented itself with an empty continuation of the style of forty years before. Not only were innumerable examples of designs of the 1870s and 1880s still being repeated in the 1920s, but even Dearle's new designs — often adaptations of Burne-Jones's — were still in the mood and spirit of an earlier generation, though weakened and softened in sentiment, and deprived of all passion and drama. The initiative, in terms of style and technique, had already passed to others, especially to artists like Christopher Whall, who were more responsive to fresh influences.[3]

Dearle died in 1932, and was succeeded in his capacity as chief designer for windows by W.H. Knight, who, as we have seen, had entered the stained-glass department early in 1899 and had been employed for many years in the designing of treework, tracery ornament, landscape and curtain backgrounds, shields, foliage, angels and seraphim for tracery lights, quarries, emblems, borders, foregrounds, canopies, inscriptions and similar subordinate parts. He does not appear to have been a glass-painter at first, but began to take a share in glass-painting, with minor parts such as Emblems of the Evangelists, in 1916. He collaborated with Dearle in the design of the Jacob's Dream, adapted from an old engraving, for a window at St Lawrence, Warslow, Staffordshire, in 1923. His first major figure designs were of Samuel and an angel for a window at Dornoch Cathedral, Sutherland, in 1931, and the central figure in the Nativity window at All Saints, Winnipeg, in 1932. In 1932 also he designed the St Augustine window for Stoke St Gregory, Somerset; and his most ambitious designs were of the Holy Family outside the Temple, made in 1937 for a no longer existing window at St Alban's, Streatham Park, and Christ among the Doctors in the Temple, for St Mary's, Nelson, Lancashire, in 1940.[4]

Knight was evidently a skilful and sensitive draughtsman, and some of his early tree-work backgrounds are equal in quality to those of Pozzi, Dearle and Bowman; but the decades of practice in the style of Dearle had killed any original creativity which he might have possessed, and these late designs are entirely without force or individuality.

Many years ago I was told by the late David Rees, who had been employed by the firm as a glass-painter in the 1930s, that he was occasionally called upon to design minor parts of windows, such as tracery ornaments and inscriptions; but this is not recorded in the Catalogue of Designs, and Mr Rees himself said that his principal design activities for the firm were connected with memorial tablets. He also told me that Charles O'Neill occasionally designed windows, generally of an heraldic nature. O'Neill's name does not occur at all in the Catalogue of Designs, but according to Mr Rees he was responsible for a number of lancets with arms of the Cinque Ports for Saltwood Castle, near Hythe, Kent, to the order of Lady Conway, and for an heraldic window for the Sitwell family, presumably at Renishaw Hall, Nottinghamshire.

When the firm closed down in 1940, the stained-glass department was sold to Duncan W. Dearle, the son of J.H. Dearle. Duncan Dearle made no windows during the war years, but resumed production in 1947, and a list of his works from that date until his death at the age of sixty-one in 1954 will be given in an appendix to the catalogue in the forthcoming second volume of this work.[5]

The extent to which the later productions of the firm fell away from the high ideals of its early years may be seen most vividly in certain windows which reverted to the early nineteenth-century practice of copying paintings. The Boy Scout window of 1907 at Roch, Pembrokeshire — certainly the worst Morris window which I have seen — is a version drawn by W.H. Knight from a painting called *The Pathfinder* by E.S. Carlos; the panel of Sir Galahad in the Holy Grail window of 1919 at St Paul's, Fairlie, Ayrshire, is copied from a painting by G.F. Watts; William Holman Hunt's painting *The Light of the World* was translated into glass for a window at Unley Park church, Adelaide, Australia, in 1930–31; and in 1931 Sir Frank Dicksee's painting *Harmony* was copied in a window for Vancouver Art Gallery, British Columbia.[6] One can only too easily imagine with what outbursts of rage and indignation such a betrayal of their principles would have been greeted by Morris, Burne-Jones and Madox Brown! Burne-Jones had been known to threaten to smash furniture at far less provocation.

The large number of Morris windows to be described in the forthcoming catalogue will possibly come as a surprise to most students, as will their wide geographical distribution over five continents. The numbers have already been appreciably reduced, however, by architectural changes in churches, by accidental damage, by demolitions, by the destruction of wartime bombing, and by other causes. A high proportion of the windows made for private houses, especially, has been lost.[7] Many of the Victorian houses for which they were made have been demolished, or the original owners, when they or their families moved elsewhere, took the glass with them to untraced new addresses, or sold it. Several whole sets of church windows, too, such as those at Fulford, Lamerton, Benhilton, and Crescent Street Montreal, have been destroyed by fire. Windows at Abinger, Butcroft, Camberwell, Cranleigh, St Cyprian's Chapel (Eastbourne), St Paul's Vicarage Gate (Kensington), Keston, the Savoy Chapel (London), St James's Piccadilly, St Michael's Bread Street, St Peter's London Docks, Forest School (Walthamstow), and elsewhere have fallen victims to wartime bombing. On the other hand, there are some instances where, upon the demolition of a building or the removal of an institution to new premises, praiseworthy efforts were made to save the windows and to reincorporate them in new settings. Aldenham School and Whitelands College (formerly at Chelsea, now at Putney) are the best examples of this; but it must be emphasized that the use of stained glass in situations for which it was not specifically intended almost inevitably results in some loss of effectiveness. In one case, however, that of the Bradford Cathedral east window — removed from its original setting, cleaned, releaded, repaired, divided into three windows, and refitted in the Lady Chapel designed by Sir Edward Maufe — the effect is now possibly even more splendid than before, and this is due not only to the sensitiveness and restraint with which the repairs were handled, but also to the brilliance of the architect's design, which allows the glass to be seen from the whole interior of the Cathedral, over the stone screen dividing the Lady Chapel from the choir.[8]

With the wholesale reorganization of parishes due to shifting populations, a great many Victorian churches are becoming redundant, or else inadequate to the needs of growing communities. Closures and demolitions are taking place in such numbers and with such frequency that it is difficult to keep pace with information, let alone to act effectively to save the most worthy examples among the threatened windows. In a book like this, which will take a year or more to go through the press, it would be hopeless to attempt to indicate all the current dangers to which Morris windows are exposed. The situation changes rapidly and continually, and great vigilance will be required on the part of all interested persons if wholesale destruction is to be averted. But a mention of some recent and present losses and dangers may serve to identify the nature of the factors which have to be contested. One ever-present danger arises from the lack of records of many nineteenth-century works of art in churches, at a parish level, and the resulting ignorance of the responsible clergy as to what their churches actually contain. One case, that of the east window of St Wilfrid's, Haywards Heath, made by the Morris firm in 1868, and destroyed in 1962 to make way for a modern work, may serve as a warning of what can only too easily happen (*280*). Park Parish church, Glasgow, was demolished in 1968, and no attempt to save the Morris glass appears to have been made. But the stories are not all so depressing. St Cuthbert's, Newcastle-on-Tyne, has been demolished, but the Morris windows were saved and are now in store at the Laing Art Gallery, though I have not heard of any moves either to find a new home for them or to exhibit them in the Gallery. The windows from St James's, Brighouse, declared redundant, have been removed to storage at the Bradford City Art Gallery (*469*, *470*). The east window of St Michael's, Torquay, made in 1878, has also been taken out and is stored at the Victoria and Albert Museum. The Royal Hospital at Ventnor has been demolished, but the Morris window from the Chapel has been saved, and the three lower panels from it have been inserted in a specially opened window at St Lawrence church, nearby (*379–82*). Onecote Vicarage, Staffordshire, is to be sold out of ecclesiastical use, but the windows have been removed into diocesan store, and may be sold. All Saints, Dedworth, Berkshire, has been under threat of demolition for several years, to make way for a larger church, but in this instance it seems likely that the glass will be saved (*149*, *150*).[9] St Paul's, Boughton, Chester, may become a victim of parochial reorganization; and Christ Church, Tunbridge Wells, is to be demolished, though there is a possibility that the Morris window may be saved. All Saints, Cambridge, also redundant, has been threatened for some years, and its fate remains uncertain, despite some interesting proposals for its re-use. St Faith's, Wandsworth, is due for demolition, and I have not heard of any arrangements for the rescue of the Morris windows. Doubtless there are many more cases of danger. Fortunately, such organizations as the Victorian Society, with its regional groups in Liverpool, Manchester and the West Midlands, the Council for the Care of Churches, the Advisory Board for Redundant Churches, and many other bodies, are becoming increasingly aware of the hazards, and persistently active in their efforts to ward them off.

Not all losses, of course, are of equal importance, and it may well prove impracticable to save every Morris window which is threatened. The most worthy candidates for preservation are those windows for which special cartoons were designed, even if, as was the case with the windows of the Savoy Chapel (destroyed by bombing during the Second World War), the subjects were repeated later in other places. The loss of the Camberwell window, with some of the finest of Morris's figure designs, and a pair of Webb's most elaborate Decorated Gothic canopies, was a major tragedy; and it may certainly be hoped that nothing else of such outstanding quality will in future be allowed to suffer destruction. It is a part of the intention of the catalogue which forms the second volume of this book to provide information in the battle for preservation by indicating clearly which are the windows where designs first appear, which is generally the same thing as saying where they are most suited to their situation, and best integrated into the total architectural effect.

The problems presented by preservation are often of great difficulty. Many windows are very large, and contain a whole series of subjects and figures. To preserve the whole intact may often prove impossible because of sheer scale. On the other hand, when windows are divided into their component parts, some essential quality in the composition as a whole is necessarily lost. To find alternative positions in which entire windows can be reinserted may often necessitate alterations in the masonry of the receiving church — an extremely expensive operation which is seldom feasible. It is good to see that in the last few years several museums and art galleries have begun to play a part in the processes of preservation; but the handling and display of large panels of stained glass entail technical problems for museums, which very few of them as yet have the experience or the finances to deal with properly. In any case, the cleaning, repair and releading of rescued windows demand the expenditure of substantial sums of money, which committees can be persuaded to vote only if they are assured of interest and response from the public. The result is that, though some glass is being saved, it is liable to lie for years inaccessible in packing-cases in museum basements. Paradoxically, one of the factors which may in the long run serve most to help the cause of preservation is the rapidly rising market appreciation of Morris's and Burne-Jones's works. If museum committees have to pay substantial sums to obtain possession of windows, they are much more likely to be willing to spend money on restoring and displaying them, than if they had picked up the windows for nothing like foundlings on their doorsteps.

Another danger to which windows are increasingly likely to be subjected is that of clumsy and tasteless restoration. A sad example of this may be seen at St James's, Muswell Hill, where one of the four figures in the windows on the north side of the chapel north of the chancel was destroyed in 1941 and replaced by a poor imitation. At the same time that this was done, the remaining three figures, made by Morris & Co. in 1919, were deprived of their backgrounds of drapery and foliage, and reset crudely in plain quarries, with the result that no proper tonal relationship now exists between the figures and their surrounds. Almost equally regrettable is the ill-chosen frosted-glass border added to the windows of 1902 from College Road Presbyterian church, Newcastle-on-Tyne, now refitted at St Andrew's Presbyterian church, Hebburn. Fortunately, restorations and removals are sometimes carried out with admirable tact and skill, as in the already mentioned case of the Bradford Cathedral east window, which was handled by Messrs Pickett of Leeds, after it had been ruthlessly hacked out of its original setting, with quite unnecessary destruction of much of the bordering and pattern-work; or that of the windows from the Green Dining Room at the Victoria and Albert Museum, most admirably repaired in the Museum's own Department of Conservation (*267–70*).[12]

What was done at Muswell Hill is an example of a practice which has unhappily become common in recent years, that of extracting the figures in Victorian windows from their backgrounds and surrounds of pattern-work, and resetting them in plain glass. This procedure may admittedly produce the advantage of admitting a more generous light into the interiors; but the effect, so far as the windows themselves are concerned, is generally disastrous. Not only do figures treated in this way appear outlined with excessive harshness against their transparent backgrounds, but in the great majority of Victorian windows the very parts thus discarded are apt to be the best, and what is kept is too often the weakest. This would not generally be the case with Morris windows; nevertheless, any proposals to treat Morris windows in this way should certainly be strenuously opposed, in spite of the undeniable fact that some of the later Morris work, with backgrounds and bases of dense foliage, does not admit a great deal of light. The darker the overall tonality of a window, the more damaging to the total effect is the insertion of plain glass in place of the coloured background.

Conclusion

At the beginning of this book I suggested that the best windows produced by Morris and the artists associated with him attained a higher level of quality than any others since the sixteenth century. We are now in a position to see just how and why such a claim can be made.

In 1864 Charles Winston had written, 'In designing windows for mediaeval churches there are but two courses which experience shows are available — either to adopt modern art (and this is the wise course when *figures* are required), or else to adopt mediaeval art; and I am persuaded that this is only good advice when the donors will be content with pattern-work. There is no third course.'[1] With very few exceptions, up to that time, Victorian stained-glass artists had attempted, usually with only moderate success, to 'adopt mediaeval art', and without restricting themselves to pattern-work. Morris and his designers, on the other hand, almost from the beginning, worked in an essentially modern style. It is true that some of Morris's own very early designs, such as the Ascension at Selsley, had been perhaps too closely modelled on mediaeval sources; and the Gothic canopies designed by Webb in the 1860s were open to the same objection. But these relics of mediaevalism were soon left behind; and from the date of his window at Topcliffe, and the rose-window of the Creation at Waltham Abbey, Burne-Jones had been a resolute modernist.

The great difficulty which a modernist faced, when working in such a medium as stained glass, was that the subject-matter required of him bore no resemblance to that of the mainstreams of modern art; and if he needed some guidance in ways of treating it, he had to turn either to mediaeval art, or, in the case of certain Christian themes which had continued in use during the Renaissance and the subsequent centuries, to paintings which had developed in techniques whose entire principles, as Winston had warned, were inimical to the special qualities and requirements of the stained-glass medium. Only artists of real imagination and individuality could find a way out of this dilemma. Such men as Hedgeland, Hughes, Wailes, Clayton and Bell, Warrington, and even Michael and Arthur O'Connor, were not of that calibre. Burne-Jones, Rossetti, Madox Brown and Morris himself were. And if Burne-Jones's figures, and especially his draperies, sometimes showed a pronounced influence from Botticelli or Mantegna, he at least avoided the faults of excessive chiaroscuro, and of too much insistence upon roundness of form and three-dimensional space which might easily have resulted from a reliance upon later Renaissance styles.

The recovery of the full iconography of Christian art, much of which had been virtually extinct for at least two hundred and fifty years, was in itself a major achievement of Victorian art, and in this field more credit is due to Burne-Jones than to any other artist. One of the most striking characteristics of the treatment of subject-matter in his windows, when compared with other Victorian work, is the clarity and directness of his exposition. There is never any doubt what the subject is.[2] His grasp of the subtle relationships between New Testament themes and their Old Testament ante-types was sure and unforced; and on occasions he was capable of such new and completely convincing conceptions as the series of Days of Creation, at Manchester College Chapel, Oxford, for which there are no close prototypes in either mediaeval or Renaissance art (*629*).[3]

As regards colour, where the credit, of course, belongs to Morris himself, no other stained glass of the nineteenth century, or of the previous two hundred years, can for one moment be compared to the splendour of his work in such churches as Bloxham, King's Walden, Lytham, Meole Brace, Staveley, Sunderland, Tadcaster or Tilehurst (to mention only a few), or in the Chapel of Jesus College, Cambridge. Of the other leading Victorian artists in stained glass, the best colourists were perhaps O'Connor, and Lavers and Barraud; but the colour-schemes of the latter, with their varieties of blues, purples, mauves and pinks, tended always towards a confectionery sweetness; and the former could seldom get away from a hackneyed chord of blue, ruby and gold. The limited and controlled scheme of white, red and cold blue which gives such expressive force to the east window at Easthampstead, with Burne-Jones's Last Judgement, belongs altogether to another level of artistic creation. In his early windows, such as those at the eastern end of St Michael's, Brighton, Morris's chords of deep green, dull ruby, blue and pale gold have a boldness of contrast and a subtlety of tonal balance which are not only entirely personal, but quite beyond the capacities of any of his competitors (*V*). And already as early as the west windows of the same church he dared, as no one else did, to give a bold predominance to one colour. These golden archangels at Brighton, the orange-gold trumpeting angels at Cheddleton (*X*), the preponderantly green windows at Nun Monkton, and many others, reveal a feeling for the expressive power of colour which was unique in the nineteenth century, and rare indeed in the whole history of the art. Effects of such boldness needed the imagination and courage of genius. Since the days of Dirk Crabeth and Bernard van Linge, at the latest, to what glass-painters could such a phrase be applied?

Finally, Morris's best windows displayed a mastery of composition, and an understanding of the possibilities and necessary limitations of stained glass, which enabled him to create masterpieces once more in a medium which had produced scarcely any for centuries.

At the end of the century a new generation, which owed an enormous debt to Morris's ideas rather than to his example, adopted an attitude which implied some criticism of his practice. The tendency of the Arts and Crafts Movement was to attempt to unite the entire processes of the art, from the manufacture of the glass itself to the completed window, in the hands of a single artist-craftsman; and, rightly or wrongly, this tendency superseded Morris's practice of separating the production in the hands of specialists, with the designer on the one hand, and the craftsman glass-painter on the other. It is odd, and rather surprising, to find Morris's old associate Philip Webb expressing this reaction, in a letter dated 19 December 1904, in which he complained that Morris's 'never could be right good craftsmen's glass, because there were no draughtsmen who could translate the beautiful pictures into effective painting *for* glass', and objecting to the fact that Morris had never made his own glass, but bought it ready-made from the trade.[4] These criticisms are not altogether just: one would have to be hypercritical to find any substantial grounds for objection to the skills of Morris & Co.'s best glass-painters — Fairfax Murray, Pozzi, Dearle, Bowman, or even, in the 1920s, Seeley and Chadwick.

The great secret of Morris's success, apart from his own personal gifts as a creative artist, was his respect for the craftsman. 'You whose hands make those things that should be works of art,' he wrote, 'you must be all artists, and good artists too . . . the handicraftsman, left behind by the artist when the arts sundered, must come up with him, must work side by side with him: apart from the difference between a great master and a scholar, apart from the differences of the natural bent of men's minds, which would make one man an imitative, and another an architectural or decorative artist, there should be no difference between those employed on strictly ornamental work; and the body of artists dealing with this should quicken with their art all makers of things into artists also. . . .'[5] That is exactly what he had done in Morris & Co.'s stained-glass workshops.

Notes

CHAPTER 1

[1] See J.A. Knowles, 'Glass-Painters 1750–1850', *Journal of the British Society of Master Glass-Painters*, XIII (1959–63), 405.

[2] F.W. Oliphant, *A Plea for Painted Glass* . . . (Oxford, 1855), pp. 20–22.

[3] E. Milner-White, 'William Jay Bolton', *Journal of the British Society of Master Glass-Painters*, VI (1937), 212.

[4] There is as yet no adequate account of Georgian and early Victorian stained glass, but some useful notes may be found in M. Whiffen, *Stuart and Georgian Churches outside London* (London, 1947/48), pp. 100–05; and a few short paragraphs in C. Woodforde, *English Stained and Painted Glass* (Oxford, 1954) and in T.S.R. Boase, *English Art 1800–1870* (Oxford, 1959). The compilation by Knowles referred to in note 1 includes some valuable source materials but makes no attempt to connect these with surviving windows.

[5] Woodforde, p. 52.

[6] F.M. Drake, *History of English Glass-Painting* (London, 1912), p. 103.

[7] *Great Exhibition of the Works of Industry of all Nations, 1851. Official Descriptive and Illustrated Catalogue* (London, 1851), II, 706.

[8] Both papers appeared in Weale's *Quarterly Papers on Architecture* (London, 1844).

[9] For example, E.O. Fromberg's *Handbuch der Glasmalerei* (Leipzig, 1844) was translated and published also in *Quarterly Papers on Architecture*, before appearing as a volume entitled *An Essay on the Art of Painting on Glass* (London, 1851); the two volumes of F. de Lasteyrie's *Histoire de la Peinture sur Verre* appeared in Paris in 1853; and among several such monographs may be mentioned M.M. Descamps, *Les Vitraux de la Cathédrale de Tournai* (Brussels, 1848). Also, the importance should not be underrated of the many articles on stained glass which were published in *The Gentleman's Magazine*, *Art Journal*, *The Builder*, *Ecclesiologist* and other magazines.

[10] See A.C. Sewter, 'The Place of Charles Winston in the Victorian Revival of the Art of Stained Glass', *Journal of the British Archaeological Association*, 3rd ser. XXIV (1961), 80–91.

[11] [C. Winston], *An Inquiry into the Difference of Style observable in Ancient Glass Paintings, especially in England: with Hints on Glass Painting*, 2 vols. (Oxford, 1847), I, 248.

[12] Ibid., I, 255.

[13] Ibid., I, 4.

[14] Ibid., I, 278, note s.

[15] Ibid., I, 281, note y.

[16] Ibid., I, 280.

[17] Ibid., I, 283.

[18] Winston's text was based on the Paris edition of 1843, with a French translation by Charles de l'Escalopier.

[19] A complete translation of the three books of Theophilus, from the Latin text in the Harleian MSS at the British Museum, by Robert Hendrie, was also published in 1847 (London). Neither Hendrie nor Winston made any reference to the other's edition, from which one may conclude that they were in preparation simultaneously. It is hardly likely that Winston's publisher would have gone to the expense of printing this long appendix had Hendrie's more complete work been available at the time of going to press.

[20] For some brief remarks on Willement see Knowles, 'Glass-Painters 1750–1850', XIII (1959–63), 522–23; Woodforde, p. 56, also *Journal of the British Society of Master Glass-Painters*, XIV (1964), 50–51.

[21] Woodforde, p. 52; and 'Modern Glass-Painting', *Edinburgh Review*, CXXV (1867), 163, 175.

[22] *Ecclesiologist*, X (1850), 81.

[23] Winston, I, 270.

[24] Add. MS 33851, fols. 108–14. Two of these are reproduced in Sewter, 'The Place of Charles Winston', pl. xxiv.

[25] Hendrie, pp. 163, 166, 168; and Mrs Merrifield, *The Art of Fresco Painting*, ed. A.C. Sewter (London, 1952), pp. xxxiv-li, esp. p. xliii. Fromberg, however, had been right in stating that black oxide of cobalt was used to colour glass blue; see *An Essay on the Art of Painting on Glass*, pp. 114–15.

[26] C. Winston, *Memoirs Illustrative of the Art of Glass-Painting* (London, 1865), p. 11.

[27] T.H. Baylis, *The Temple Church* (London, 1893), p. 12. The project was evidently closely directed by Winston himself, for he says, 'I tried the experiment . . . of having several figures copied from Greek designs, and the ornament borrowed quite as much from classical Greek work as from that of the twelfth century' (*Memoirs*, p. 19).

[28] Woodforde, p. 57.

[29] 'Modern Glass-Painting', p. 184. This important article is actually a review of Winston's *Memoirs*, and of C.H. Wilson's *Descriptive Catalogue of the Painted Glass Windows in Glasgow Cathedral* (Glasgow, 1866).

[30] A great deal was written about the Glasgow windows, but see especially G. Eyre-Todd, ed. *The Book of Glasgow Cathedral* (Glasgow, 1898), which has illustrations. The Munich windows, now all except one replaced by modern glass, are stored in racks in the triforium.

[31] *The International Exhibition of 1862. The Illustrated Catalogue of the Industrial Department*, British Division, Class XXXIV (London, 1862), II, 67. On Chance, see T. Stokes, 'W.E. Chance and the Revived Manufacture of Coloured Glass'. *Journal of the British Society of Master Glass-Painters*, V (1933–34), 170–76.

[32] *The International Exhibition of 1862*, II, 70.

[33] *The Gentleman's Magazine* (July 1842), p. 81.

[34] Winston, *An Inquiry*, p. 237.

[35] See J.D. Le Couteur, *Ancient Glass in Winchester* (Winchester, 1920). Two details of the copies by Betton and Evans are illustrated in Woodforde, pl. 65.

[36] Illustrated in Sewter, 'The Place of Charles Winston', pl. xxv.

[37] *Ecclesiologist*, IX (1849), 67.

[38] Ibid., p. 201. These important windows, of which the only figurative one, the chancel east window, was unhappily

replaced in 1891, and the remainder somewhat damaged by flying bombs in the Second World War, are not mentioned in J. Newman, *West Kent and the Weald* (Harmondsworth, 1969). It was possibly the most complete scheme of glazing which Miller left.

[39] *The Gentleman's Magazine* (January 1846), p. 84. Again, this escaped notice in N. Pevsner, *Wiltshire* (Harmondsworth, 1963).

[40] *The Builder*, XIII (1855), 418.

[41] *The Builder*, XI (1853), 650.

[42] *The Builder*, XVI (1858), 524.

[43] *The Builder*, XI (1853), 656.

[44] *Art Journal*, n.s. I (1862), 174.

[45] *The Builder*, XX (1862), 577, and *Art Journal Illustrated Catalogue of the International Exhibition* (1862), p. 25. The employment of Burne-Jones was first noticed in *The Builder*, XVIII (1860), 661.

[46] This information comes from some notes by C. Fairfax Murray preserved among the Morris & Co. documents in the library of Birmingham City Art Gallery. My attention was kindly drawn to this point by Mr Martin Harrison.

[47] A. Vallance, *The Decorative Art of Burne-Jones* (*Art Journal* Easter Annual, London, 1900), p. 2.

[48] Ibid.

[49] M. Bell, *Sir Edward Burne-Jones: A Record and Review* (London, 4th ed. 1898), p. 74, states that the Bradfield College designs were the artist's first commissions for stained glass, which seems to be contradicted by Vallance (see note 47). The cartoons for the left and centre lights, now in the Victoria and Albert Museum, are dated 1857. See also J. Gordon-Christian, 'Source Material: The Archives of the Whitefriars Studios, London', *Artifex*, I (1968), 35.

[50] Lady G. Burne-Jones, *Memorials of Edward Burne-Jones*, 2 vols. (London, 1904), I, 196; and J. Gordon- Christian, p. 38.

[51] A. Vallance, *Decorative Art of Burne-Jones*, p. 2; N. Pevsner, *Essex* (Harmondsworth, 1954), pp. 47, 371. The scale of the window is suggested by the measurements of the cartoons for Christ in Majesty and one of the Days of Creation, for the circles of the rose tracery, now in the Victoria and Albert Museum, which have a diameter of 52 inches.

[52] Quoted by P. Henderson, *William Morris, His Life, Work and Friends* (London, 1967), p. 70.

CHAPTER 2

[1] The basic account is that given by J.W. Mackail, *The Life of William Morris*, 2 vols. (London, 1912), I, 149–59.

[2] Burne-Jones's account-books are in the Fitzwilliam Museum, Cambridge, and Philip Webb's belongs to Mr John Brandon-Jones, Hampstead. J.R. Holliday made a transcription of the latter, and it was among materials bequeathed by him to Birmingham City Art Gallery in 1927. This has the advantage of an index of places and persons, added by Holliday. Similar account-books were presumably kept by all the partners. Extracts from Ford Madox Brown's, relating to designs for stained glass, were printed as Appendix C in F. M. Hueffer, *Ford Madox Brown: A Record of His Life and Work* (London, 1896); but the original seems now to be lost, as also do the account-books of Rossetti and the others. On Bodley, see F.M. Simpson, 'G.F. Bodley, R.A.', *Royal Institute of British Architects Journal*, 3rd ser. XV (1907–08), 145–58; Victoria and Albert Museum, *Victorian Church Art* (London, 1971), Section L; and D. Verey, 'Two Early Churches by Bodley', *Country Life*, CXLIX (1971), 1246–49.

[3] See Hueffer, pp. 142, 148, and unnumbered plate; and J. Gordon-Christian, 'Source Material: The Archives of the Whitefriars Studios, London', *Artifex*, I (1968), 35.

[4] Webb's sketch-book containing his studies after the Merton College Chapel windows belongs to Mr John Brandon-Jones.

[5] H.J. Powell, *Glass Making in England* (Cambridge, 1923), p. 130.

[6] The evidence is contained in an entry in Burne-Jones's account-book dated 27 November 1862: 'Alteration in St John Baptist designs 5s. Altering a figure for poor Topsy — this I won't charge for — I'll give it poor Topsy. N.B. To threaten to charge this if the firm behaves meanly in any case!'

[7] Some further comments on Rossetti's short-comings in this respect are made in chapter 5.

[8] A. Vallance, *William Morris, His Art, His Writings and His Public Life: A Record* (London, 1909), p. 65.

[9] The name of Arthur Hughes actually appeared with those of the partners on the firm's first prospectus, but he had withdrawn before the firm was formally registered. See Mackail, I, 152.

[10] Ibid., I, 179–80.

[11] Ibid., I, 180.

[12] Ibid., I, 153, and Vallance, p. 57. R. Watkinson, *William Morris as Designer* (London, 1967), p. 36, states that Campfield had been employed as a glass-painter by the firm of Heaton, Butler and Bayne, without quoting his authority for this statement.

[13] Vallance, pp. 59, 63.

[14] Mackail, I, 153.

[15] Ibid., II, 45. The testimony was that of George Wardle, who succeeded Warrington Taylor as manager at Queen Square in 1870. The last part of his statement is amply confirmed by one of Morris's sketch-books (British Museum, Add. MSS 45336), which contains two pages of notes for the final revision of the Scarborough east window of 1861–62. They are of such interest that it is worth giving them here in their entirety. The extent of the revisions which he demanded is impressive evidence of Morris's thoroughness:

Scarboro East W — alteration.
Vine dressers — Touch up wh. spots. Lighter green leaves in basket. Lighter green man fastening one to pole.
Heir before rebels — New head of heir. cover over wh. specks. lead across fur gown.
Lord taking leave — All right, except border.
Dancing scene — Cover all wh. specks. All right.
Captive — Turn brown hood — bright red. Turn orange sleeve bright red. Mend cracks.
Messenger — all right — cover spots.
Death of son — make saddle of King red, belt light yellow, armour deep stained orange. Second figure saddle to be made P–O. Better orange dress to dead son. New yellow flag with crowns on. Arms of son red instead of green.
Xifixion — Right arm new. Cutt of [*sic*] bottom brown dress, & remake. 3 pieces of backgd. over virgin's head, fresh. Fire again pieces of cherubs.

[16] *The Morris Exhibit at the Foreign Fair, Boston* (Boston, 1883), pp. 29–30. I am indebted to Mr Ray Watkinson for drawing my attention to this pamphlet by his quotations from it in *William Morris as Designer*, pp. 39, 53–57. Mr Watkinson thinks it was probably written hurriedly on the spot by George Wardle; however, in spite of many signs of haste, it seems to me that the most important passages bear all the marks of Morris's own style.

[17] *Work, and Other Paintings by Ford Madox Brown*, exhibition catalogue (London, 1865).

[18] Herbert Read, *English Stained Glass* (London, 1926), p. 222.

[19] Ibid.

[20] Ibid.

[21] Some doubt might appear to be thrown on this statement by the series of sketches of the Selsley windows which occur in Morris's notebook at the British Museum (Add. MSS 45305, 613D, pp. 215rev.–120), but the purpose of these sketches had nothing to do with the design and layout of the subjects. They merely record the shapes and measurements of the openings to be filled, and the numbers of saddle-bars required. Annotations subsequently added indicate the main subjects; and, each opening having been numbered, the same sketches probably served as guide to the glaziers who finally fitted the glass into position.

[22] W.R. Lethaby, *Philip Webb and His Work* (London, 1935), pp. 37–38.

[23] Built by G.F. Bodley, 1862, in thirteenth-century French style.

[24] The idea of this arrangement was said by J.R. Holliday to have been derived from the windows of Merton College Chapel, Oxford. See notes among H.C. Marillier's MSS at Birmingham City Art Gallery.

[25] Bodley's church, built in 1858–62, was enlarged and completed by W. Burges in 1893.

[26] St Martin's-on-the-Hill, another of Bodley's churches, consecrated in 1863.

[27] The window is illustrated in Vallance, opp. p. 68.

[28] Yet another of Bodley's churches, built in 1863–65.

[29] St Edward the Confessor, a mainly mediaeval church of the fourteenth and fifteenth centuries, restored by Gilbert Scott in 1863–64.

[30] Since the removal of the window from its original setting in 1958, and its division into three smaller windows, it is no longer possible to judge the original compositional effect, except from photographs.

[31] By Bodley, 1864. The church is in danger of redundancy, but there is some hope of saving it. See *The Victorian Society Annual 1970–71* (London), p. 16.

[32] By James Murray, 1862–64.

[33] A small church of the late twelfth and fourteenth–fifteenth centuries, with new east end and south aisle of 1864.

[34] A remarkable church by William White, begun in 1860.

[35] A mostly fourteenth-century church, much restored by Gilbert Scott in 1865. See N. Pevsner, *Northamptonshire* (Harmondsworth, 1961), p. 294.

[36] The chancel is of the thirteenth century. G.E. Street carried out restorations in 1866.

[37] It may be useful here to list other places for which windows were supplied in the 1860s: Amington, Antingham, Bicester, Bishop's Tachbrook, Bournemouth (St Peter's), Bradford (Cathedral), Bradford (St Paul's, Manningham), Brighton (Annunciation), Cambridge (Peterhouse), Cardiff, Catton, Cawthorne, Cheddleton, Coddington (Notts.), Coity, Cranborne, Dalton, Dedworth, Doddington, Farnham Royal, Fawley, Furneaux Pelham, Gatcombe, Guernsey, Harden, Haywards Heath, Henley-in-Arden, King's Walden, Ladock, Langton Green, Liverpool (St John the Baptist, Tuebrook), Llandaff, London (Christ Church, Albany Street; Kentish Town Parish Church; Victoria and Albert Museum), Marple, Onecote (Vicarage), Oxford (St Edmund Hall), Peterborough, Rodbourne, St Michael Penkevil, Sculthorpe, Southgate, Tilehurst, Torquay (St John the Evangelist), and Wigan. Some of these are briefly discussed in the following paragraphs.

[38] On the domestic glass, see A.C. Sewter, 'Notes on Morris & Co.'s Domestic Stained Glass', *Journal of the William Morris Society*, I (1961), 22–28.

[39] By G.E. Street. Two years earlier, in the Lyndhurst east window, there were foliage backgrounds, but they have far less importance than those at Amington.

[40] This commission followed a reconstruction of the church by G.E. Street in 1862.

[41] G.E. Street had carried out restoration work also at Catton.

[42] This large and slightly forbidding church is the work of Bodley, 1868–71.

[43] See Mackail, II, 44.

[44] See Peter Floud, 'Dating Morris Patterns', *Architectural Review*, CXXVI (July 1959), 15–20.

[45] Morris's drawing for the figure of Jesse belongs to Mr Sanford Berger.

[46] See H.T. Kirby, 'The Jesse Tree Motif in Stained Glass', *Journal of the British Society of Master Glass-Painters*, XIII (1959–63), 313–20, 434–41.

CHAPTER 3

[1] Only the Absalom was a newly designed figure; the Samuel and Timothy had been designed earlier in the same year for the Vyner window at Christ Church Cathedral, Oxford.

[2] The story is told in 2 Samuel 18:9–15.

[3] The branches and foliage were later extended upwards to provide backgrounds also for the figures of Enoch, Solomon and David in the upper lights, added in 1890.

[4] BLA 407.

[5] E.2791–1927.

[6] St Michael's, Waterford is unaccountably omitted from N. Pevsner, *Hertfordshire* (London, 1953). It is by Henry Woodyer, 1875.

[7] The exception is the east window of the chapel at St Edmund Hall, Oxford, inserted in 1865. There, however, it had been possible to alter the form of the tracery. See A.B. Emden, *An Account of the Chapel and Library Building, St Edmund Hall, Oxford* (Oxford, 1932), p. 37 and pl. opp. p. 34.

[8] The best of many repetitions of these figures, but still far from equalling the Cheddleton example, is at All Saints, Bingley, Yorks., 1874; but this window is now obscured by the organ. The figures are again robed in white and gold, but the wings are pink, blue and red.

[9] This design was repeated only at St Luke's (formerly St Wilfrid's), Farnworth near Widnes, Lancs., in 1876, where the figures were clothed instead in light-toned robes, and much of the effect thereby lost.

[10] Again there is a later repetition of this design, at All Saints, Leigh, Staffs., made in 1913. It is very inferior to the Lytham original, both because the colouring is less brilliant, and because the elaborate decoration introduced on the robes detracts from the simplicity and impressiveness of the figures.

[11] Actually, quite a number of Morris's windows made in the years ca. 1869–ca. 1880 have deteriorated in this way. In Mackail, *Life of Morris*, II, 59–60, and in P. Henderson, ed., *The Letters of William Morris to His Family and Friends* (London, 1950), pp. 162–63, are printed extracts from two of Morris's letters to the Hon. George Howard (later Earl of Carlisle) which explain how Morris, along with many other glass-painters, had been misled by a pigment, marketed as suitable for the purpose and having the advantage of fusing at a lowish temperature, which turned out to contain borax; but unluckily glass of borax is soluble in water. The windows are

often apparently sound until, during some redecoration or restoration, they are washed, when the colour simply washes off. Whenever Morris received complaints of this having happened, he renewed the affected parts. It would not be so easy to get them adequately replaced today.

12 Ford Madox Brown's designs are further discussed in chapter 5 below.

CHAPTER 4

1 Mackail, *Life of Morris*, I, 315–17.

2 Ford Madox Brown retained the copyright to all his cartoons made for the firm, excluding only their use for stained glass, and retained also their absolute ownership; so they were probably returned to him at the dissolution of the partnership. Several windows made from his designs after 1874 were in fact repetitions of earlier cartoons: e.g., the St Anne used at Middleton Cheney in 1880 and at Coddington, Notts., in 1881 repeated a cartoon of 1863; and the St Michael originally designed for St Michael's, Brighton, in 1862 was repeated several times after 1900, the cartoon having been purchased by the firm after Brown's death.

3 Mackail, I, 317.

4 Webb's account-book, which continues until 1 January 1878, contains entries for new designs down to 1 July 1876.

5 Even one of these appears to be the same as a figure used already at Tilehurst in 1869.

6 *Sigurd the Volsung* was published in November 1876. This was the period in which Morris was also beginning to weave brocades and damasks, and was designing many patterns for printed and woven fabrics.

7 As early as the meeting of the partners on 28 January 1863, it was agreed 'that the next meeting be employed in the discussion of the right of ownership of cartoons'. But in fact the subject was not regulated until 27 February 1871, when 'Mr Brown proposed that on all future cartoons a royalty of 10 p.c. of their value should be paid upon any occasion of their use after the first — but this should not apply to designs which by their nature would be subject to frequent repetition, as common tiles &c. passed unam. Mr Brown further proposed a tariff of prices to be paid to members for first use of their cartoons, as follows:

Single cartoons over 4 ft high	£15
,, ,, ,, 2′6″ and up to 4 ft	£12
,, ,, ,, 1′8″ up to 2′6″	£10

and less sizes by special arrangement. Subjects also to be paid by special arrangement.' See Minute Book. It had been Madox Brown's practice, in any case, to assign the copyright of his cartoons for stained glass only to the firm, and to reserve the copyright otherwise to himself. Many of his cartoons have written on them a note to this effect. The scale of charges was amended many times without such formal resolutions as those recorded of the meeting of 1871.

8 M. Bell, *Sir Edward Burne-Jones: A Record and Review* (London, 1892, and subsequent eds.), Appendix III. These lists are incomplete and often very inaccurate, but useful nonetheless.

9 Lady G. Burne-Jones, *Memorials of Edward Burne-Jones*. 2 vols. (London, 1904).

10 The case of the St Helena, however, is the most specific. The first entry for it, in 1875, says: 'S. Helena. Mr Newman's window in small. Not including touching up — nor will any small design include touching up. £6', and a pointing hand is drawn in the margin, to call special attention to this remark. The second entry, in 1876, reads: 'Redrawing head on large photograph of S. Helena. £1'.

11 Such entries begin in 1864, and become more frequent from the beginning of 1866. For instance, the first entry for that year, dated 1 January, reads: 'To wholly redoing Faith Hope & Charity because of their useless condition when they came to be touched — £5.' There are two possible explanations: first, that the cartoons which required touching up were the Sculthorpe designs of 1865, which had been previously used, and wanted some repair; or, second, that they were cartoons produced in the firm's studio, as enlargements or reductions from Burne-Jones's originals, or from small drawings. After September 1869, these references to retouching disappear; and the coincidence of the date with the arrival of T.M. Rooke in the artist's studio suggests that the task of enlarging designs was transferred from the firm's studio to him, and that he continued to be responsible for this work when, later in the same year, he himself transferred to the firm's employment. See note 13 below.

12 Charles Fairfax Murray (1849–1919) was an artist, collector, connoisseur, and friend of Rossetti and the whole Morris circle. He bequeathed a number of English eighteenth-century portraits to the Dulwich Gallery.

13 Thomas Matthews Rooke (1842–1942) studied at South Kensington and in the Royal Academy. He joined Burne-Jones's studio in 1869, and began exhibiting in 1871. After 1884, on Ruskin's advice, he devoted himself to the representation of historic architecture. He was elected a member of the Royal Watercolour Society in 1903, and his work is represented in the Birmingham City Art Gallery, the Graves Art Gallery, Sheffield, and in the Tate Gallery.

14 City of Birmingham Art Gallery, *Catalogue of the Permanent Collection of Paintings* (Birmingham, 1930), p. 33.

15 Ibid., p. 31. J.M. Strudwick and R. Spencer Stanhope probably also worked at times in Burne-Jones's studio.

16 City of Birmingham Art Gallery, *Catalogue of the Permanent Collection of Drawings* (Birmingham, 1939), pp. 140–41, nos. 411'27, 1–10.

17 E.1844-1946.

18 A.23. The *Catalogue of the Morris Collection* (Walthamstow, 1969), p. 6, dates this cartoon ca. 1862, and identifies it as 'for window representing the Three Marys at the Tomb, at St Martin's-on-the-Hill, Scarborough and at St Michael and All Angels, Brighton.' But there is no window of this subject at Scarborough.

19 A.E. Whitley, in the Birmingham *Catalogue of Drawings*, p. 135, suggested that one cartoon (533'04), of the Nativity for the east window at Amington, drawn in 1864, 'is probably a copy *after* Burne-Jones, by some other hand.' I do not agree. On the contrary, the cartoon of Christ Blessing Children (432'27), for the 1862 window at Selsley, which Whitley catalogued as by Burne-Jones (p. 145), is in my opinion a scale-reduction of Burne-Jones's cartoon, most likely by Philip Webb.

20 There is some confusion over this subject in the Birmingham *Catalogue of Drawings* (p. 124). The cartoon (186'00) which is there entitled Fra Angelico is in fact inscribed as St Luke, which is probably correct, though the occasion of its use remains unidentified. On the other hand, the cartoon for the Fra Angelico in St Saviour's, Leeds (187'00) is catalogued as St Luke, and dated four years too early.

21 Account-book, undated entry between March and August 1878.

22 There is unfortunately no documentary evidence as to the authorship of the designs for the foliage background of the Salisbury angels, but they may very well have been by Pozzi.

23 Account-book, undated entry, opposite one dated 29 September 1882.

[24] Ibid., entry dated July 1883.

[25] See H.-R. Hitchcock, *The Architecture of H.H. Richardson and His Times* (rev. ed. New York, 1961), pp. 136 ff.

[26] Account-book, entry dated May 1882.

[27] See J. White, *The Birth and Rebirth of Pictorial Space* (London, 1957), esp. chapter 12, on Filippo Lippi, which refers also to Fra Angelico's Coronation of the Virgin.

[28] Account-book, entry dated July 1883.

[29] Ibid., entry dated March to November 1887.

[30] See [H.C. Marillier], *A Note on the Morris Stained Glass Work* (London, 1913); also, for example, F. de Lisle, *Burne-Jones* (London, 1904), p. 157, where she writes: 'Admirable as Burne-Jones's windows are, none are finer than those in St Philip's Church, Birmingham . . . works which are probably the highest attainment of modern times in this branch of art'.

[31] N. Pevsner and A. Wedgwood, *Warwickshire* (Harmondsworth, 1966), p. 108.

[32] Ibid.

[33] An excellent account of the formation of 'Anti-scrape' and of Morris's connections with it is given by A. Vallance, *William Morris*, pp. 267–99.

[34] Ibid., p. 293.

[35] From a letter to *The Times*, 15 August 1890, printed in full by A. Briggs, ed., *William Morris: Selected Writings and Designs* (Harmondsworth, 1962), p. 83.

[36] This criticism of the Sloane Street window was anticipated by Vallance, pp. 78–79.

[37] M. Bell, *Burne-Jones* (1898 ed.), p. 52, stated that the Angels of Creation 'were originally designed for a window erected in 1874 in Tamworth Church'. They do indeed occur in that window, but the Middleton Cheney window of 1870 was their first appearance. The relevant entry in Burne-Jones's account-book is dated July 1870.

[38] The Days of Creation designs are the subject of a detailed study by Miss Beth Mandelbaum of the Fogg Art Museum, as yet unpublished, which she very kindly allowed me to see in typescript.

[39] De Lisle, *Burne-Jones*, pp. 165–67, gives a concise summary of these honours.

[40] Lady G. Burne-Jones, *Memorials of Edward Burne-Jones*, II, 317.

CHAPTER 5

[1] Mackail, *Life of Morris*, II, 44.

[2] 534'04. See the Birmingham *Catalogue of Drawings*, p. 287.

[3] See bibliography nos. 4–6.

[4] See bibliography no. 5.

[5] See bibliography no. 11.

[6] Only eight or nine of the many quarry designs used can be shown from Webb's account-book to have been designed by Webb; and there is no evidence, so far as I know, that Madox Brown or Burne-Jones designed any quarries.

[7] For an example of this direction in operation, see chapter 2, note 15.

[8] A 24. Illustrated in A.C. Sewter, 'William Morris's Designs for Stained Glass', *Architectural Review*, CXXVII (March 1960), 198.

[9] Several studies for this design will be found in Morris's sketch-book in the British Museum, Add. MSS 45336, fols. 13–14. For Queen Mary's Psalter, see Sir George Warner, *Queen Mary's Psalter* (London, 1912). The figures on the left of fol. 13 in the sketch-book, facing right, are taken from Warner pl. 311, and those on the right, facing left, are from Warner pl. 312. The lower figure on fol. 14 is copied from the St Stephen in the lower marginal illustration, Warner pl. 240; and the upper figure is again from pl. 311. The disappearing feet of the ascending Christ do not occur in Queen Mary's Psalter; this way of representing him was an Anglo-Saxon invention (see for example the Bury St Edmunds Gospels, Pembroke College, Cambridge, fol. 5v.), which became a convention in the Gothic period. I am indebted to my colleague Professor C.R. Dodwell for help in identifying these sources.

[10] William Morris Gallery, Walthamstow, A 7.

[11] Possibly Morris's best drawing, from the point of view of an academic grasp of anatomy, is the cartoon of Artemis in the Carlisle Art Gallery, perhaps designed for tapestry.

[12] Both panels were repeated at Knaresborough and Marple (1873), and the left one only at Llandaff Cathedral (1869). The cartoons are at the William Morris Gallery, Walthamstow, A 13–14. The left one is illustrated in Sewter, 'William Morris's Designs', p. 199.

[13] The cartoon for the left panel is in the Tate Gallery, 5223. It is illustrated in ibid., p. 199. The same figures were later used in a small single-panel version of the subject at St Olave's, Gatcombe, Isle of Wight, ca. 1865–66. The relationship between the two versions is puzzling, as it is easier to see the Brighton diptych as an expansion of the Gatcombe design than to conceive the reverse order of date.

[14] Cartoon in the William Morris Gallery, Walthamstow, A 11.

[15] A 18.

[16] In fact there are two cartoons of this design in the William Morris Gallery, A 16 and A 17; one of them must be for a later use of the subject at Coddington, Notts., Guernsey, Knaresborough or Scarborough.

[17] A 261.

[18] William Morris Gallery, Walthamstow, A 8.

[19] I have not identified Morris's exact sources, but a somewhat similar type of thick, heavy drapery may be observed in the weepers of the tomb of Philip the Bold, by Claus Sluter and others, now in the Musée de Dijon and the Musée de Cluny. Burne-Jones also designed a set of the Four Seasons ca. 1864, to be executed in Della Robbia ware; see de Lisle, *Burne-Jones*, p. 192. Drawings for two of these, Spring and Summer, were exhibited in 1971 by Hartnoll & Eyre, London (*Drawings, Studies and Paintings by Sir Edward Burne-Jones*, 1a and 1b, illus.); and there are studies for the figure of Spring in the Fogg Museum, Harvard, and in the Ashmolean Museum, Oxford. They are quite different from the stained-glass set.

[20] The most frequently repeated designs were those of St George and St Martin, of 1878 and 1880 respectively, both of which were used at least thirty-eight times; in third place comes a Mary Virgin designed in 1874 and used at least thirty-six times; and fourth, a figure of Humility designed in 1883 and made at least thirty-five times.

[21] In these comparisons I have used the article by Peter Floud, 'Dating Morris Patterns', *Architectural Review*, CXXVI (July 1959), 15–20.

[22] Lewis F. Day, *William Morris and His Art* (*Art Journal*, Easter Number), London, 1899, p. 19.

[23] For an annotated list of Rossetti's designs for stained glass see A.C. Sewter, 'D.G. Rossetti's Designs for Stained Glass', *Journal of the British Society of Master Glass-Painters*, XIII (1960–61), 419–24; reprinted (with some misprints) as an appendix in R.G. Grylls, *Portrait of Rossetti* (London, 1964). That list, however, is no longer complete, and is superseded by the one included in the forthcoming catalogue volume of this work.

[24] H. C. Marillier, *Dante Gabriel Rossetti: An Illustrated Memorial of His Art and Life*, 3rd ed. (London, 1904). p. 75.

[25] Hueffer, *Ford Madox Brown*, p. 343.

[26] In the William Morris Gallery, Walthamstow, A 263 – A 269. All are illustrated in V. Surtees, *The Paintings and Drawings of Dante Gabriel Rossetti*, 2 vols. (Oxford, 1971), pls. 202–08.

[27] C.315–320–1927. The purpose for which these panels were made is not known. They were bequeathed to the museum in 1927 by J.R. Holliday. The cartoons in the Birmingham City Art Gallery (241–245'04 and 494'04) are described and illustrated by Surtees, I, nos. 145–151, pls. 212–18, together with replicas and variants.

[28] In the Williamson Art Gallery, Birkenhead. Illustrated in Sewter, 'Rossetti's Designs', opp. p. 422, and in Surtees, pl. 256.

[29] C.197–1918. It is only fair to note that the subject was originally designed not for stained glass but for the decoration of a cabinet; this cartoon, however, is an adaptation intended specifically for stained glass.

[30] The cartoon belongs to Leeds City Art Gallery, and hangs at Temple Newsam; see Surtees, no. 142A. The note on it is as follows: 'Dear Top [an affectionate nickname for Morris] If you have to reduce it do it in pencil and then I'll draw it again. It strikes me now it's done there's no space left for the lead-lines, is there? Don't spoil this one as I'll make some use of it if you find it too big. I'm waiting for the reduction to do the others, as then I'll get them the exact size. Note that I've added a little bit at the bottom to get Christ in.' The redrawn cartoon is in the William Morris Gallery at Walthamstow, A 210; see Surtees, no. 142, pl. 210.

[31] The original sketch-design in watercolour and gouache is in the Birmingham City Art Gallery, 417'04, illustrated in Surtees, pl. 222.

[32] The Gatcombe version is illustrated in Sewter, 'Rossetti's Designs', opp. p. 423. The cartoon, in the possession of Mrs Imogen Dennis, is described and illustrated in Surtees, no. 140, pl. 209. The window originally at All Saints, Langton Green, is now at St Mary's, Doddington, Cambs.

[33] The only known repetition of it is in the chancel south window at St Mary's, Antingham, Norfolk (1865). The cartoons are untraced.

[34] Entry in the firm's minute-book; see bibliography no. 7.

[35] The cartoon of the Annunciation, formerly in the collections of Theodore Watts-Dunton and Algernon Charles Swinburne, has recently appeared on the art market; see the exhibition catalogue of Stone Gallery, Newcastle-on-Tyne, *Some Pre-Raphaelite Works* (Summer 1971), no. 6, illus., and Surtees, Appendix no. 5. The same exhibition also contained Rossetti's cartoon of Joshua, the occasion for which remains unknown; see Surtees, no. 157.

[36] Hueffer, p. 178.

[37] Ibid., Appendix C, pp. 445–47, listed 106 designs for stained glass, on the basis of information extracted from Brown's account-book with the firm. Hueffer was aware that this list was incomplete, and in a footnote on p. 445 he mentioned four others, the cartoons for which were in his possession. The figure of 150 was no more than a guess.

[38] See A. C. Sewter, 'A Check-list of Designs for Stained Glass by Ford Madox Brown', *Journal of the William Morris Society*, II, (Summer 1968), 19–29. This list is no longer quite complete, and is superseded by the one in the forthcoming volume 2 of this work.

[39] Quoted by Vallance, William Morris, pp. 69–70.

[40] This design has been the subject of much confusion. It was illustrated by Hueffer incorrectly titled as the Archangel Michael. The original cartoon in the Victoria and Albert Museum (E.2906–1927) was catalogued as by Burne-Jones. The same figure was also used as Sir Lancelot in the last of the panels of the Story of Tristram series now in the Bradford City Art Gallery, and the cartoon for this, in the William Morris Gallery, Walthamstow (A262), containing also the figure of King Arthur by Morris, shows a slightly simplified version of the armour, and a straightened shield.

[41] The cartoon by Ford Madox Brown for Uriel is illustrated by Hueffer, last plate.

[42] The cartoon for the right-hand panel, St Martin in Heaven, was reproduced by Rathbone, pl. 11; see bibliography, no. 108.

[43] Madox Brown painted a water-colour of the same design in 1863, and a version in oils on canvas in 1864 for George Rae, which now belongs to the Birmingham City Art Gallery (26'16), and is illustrated by Hueffer opp. p. 200. See the Birmingham *Catalogue of Paintings*, pp. 23–24.

[44] Christ carrying the Cross was designed in 1872 for a window at Haltwhistle; Christ laid in the Sepulchre was designed in 1865 for a window at Gatcombe; Christ scourged at the Pillar and the Agony in the Garden were designed in 1872 for Jesus College Chapel, Cambridge.

[45] This design was not documented in the account-book, if Hueffer's list is to be trusted; but a version of the same design was published as a wood-engraving in John Leighton, *Lyra Germanica* (London, 1867), illustrated by Hueffer, p. 222; and another version was executed as a painting, illustrated ibid., opp. p. 222.

[46] Two of the original cartoons, for the Birth of St Oswald, and St Oswald crowned King of Benucia, are in the Victoria and Albert Museum 231–1894 and E.1853–1910.

[47] This can be appreciated more easily in the cartoons for these lights, now in the Whitworth Art Gallery, University of Manchester, than in the very unapproachable windows at Tamworth.

[48] This feature of Brown's style was possibly due to the influence of his early training under Baron Wappers at Antwerp.

[49] The canopies and borders are also closely related to the fourteenth-century windows in Merton College Chapel, Oxford, of which careful water-colour studies are in Webb's notebook belonging to Mr John Brandon-Jones.

[50] The fine cartoon for this figure, in the Walker Art Gallery, Liverpool, is inscribed: 'This cartoon is the property of the artist copyright for stained glass only granted to the firm of M.M.F. & Co.'

[51] Most of these figures were repeated in the series of cartoons of 'Twelve Worthies' drawn in 1878–79 for the 'Museum for the People' at Old Trafford, now in the possession of the University of Manchester.

[52] The cartoon of St Simon is in the Birmingham City Art Gallery 150'12; that of St Jude is in the Walker Art Gallery, Liverpool.

[53] Mackail, II, 44.

[54] The cartoon is at the Victoria and Albert Museum, E.1289–1931.

[55] The cartoon for one section of the Banners of the Tribes of Israel is in the Victoria and Albert Museum, E.2940–1927.

[56] Entries dated 1 January 1864.

[57] The cartoon is at the Victoria and Albert Museum, E.1166–1940.

[58] The cartoon for Joshua is in the Victoria and Albert Museum, E.1167–1940; that for Moses is in the William Morris Gallery, Walthamstow, A 12.

[59] The Daniel cartoon is in the Victoria and Albert Museum, E.1168–1940.

[60] Entries in the firm's minute-book. One of my students, Miss Jane Sellars, has, since the text of this book was already in type, succeeded in tracing Mr Hastings, a Bradford manufacturer who lived at Silsden House near Keighley, Yorks., where the windows were. The house, however, was demolished in 1903, and the windows are untraced.

[61] Ibid., entries dated 11 February and 6 May 1863.

[62] See also O.G. Destrée, *Les Préraphaélites: Notes sur l'art decoratif et la peinture en Angleterre* (Brussels, 1894).

[63] See *Catalogue of Drawings*, p. 285.

[64] See N. Pevsner, *Northamptonshire* (Harmondsworth, 1961), p. 295.

[65] I am indebted to the present rector, the Rev. G.E. Glynne-Jones, for this information.

[66] The cartoon is in the Birmingham City Art Gallery, 39'12; see *Catalogue of Drawings*, p. 237.

[67] Valentine Cameron Prinsep studied at the Royal Academy Schools and under Gleyre in Paris. He was elected Associate of the R.A. in 1879, full member in 1894, and Professor of Painting for 1900–03.

[68] Frederic Shields was actually approached, via Rossetti, in January 1865, but on this occasion declined on the grounds of other commitments. See O. Doughty and J.R. Wahl, eds., *The Letters of Dante Gabriel Rossetti*, 5 vols. (Oxford, 1965–67), II, 541, 543.

[69] Walter Crane, *An Artist's Reminiscences* (London, 1907), p. 375.

[70] The Adcote windows were first recognized as the work of Morris & Co. by Mark Girouard; see *Country Life* (22 October 1970), p. 1058. The attribution of the designs to Crane, however, is mine.

[71] Another example, by an unidentified maker, dated 1914, exists in St Paul's, Stalybridge, Cheshire; and one signed by E.J. Salisbury is at St Oswald's, Sowerby near Thirsk, Yorks.

[72] See *The Builder*, XIII (1864), 439; *Ecclesiologist*, XXV (1864), 191, 249; *Art Journal*, III (1864), 260.

CHAPTER 6

[1] Day, *William Morris and His Art*, p. 30.

[2] A John H. Dearle who exhibited eighteen landscapes at the Royal Academy between 1878 and 1900 was probably the same person; but the John Dearle who also showed landscapes at the Royal Academy from 1852 to 1871 must have been another, possibly his father. See A. Graves, *The Royal Academy of Arts*, 8 vols. (London, 1905–06). The chief printed source of information on J.H. Dearle is a note inserted between pp. 50 and 51 of the 1912 pocket edition of Mackail, *Life of Morris*, II. This corrects his original text references, based upon notes by George Wardle, by means of information supplied by Dearle himself. According to this note, Dearle entered the service of the firm when very young, from a post in an insurance office. He was employed for several years in the glass-painting shop, and was then picked out by Morris to help on the high-warp tapestries. Later he became manager and chief designer at the Merton Abbey works, and a partner in 1894. Dates are supplied by the Victoria and Albert Museum, *Catalogue of an Exhibition of Victorian and Edwardian Decorative Arts* (London, 1952), p. 138, according to which Dearle was born in 1860, joined the firm in 1878, and died on 15 January 1932.

[3] Christopher Whall (1850–1924), who, together with Louis Davis (1861–1941) may be considered the best representative artist of the Arts and Crafts style in stained glass, would be worth a proper investigation, especially for his use of iridescent glass. Both his well-known book, *Stained Glass Work* (London, 1905) and his works exerted an important influence on artists of the next generation, including Karl Parsons and Douglas Strachan. See C. Woodforde, *English Stained and Painted Glass* (Oxford, 1954), p. 63 and pl. 73; and E.L. Armitage, *Stained Glass* (London, 1959), p. 66 and pl. 47.

[4] This information on W.H. Knight comes entirely from entries in the Catalogue of Designs, now in the possession of Mr Sanford Berger.

[5] For information concerning Duncan Dearle I am indebted to his widow, Mrs Frances Dearle, and to the Catalogue of Designs.

[6] All the facts cited in this paragraph are derived from the Catalogue of Designs.

[7] See Sewter, 'Notes on Morris & Co.'s Domestic Stained Glass'.

[8] Other windows which have been moved to new positions are in the Council Chambers at Dundee; at Ingatestone; Ullet Road, Liverpool; Maidstone Grammar School; Queen Elizabeth Grammar School, Blackburn; Blackburn Cathedral; St Paul's, Montreal; Doddington; and Frinton-on-Sea.

[9] *The Victorian Society Annual 1969–70* (London, 1971), p. 26.

[10] Ibid., pp. 19, 27.

[11] The Camberwell window is illustrated in Vallance, *William Morris*, opp. p. 68.

[12] See J. Lowe, 'Restoration of Morris Windows at the Victoria and Albert Museum', *Museums Journal* (August 1960), pp. 121–22.

CONCLUSION

[1] Winston, *Memoirs*, p. 61.

[2] Almost the only exception I can think of is the very early window of 1862–63 at Kentish Town parish church.

[3] These Manchester College windows, made in 1895, were enlarged versions of designs originally prepared in 1870 for the tracery lights of a window at Middleton Cheney, and used also at St Editha's, Tamworth, in 1874. Burne-Jones had in the meantime painted a series of large versions of them, now in the Fogg Art Museum, Harvard. They are the theme of a paper by Miss Beth Mandelbaum, as yet unpublished, which she kindly allowed me to see in typescript.

[4] Lethaby, *Philip Webb and His Work*, pp. 61–62.

[5] From a lecture on 'The Lesser Arts' (1878), reprinted in Briggs, ed., *William Morris: Selected Writings and Designs*, pp. 93–94.

Glossary

BAR-LINES. The metal bars used to support and join the rectangular panes of glass in windows painted in the eighteenth- and early nineteenth-century manner; usually unrelated to the design of the painting.

CANOPY. The representation of a roof-like projection above a figure, as used in late mediaeval architectural sculpture, and in stained glass; normally used in conjunction with a pedestal on which the figure stands.

CARTOON. A drawing, usually on paper, showing the complete design for a window or section of a window, on the full scale of the space to be filled.

CUT-LINES. The lines, usually indicated on the cartoon or on a tracing from it, to show the shapes and positions of the small pieces of glass which will make up the window; also, of course, the lines of the lead joints.

DIAPER. A geometrical or conventional pattern based upon intersecting diagonal lines forming diamond shapes; the term is often loosely used in connection with stained glass to mean any repeating or subordinate patterning of backgrounds or of represented fabrics.

ENAMEL COLOURS. Colours consisting of coloured glass ground to a fine powder and mixed with a medium of oil or gum, which are painted on the surface of glass and fired in a kiln so that the medium is burnt away and the particles of colour melt and adhere to the surface of the glass. Colours produced by this process are always less translucent, less pure and rich than pot-metal or flashed colour.

FLASHED GLASS. Glass in which a thin layer of deeply coloured glass, most frequently ruby, is fused with glass of a different colour, usually white. The purpose of this technique is to avoid the excessive depth of tone of glass coloured throughout its thickness.

GRISAILLE. Pattern-work, generally geometrical, in which a background of white, grey or pale-tinted glass, usually in the form of quarries, is enriched with diaper pattern, borders or bands of colour; sometimes a grisaille window may contain small panels or medallions of figurative work.

LANCET. A tall narrow window with a pointed head; sometimes loosely used for tall narrow lights with heads of trefoil or other forms.

LEADS, LEAD-LINES. The joints consisting of H-section strips of lead, by means of which the pieces of glass composing a window are held together; the lead-lines are marked, in the first place, on the cartoon (or tracing from it) which later serves as a guide to the workman who assembles the pieces. Since the lead-lines form an integral part of the whole, they must be allowed for in the designing of the cartoon.

LIGHT. A window-opening, or a principal division of a window between the stone-work.

PEDESTAL. See CANOPY.

POT-METAL. Glass which is coloured in the molten state, and is therefore tinted all through its substance.

QUARRY. Properly a square stone, tile or brick, but used in connection with stained glass to indicate a regular geometrical piece of glass, square, rectangular or diamond shaped; usually decorated with conventional ornament; used sometimes for whole lights, for panels above or below figured subjects, or as a background.

ROUND-GLASS. A type of quarry ground consisting of small circles separated by four-pointed pieces of glass.

SADDLE-BAR. An iron rod, inserted into the stone-work on either side of a window, on the inside, to which the lead joints or edges of a glass panel are attached by copper wires for purposes of support.

STAINED GLASS. This term is used in most of the literature on the subject, and in this book, as a convenient shorthand term for stained and painted glass. All the works described and discussed here consist of glass prepared in one or more of three ways, i.e., coloured pot-metal, yellow-stained glass, or enamelled glass.

STREAKY GLASS. Glass in which the hue or intensity of colour is not even, but varies in streaks, due usually to small variations in the thickness of the metal.

TEMPLATE. A piece of paper, card or other material cut to fit exactly into the opening of a light or window, and therefore indicating the size and shape of the glass to be made.

YELLOW-STAIN. The process, discovered in the fourteenth century, of painting white glass with a solution of silver, usually silver nitrate, which when fired in the kiln produces a pure transparent stain of yellow, varying according to the strength of the solution and the heat of the kiln from pale lemon to deep golden-orange. The process superseded pot-metal yellows, which were generally harsh.

Appendix: Glass-Painters and Glaziers in the Morris Firm

The following is a list of glass-painters and glaziers employed by the firm, and their dates of employment, as recorded in the so-called Catalogue of Designs, now in the possession of Mr Sanford L. Berger, Berkeley, California. Some of them, of course, and particularly Pozzi and Bowman, may very well have been with the firm for some time before their names occur in the records, as we know was the case with Campfield.

Bowman	1877–1909
Brown	1892–1902
Brown, H.	1907
Burrows	1911
Campfield, George	1861–98
Chadwick*	1916, 1919–33, 1939
Cory	1902
Crabbe	1907–08
Cutting	1895
Davis (or Davies)	1909, 1912, 1916, 1926–28
Drake	1920–21
Edge	1912–14
Egan	1877, 1884, 1893
Fletcher	1877
Glasby	1909–11, 1913–23
Howard	1908–10, 1920
Howarth	1920
Jennings	1921–22
Knight, W. H.	1899–1924, 1930, 1932–35, 1937, 1939–40
Markham, W.	1917–18
Mears, S. G.	1936–38
Potts	1908–09
Pozzi	1876–78, 1881–83, 1886–88
Rees, D.	1939
Riviere, G. and W.	1886, 1889, 1892, 1898, 1901, 1909
Rogers	1903–04
Seeley	1921–38
Simmons	1935
Singleton	1880–82
Stokes	1880–1915
Taylor	1936
Titcomb	1896–97, 1899–1928, 1930
Trinick	1921
Veal	1895–97
Walters	1893–1902
Watson	1902–04, 1907–24
Wills	1898, 1910
Wilson	1902–03
Wren	1893–1907

* There were, in fact, two glass-painters named Chadwick, one of whom had the initial H., but they are not clearly distinguishable.

Selected Bibliography

The following lists do not attempt to be complete or exhaustive; they merely indicate the items most likely to be of use to the student of Morris stained glass. It must be added that the excellent volume by W.E. Fredeman, *Pre-Raphaelitism: A Bibliocritical Study* (Cambridge, Mass., 1965), is an essential tool for all serious study in this field.

MANUSCRIPT AND UNPUBLISHED SOURCE MATERIAL

1 British Museum. The Department of Manuscripts has an extensive collection of William Morris MSS, including poems, letters, journals and sketch-books, briefly described by Fredeman, p. 45.

2 Burne-Jones. Two MS volumes containing his accounts with the Morris firm in 1861–96, and illustrated with several humorous sketches. Now in the Fitzwilliam Museum, Cambridge.

3 Dearle Papers. One letter from William Morris and eleven letters from Burne-Jones addressed to J.H. Dearle. They were lent by Mrs F.A. Dearle to the Burne-Jones Commemorative Exhibition at Fulham Public Library, 1967, nos. 80–85, and briefly (and not very accurately) described in the catalogue. Now in the possession of Mr Sanford L. Berger, Berkeley, California.

4 Marillier, H.C. 'Record of Stained Glass Windows executed by Morris & Co.' A MS volume of notes, arranged in alphabetical order by place, with dates, details of subjects, designers and cartoon reference numbers in many cases; and lists of 'Ancient Sketches from Merton', and of windows supplied to private persons. Now in the library of Birmingham City Art Gallery (603'40). Mostly compiled from no. 8 below, but with some additional information; many minor works, however, are omitted, as well as certain early windows not included in no. 8; and the latest windows included are of about 1920.

5 Marillier, H.C. 'An Alphabetical Index of Subjects and Cartoons for stained glass made by Morris & Co.' Now in the library of Birmingham City Art Gallery (604'40). A useful MS index which provides the basis for the index of subjects and cartoons in the forthcoming second volume of the present work, but incomplete in the same respects as no. 4 above.

6 Morris & Co. The Window-Book. An album of photographs of windows and cartoons made and designed by Morris & Co., and formerly used in the firm's London show-rooms. Now in the library of Birmingham City Art Gallery.

7 Morris, Marshall, Faulkner & Co. 'Minute Book', 10 December 1862 to 23 October 1874. Lent by Mrs F.A. Dearle to the Burne-Jones Commemorative Exhibition, Fulham Public Library, 1967, no. 76, and described in the catalogue. Now in the possession of Mr Sanford L. Berger, Berkeley, California.

8 Morris & Co. 'Catalogue of Designs used for Windows Executed from June 1876 to 30 June 1916'. A detailed list of all the stained-glass work executed by the firm, in order of date, giving the subjects, cartoon reference numbers, and in later years the names of the glass-painters responsible for the various parts. Now in the possession of Mr Sanford L. Berger, Berkeley, California.

9 Morris & Co. 'Windows Executed from 1st July 1916'. A continuation of the records kept in no. 8 above; it also includes lists of windows executed by Duncan W. Dearle. In the possession of Mr Sanford L. Berger, Berkeley, California.

10 Powell's Whitefriars Studios. Account-books, window-glass order books, notebooks, ledgers, letters, press-cuttings, etc., connected with their business as manufacturers of coloured window-glass and of stained and painted glass windows. These extensive archives, in the firm's offices in Wealdstone, Middlesex, are usefully described by J. Gordon-Christian, in 'Source Material: The Archives of the Whitefriars Studio, London', *Artifex*, I (1968), 30–46.

11 Philip Webb. A small MS notebook containing his accounts with the Morris firm in 1861–78. Now in the possession of Mr John Brandon-Jones, A.R.I.B.A., Hampstead. A MS transcription by J.R. Holliday, with the useful addition of indexes of persons and places, is in the library of Birmingham City Art Gallery.

12 Philip Webb Letter-book. A MS volume containing drafts or copies of more than 300 of Webb's letters connected with his architectural practice from 1874 to 1882. In the possession of Mr John Brandon-Jones, A.R.I.B.A., Hampstead.

CATALOGUES OF PRINCIPAL PUBLIC COLLECTIONS

13 City of Birmingham Art Gallery. *Catalogue of the Permanent Collection of Paintings in Oil, Tempera,*

Watercolour, etc., 1930; and *Supplements*, 1935, 1935–39 and 1939–50.

14 CITY OF BIRMINGHAM ART GALLERY. *Catalogue of the Permanent Collection of Drawings*, 1939.

15 LIVERPOOL. *Walker Art Gallery: Catalogue of the Permanent Collection*, 1929.

16 LONDON, TATE GALLERY. M. Chamot. *The Tate Gallery. British School. A Concise Catalogue*, 1958.

17 PORT SUNLIGHT. R.R. Tatlock *et al. A Record of the Collections in the Lady Lever Art Gallery*. London, 1928.

18 WALTHAMSTOW. *The William Morris Gallery: Catalogue of the Morris Collection*, 1958. 2nd rev. ed. 1969.

PRINCIPAL EXHIBITIONS

19 *The International Exhibition of 1862. The Illustrated Catalogue of the Industrial Department*. London, 1862.

20 *Work, and Other Paintings by Ford Madox Brown*. Catalogue of the Exhibition at 191 Piccadilly. London, 1865.

21 *The Morris Exhibit at the Foreign Fair, Boston*. Boston, 1883.

22 *Drawings and Studies by Sir Edward Burne-Jones*. Burlington Fine Arts Club, London, 1899.

23 *Loan Exhibition of Works by Ford Madox Brown and the Pre-Raphaelites*. Manchester City Art Gallery, Manchester, 1911.

24 *Centenary Exhibition of Paintings and Drawings by Sir Edward Burne-Jones, Bart*. National Gallery, Millbank, London, 1933.

25 *Catalogue of an Exhibition in Celebration of the Centenary of William Morris*. Victoria and Albert Museum, London, 1934.

26 *Centenary Exhibition of Works by the Pre-Raphaelites, Their Friends and Followers*. Lady Lever Art Gallery, Port Sunlight, 1948.

27 *The Pre-Raphaelites: A Loan Exhibition of their Paintings held in the Centenary Year of the Foundation of the Brotherhood*. Whitechapel Art Gallery, London, 1948.

28 *Catalogue of an Exhibition of Victorian and Edwardian Decorative Arts*. Victoria and Albert Museum, London, 1952.

29 *Morris and Company 1861–1940: A Commemorative Centenary Exhibition*. Arts Council of Great Britain, London, 1961.

30 *Ford Madox Brown 1821–1893*. Exhibition organized by the Walker Art Gallery, Liverpool, 1964.

31 *The Pre-Raphaelites: A Loan Exhibition of Paintings and Drawings*. Herron Museum of Art, Indianapolis, and Gallery of Modern Art, including the Huntington Hartford Collection, New York, 1964.

32 *Sir Edward Burne-Jones Commemorative Exhibition*. Fulham Public Library, London, 1967.

33 *Paintings and Drawings from the Leathart Collection*. Laing Art Gallery, Newcastle-on-Tyne, 1968.

34 *Burne-Jones*. Mappin Art Gallery, Weston Park, Sheffield, 1971.

35 *Victorian Church Art*. Victoria and Albert Museum, London, 1971.

GUIDE-BOOKS AND WORKS ON PARTICULAR BUILDINGS AND PLACES

36 BAYLIS, T.H. *The Temple Church*. London, 1893.

37 BETJEMAN, J. and PIPER, J. *Murray's Berkshire Architectural Guide*. London, 1948.

38 ——— eds. *Murray's Buckinghamshire Architectural Guide*. London, 1948.

39 *Birket Foster*. *Art Journal* Christmas Number, London, 1890.

40 BOGGIS, R.J.E. *History of St John's, Torquay*. Torquay, 1930.

41 CLARKE, B.F.L. *Anglican Cathedrals outside the British Isles*. London, 1958.

42 ——— *Parish Churches of London*. London, 1966.

43 DODD, E.E. *Bingley, A Yorkshire Town through Nine Centuries*. Bingley, 1958.

44 EMDEN, A.B. *An Account of the Chapel and Library Building, St Edmund Hall, Oxford*. Oxford, 1932.

45 FLEETWOOD-HESKETH, P. *Murray's Lancashire Architectural Guide*. London, 1955.

46 HITCHCOCK, H.-R. *The Architecture of H.H. Richardson and His Times*. Rev. ed. New York, 1961.

47 KENT, W. *The Lost Treasures of London*. London, 1947.

48 *Liverpool Cathedral. The Official Handbook of the Cathedral Committee*. 11th ed. Liverpool, 1951.

49 PETER, F. *Berkeley Castle. An Illustrated Survey*. Derby, n.d.

50 PEVSNER, N., *et al. The Buildings of England*. A series of invaluable architectural guides, due eventually to cover all the counties of England. The volumes issued to date are: *Bedfordshire and the County of Huntingdon and Peterborough, Berkshire, Buckinghamshire, Cambridgeshire, Cheshire, Cornwall, Cumberland and Westmorland, Derbyshire, North Devon, South Devon, Durham, Essex, Gloucestershire: The Cotswolds, Gloucestershire: The Vale and the Forest of Dean, Hampshire and the Isle of Wight, Herefordshire, Hertfordshire, North East and East Kent, West Kent and the Weald, North Lancashire, South Lancashire, Leicestershire and Rutland, Lincolnshire, London: The Cities of London and Westminster, London except the Cities of London and Westminster, Middlesex, North East Norfolk and Norwich, North West and South Norfolk, Northamptonshire, Northumberland, Nottinghamshire, Shropshire, North Somerset and Bristol, South and West Somerset, Suffolk, Surrey, Sussex, Warwickshire, Wiltshire, Worcestershire, Yorkshire: The North Riding, Yorkshire: The West Riding.*

51 SPEIGHT, H. *Chronicles and Stories of Old Bingley*. London, 1898.

52 WHIFFEN, M. *Stuart and Georgian Churches outside London*. London, 1947–48.

PRE-RAPHAELITISM: GENERAL

53 BATE, P.H. *The English Pre-Raphaelite Painters*. London, 1899.

54 BOASE, T.S.R. *English Art 1800–1870*. Oxford, 1959.

55 CRANE, W. *An Artist's Reminiscences*. London, 1907. Reprint, Detroit, 1969.

56 DESTRÉE, O.G. *Les Préraphaelites: Notes sur l'art décoratif et la peinture en Angleterre*. Brussels, 1894.

57 GAUNT, W. *The Pre-Raphaelite Tragedy*. London, 1942. Re-titled *The Pre-Raphaelite Dream*, 1943 edition.

58 HILTON, T. *The Pre-Raphaelites*. London, 1970.

59 HUNT, W.H. *Pre-Raphaelitism and the Pre-Raphaelite Brotherhood*. 2 vols. London, 1905–06.

60 IRONSIDE, R., and GERE, J. *Pre-Raphaelite Painters*. London, 1948.

61 MILLAIS, J.G. *The Life and Letters of Sir John Everett Millais*. 2 vols. London, 1899.

62 MILLS, E. *The Life and Letters of Frederic Shields.* London, 1912.

63 NICOLL, J. *The Pre-Raphaelites.* London, 1970.

64 ROBERTSON, G. *Time Was.* London, 1931.

65 ROSSETTI, W.M. *Fine Art, Chiefly Contemporary: Notices Reprinted with Revisions.* London, 1867.

66 ———, ed. *Ruskin, Rossetti, Pre-Raphaelitism.* London, 1899.

67 ———, ed. *Pre-Raphaelite Diaries and Letters.* London, 1900.

68 WATKINSON, R. *Pre-Raphaelite Art and Design.* London, 1970.

69 WELBY, T.E. *The Victorian Romantics 1850–1870.* London, 1929.

70 WELLAND, D.S.R. *The Pre-Raphaelites in Literature and Art.* London, 1953.

STAINED GLASS: TECHNIQUE

71 ARMITAGE, E.L. *Stained Glass: History, Technology and Practice.* London, 1959.

72 BALLANTYNE, J. *A Treatise on Painted Glass.* London, 1845.

73 DIVINE, J.A.F., and BLACHFORD, G. *Stained Glass Craft.* London, n.d.

74 FROMBERG, E.O. *An Essay on the Art of Painting on Glass.* London, 1851.

75 GESSERT, M.A. 'The Art of Painting on Glass, or Glass Staining'. *Quarterly Papers on Architecture*, I, Part II (London, 1844), 1–34.

76 HENDRIE, R. *An Essay upon Various Arts, in Three Books, by Theophilus.* London, 1847.

77 MERRIFIELD, M.P. *Original Treatises on the arts of painting in oil, miniature, mosaic and on glass, of gilding, dyeing and preparation of colours and artificial gems.* 2 vols. London, 1849.

78 POWELL, H.J. *Glass Making in England.* Cambridge, 1923.

79 REYNTIENS, P. *The Technique of Stained Glass.* London, 1967.

80 TWINING, E.W. *The Art and Craft of Stained Glass.* London, 1928.

81 WHALL, C.H. *Stained Glass Work.* London, 1905.

STAINED GLASS: GENERAL AND HISTORICAL

82 DAY, L.F. *Windows: A Book about Stained and Painted Glass.* London, 1897.

83 HOLIDAY, H. *Stained Glass as an Art.* London, 1896.

84 KIRBY, H.T. 'The Jesse Tree Motif in Stained Glass'. *Journal of the British Society of Master Glass-Painters*, XIII (1959–63), 313–20, 434–41.

85 OLIPHANT, F.W. *A Plea for Painted Glass, being an Inquiry into its Nature, Character, and Objects, and its Claims as an Art.* Oxford, 1855.

86 PIPER, J. *Stained Glass: Art or Anti-Art.* London, 1968.

87 RACKHAM, B. *A Guide to the Collections of Stained Glass in the Victoria and Albert Museum.* London, 1936.

88 WESTLAKE, N.H.J. *A History of Design in Painted Glass.* 4 vols. London, 1881–94.

89 [WINSTON, C.] *An Inquiry into the Difference of Style observable in Ancient Glass Paintings, especially in England: with Hints on Glass Painting.* 2 vols. Oxford, 1847.

90 WINSTON, C. *Memoirs Illustrative of the Art of Glass-Painting.* London, 1865.

STAINED GLASS: VICTORIAN

91 DRAKE, F.M. *History of English Glass Painting.* London, 1912.

92 HITCHCOCK, H.-R. *Early Victorian Architecture in Britain.* New Haven, 1954. Reprint, New York, 1972.

93 KNOWLES, J.A. 'Glass Painters 1750–1850'. *Journal of the British Society of Master Glass-Painters*, XIII (1959–63), 326–28, 390–407, 514–25.

94 READ, H. *English Stained Glass.* London, 1926.

95 SEWTER, A.C. 'The Place of Charles Winston in the Victorian Revival of the Art of Stained Glass'. *Journal of the British Archaeological Association*, 3rd ser. XXIV (1961) 80–91.

96 ——— 'Victorian Stained Glass'. *Apollo*, LXXVI (1962), 760–65.

97 WOODFORDE, C. *English Stained and Painted Glass.* Oxford, 1954.

STAINED GLASS: PRE-RAPHAELITE

98 DESTRÉE, O.G. 'Some Notes on the Stained Glass Windows and Decorative Paintings of the Church of St Martin-on-the-Hill, Scarborough'. *Savoy* (October 1896), pp. 76–90.

99 [MARILLIER, H.C.] *A Note on the Morris Stained Glass Work.* London, privately printed for Morris & Co., Ltd., 1913.

100 PEVSNER, N. 'Colonel Gillum and the Pre-Raphaelites'. *Burlington Magazine* (March 1953), XCV, 78–81.

101 SEDDON, J.P. 'The Works of the P.R.B. in Llandaff Cathedral'. *Public Library Journal: Quarterly Magazine of the Cardiff and Penarth Free Public Libraries* (March, June, and September 1903).

102 SEWTER, A.C. 'William Morris's Designs for Stained Glass'. *Architectural Review*, CXXVII (March 1960), 196–200.

103 ——— 'Notes on Morris & Co.'s Domestic Stained Glass'. *Journal of the William Morris Society*, I (1961), 22–28.

104 SPARKE, A. 'Pre-Raphaelite Stained Glass'. *Notes & Queries* (December 1918), 12th ser., IV, 337.

105 WROOT, H.E. 'Pre-Raphaelite Windows at Bradford'. *Studio* (1917), LXXII, 69–73.

FORD MADOX BROWN

106 HUEFFER, F.M. *Ford Madox Brown: A Record of His Life and Work.* London, 1896.

107 IMAGE, S. 'St Michael and St Uriel: Designs by Mr Ford Madox Brown for Painted Glass'. *Century Guild Hobby-Horse* (July 1890), V, 112–19.

108 *The Cartoons of Ford Madox Brown.* London, 1895. (The collection of 20 cartoons then in the possession of H.S. Rathbone.)

109 ROWLEY, C. *Fifty Years of Work without Wages.* London, 1911.

110 SEWTER, A.C. 'A check-list of designs for stained glass by Ford Madox Brown'. *Journal of the William Morris Society*, II (Summer 1968), 19–29.

EDWARD BURNE-JONES

111 BELL, M. *Sir Edward Burne-Jones: A Record and Review.* London, 1892. Rev. eds. 1894 and 1898.

112 BURNE-JONES, G. *Memorials of Edward Burne-Jones.* 2 vols. London, 1904.

113 CARTWRIGHT, J. *Sir Edward Burne-Jones, Bart., His Life and Work. Art Journal* Christmas Number, London, 1894.

114 CONSTABLE, W.G. 'Hope by Edward Burne-Jones'. *Boston Museum Bulletin* (February 1941), XXXIX, 12–14.

115 DE LISLE, F. *Burne-Jones.* London, 1904.

116 SEWTER, A.C. 'Notes on Some Burne-Jones Designs for Stained Glass in American Collections'. *Museum Studies* (Art Institute of Chicago), V (1970), 76–81.

117 STEPHENS, F.G. 'Mr Edward Burne-Jones ARA as a Decorative Artist'. *Portfolio* (November 1889), XX, 214–219.

118 VALLANCE, A. *The Decorative Art of Sir Edward Burne-Jones. Art Journal* Easter Annual, London, 1900.

119 ——'Sir Edward Burne-Jones's Designs for Painted Glass'. *Studio* (November 1910), LI, 91–103.

120 WILSON, H. 'The Work of Sir Edward Burne-Jones, more especially in Decoration and Design'. *Architectural Review* (March, April and May, 1897), I, 171–81, 225–33, 273–81.

121 WOOD, T.M. *Drawings of Sir Edward Burne-Jones.* London, 1907.

JOHN HENRY DEARLE

122 DAY, L.F. 'A Disciple of William Morris'. *Art Journal* (March 1905), LXVII, 84–9.

123 VALLANCE, A. 'Some Examples of Tapestry Designed by Burne-Jones and J.H. Dearle'. *Studio* (October 1908), XLV, 13–24.

ARTHUR HUGHES

124 BELL, M. 'Arthur Hughes'. *Dictionary of National Biography*, Supplement II, 275–76.

125 HOUSMAN, L. 'The Illustrations of Arthur Hughes'. *Bibliophile* (July 1908), I, 231–37.

126 ROSSETTI, W.M. 'English Painters of the Present Day. X. Arthur Hughes'. *Portfolio* (August 1870), I, 113–19.

ALBERT MOORE

127 BALDRY, A.L. *Albert Moore: His Life and Works.* London, 1894.

WILLIAM MORRIS AND HIS FIRM

128 BRIGGS, A. ed. *William Morris: Selected Writings and Designs*, Harmondsworth, 1962.

129 CROWE, G.H. *William Morris, Designer.* London, 1934.

130 DAY, L.F. *William Morris and His Art. Art Journal* Easter Number, London, 1899.

131 FLOUD, P. 'William Morris as an Artist: A New View'. *The Listener* (7 October 1954), LII, 562–64.

132 ——'The Inconsistencies of William Morris'. *The Listener* (14 October 1954), LII, 615–17.

133 ——'Dating Morris Patterns'. *Architectural Review*, CXXVI (July 1959), 14–20.

134 ——'The Wallpaper Designs of William Morris'. *Penrose Annual*, LIV, 1960, 41–45.

135 GASSER, M. 'Das Prae-Raffaelitische Abenteuer'. *Du Atlantis* (Zurich, September 1965), 671–82.

136 HENDERSON, P, ed. *The Letters of William Morris to His Family and Friends.* London, 1950.

137 —— *William Morris, His Life, Work and Friends.* London, 1967.

138 HÜRLIMANN, M. 'William Morris und die Anti-Viktorianer'. *Du Atlantis* (Zurich, September 1965), 640–57.

139 LONDON, VICTORIA AND ALBERT MUSEUM. *William Morris* (Museum Picture-Book), 1958.

140 LOWE, J. 'Restoration of Morris Windows at the Victoria and Albert Museum'. *Museums Journal* LX (August 1960), 121–22.

141 MACKAIL, J.W. *The Life of William Morris.* 2 vols. London, 1899, 1912.

142 [MARILLIER, H.C.] *A Brief Sketch of the Morris Movement and of the firm founded by William Morris to carry out his designs, and the industries revived or started by him. Written to commemorate the firm's Fiftieth Anniversary in June 1911.* London, privately printed for Morris and Co., 1911.

143 MORRIS, B. 'Morris und Company'. *Du Atlantis* (Zurich, September 1965) 658–70.

144 PEVSNER, N. *Pioneers of the Modern Movement.* London, 1936. Retitled *Pioneers of Modern Design* in the revised and partly rewritten edition, Harmondsworth, 1960.

145 ——'Architecture and William Morris'. *Journal of the Royal Institute of British Architects*, 3rd ser., LXIV (March 1957), 172–77.

146 SEWTER, A.C. 'William Morris's Designs for Stained Glass'. *Architectural Review*, CXXVII (March 1960), 196–200.

147 ——'Notes on Morris & Co.'s Domestic Stained Glass'. *Journal of the William Morris Society*, I (1961), 22–28.

148 ——'Morris Windows at Dedworth'. *Architectural Review*, CXXXVI (December 1964), 457–58.

149 TAYLOR, N. and SEWTER, A.C. 'Morris in Hospital'. *Architectural Review*, CXLI (March 1967), 224–27.

150 THOMPSON, P. *The Work of William Morris.* London, 1967.

151 VALLANCE, A. *William Morris, His Art, His Writings, and His Public Life: A Record.* London, 1897.

152 WATKINSON, R. *William Morris as Designer.* London, 1967.

VAL PRINSEP

153 CHESTER, A. 'The Art of Val C. Prinsep'. *Windsor Magazine*, XXXIX (April 1914), 613–28.

154 MEYNELL, W. 'Val Prinsep, A.R.A.: Painter and Drama tist'. *Magazine of Art.* VI (1883), 405–09.

155 PRINSEP, V.C. 'Dante Gabriel Rossetti: A Chapter from a Painter's Reminiscences'. *Magazine of Art*, XXVII (1904) 281–86.

156 —— 'The Oxford Circle: Rossetti, Burne-Jones and William Morris. A Chapter from a Painter's Reminiscences'. *Magazine of Art*, XXVII (1904), 167–72.

157 STEELCRAFT, F. 'Illustrated Interviews. No. LI—Mr Val C. Prinsep, R.A.'. *Strand Magazine*, XII (December 1896), 603–15.

DANTE GABRIEL ROSSETTI

158 ANGELI, H.R. *Dante Gabriel Rossetti: His Friends and Enemies*. London, 1949.

159 DOUGHTY, O. *A Victorian Romantic: Dante Gabriel Rossetti*. London, 1949.

160 ——, and WAHL, J.R. *The Letters of Dante Gabriel Rossetti*. 5 vols. Oxford, 1965–67.

161 GRYLLS, R.G. *Portrait of Rossetti*. London, 1964.

162 HUEFFER, F.M. *Rossetti: A Critical Essay on his Art*. London, 1896.

163 MARILLIER, H.C. *Dante Gabriel Rossetti: An Illustrated Memorial of His Art and Life*. London, 1899.

164 ROSSETTI, W.M. *The Life and Work of Dante Gabriel Rossetti*. *Art Journal* Easter Number, London, 1902.

165 —— *Dante Gabriel Rossetti as Designer and Writer*. London, 1889.

166 SEWTER, A.C. 'D.G. Rossetti's Designs for Stained Glass'. *Journal of the British Society of Master Glass-Painters*, XIII (1960–61), 419–24.

167 STEPHENS, F.G. *Dante Gabriel Rossetti*. London, 1894.

168 SURTEES, V. *The Paintings and Drawings of Dante Gabriel Rossetti*. 2 vols. Oxford, 1971.

169 SYMONS, A. *Dante Gabriel Rossetti*. London, 1909.

170 WOOD, E. *Dante Gabriel Rossetti and the Pre-Raphaelite Movement*. London, 1894.

171 WOOD, T.M. *Drawings of Rossetti*. London, n.d.

SIMEON SOLOMON

172 FALK, B. *Five Years Dead*. London, 1937.

173 FORD, J.E. *Simeon Solomon. An Appreciation*. New York, 1908.

PHILIP WEBB

174 BRANDON-JONES, J. 'The Work of Philip Webb and Norman Shaw'. *Architectural Association Journal* LXXI, (June and July–August 1955), 9–21, 40–47.

175 LETHABY, W.R. *Philip Webb and His Work*. London, 1935.

Index of Illustrations

I. Windows by Morris & Co.

II. Windows by Other Makers

III. Cartoons, Drawings, Sketch-Designs and Studies (listed in order of artist and owner)

IV. Other Subjects

General Index

Illustrations

I Burne-Jones. Cartoons for Christ in Majesty, and Third Day of Creation, ca. 1860, for eastern rose window, Holy Cross and St Laurence, Waltham Abbey, Essex. Victoria and Albert Museum.

II St Columba, Topcliffe, Yorks. Chancel south window, made by Lavers and Barraud, ca. 1860. Annunciation designed by Burne-Jones; Visitation and Nativity designed by Michael F. Halliday.

III Christ Church Cathedral, Oxford. Latin Chapel east window, made by James Powell & Sons, 1859. Detail, Death of St Frideswide, designed by Burne-Jones.

CYPRVS

IV Four panels: King René's Honeymoon, 1862. (a) Music, designed by Rossetti; (b) Architecture, designed by Madox Brown; (c) Painting, and (d) Sculpture, designed by Burne-Jones. Victoria and Albert Museum.
V St Michael and All Angels, Brighton, Sussex. South aisle east window, 1862. Three Maries at the Sepulchre, designed by Morris.

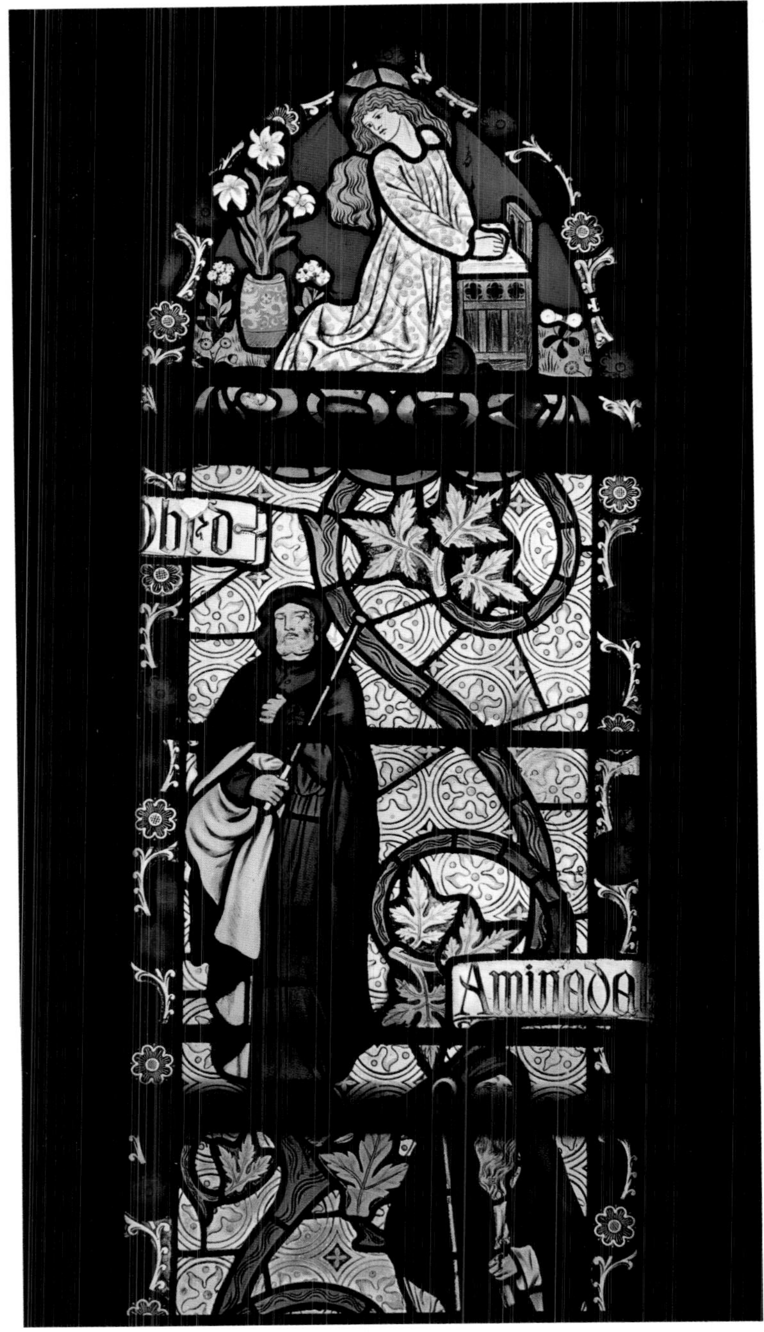

VI St Stephen's, Guernsey. West window, 1864. Tree of Jesse, detail, top of left light.

VII St Martin's-on-the-Hill, Scarborough, Yorks. South aisle west window, 1864. St Martin dividing his cloak with a beggar, and St Martin in Heaven, designed by Madox Brown.

VIII St Editha's, Amington, Staffs. East window, 1864. Detail, Nativity, designed by Burne-Jones.

IX St Mary's, Kings Walden, Herts. South aisle window, ca. 1869. Archangels Raphael, Michael, and Gabriel, designed by Morris.

X St Edward the Confessor, Cheddleton, Staffs. South aisle window, 1869. Three Angels blowing long trumpets, designed by Burne-Jones.

XI Holy Cross, Haltwhistle, Northumberland. East window, 1872. Detail, Christ bearing the Cross, designed by Madox Brown.

XII St Cuthbert's, Lytham, Lancs. South aisle window, 1875.
Transfiguration, designed by Burne-Jones.

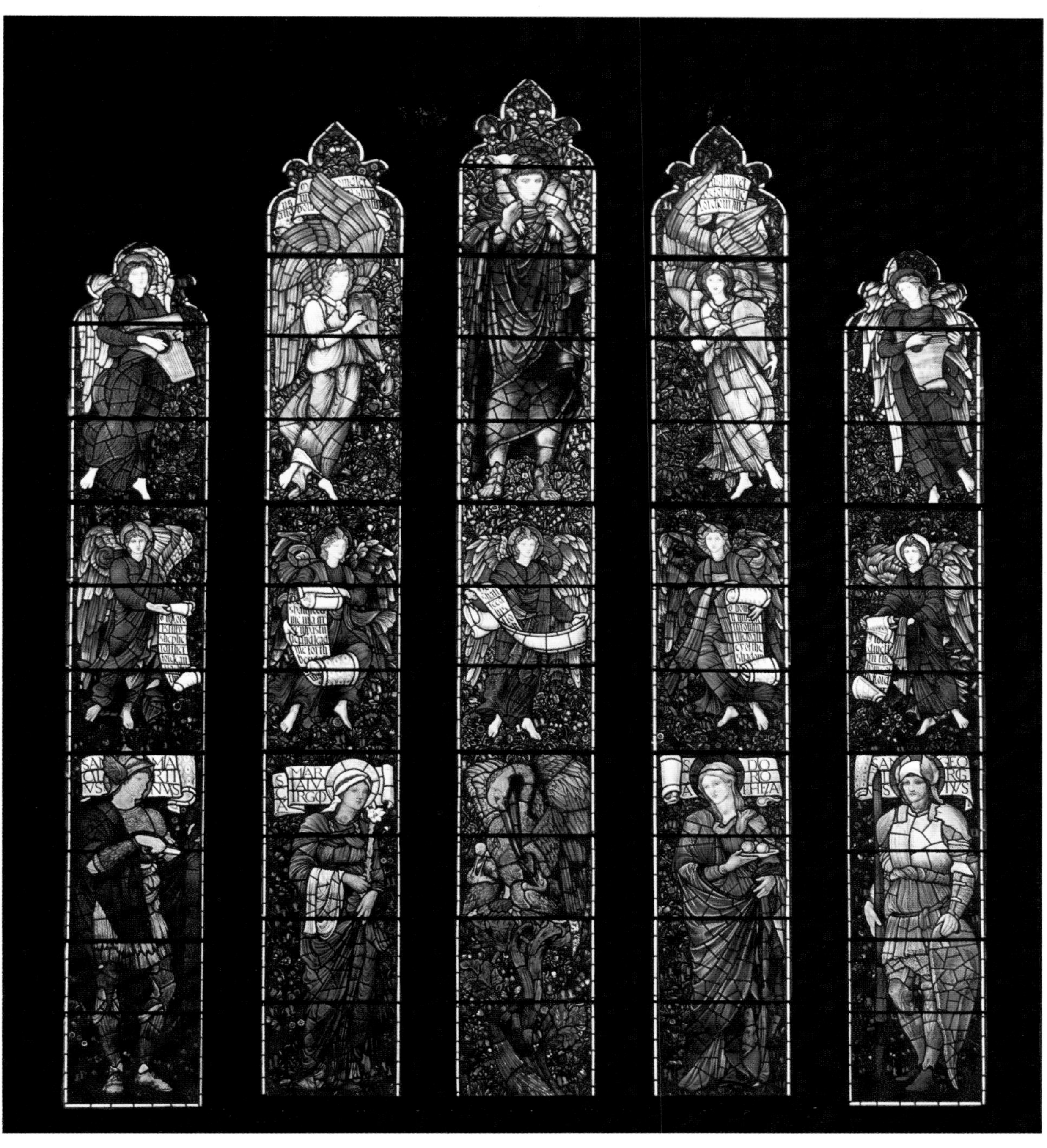

XIII St Martin's, Brampton, Cumberland. Chancel east window, 1880, designed by Burne-Jones.

XIV St John the Divine, Frankby, Cheshire. North aisle window, 1873. Adam and Eve, designed by Burne-Jones.

XV St Philip's Cathedral, Birmingham. Chancel east window, 1885. Ascension, designed by Burne-Jones.

XVI St Peter's, Swinton, Lancs. South aisle window, 1902. Calling of St Peter, designed by J. H. Dearle.

1

2

3

1 St Mary's College, Strawberry Hill, Twickenham. Window with medallions of Swiss and Flemish glass, late sixteenth and seventeenth centuries, arranged for Horace Walpole by William Peckitt.

2 St Mary's, Hulme, Manchester. Window by William Peckitt, 1769, originally in St John's, Manchester.

3 New College Chapel, Oxford. Window by Thomas Jervais, 1777–83, with Nativity after Correggio, and Virtues after Sir Joshua Reynolds.

4

5

6

4 St Alkmund's, Shrewsbury. Window by Francis Eginton, 1795, with Faith after Guido Reni.
5 Wells Cathedral. Lady Chapel east window, part, by Thomas Willement, 1843.
6 St Peter's, Chichester. Window by William Wailes, 1842.

7

8

9

7 St Andrew's, Bradfield, Berks. Grisaille-work by William Wailes, 1856, detail.
8 St Mary's, Bushbury, Staffs. Grisaille-work by Ward and Hughes, ca. 1854, detail.
9 St Leonard's, Rockingham, Northants. Watson memorial window by George Hedgeland, 1853.

10

11

12

10 Edward Burne-Jones. Cartoon for Annunciation, 1857. Birmingham City Art Gallery.

11 Burne-Jones. Cartoon for Good Shepherd, 1857. Victoria and Albert Museum.

12 Ford Madox Brown. Transfiguration, design for James Powell & Sons, 1857. Whereabouts unknown. (After Hueffer)

13 Burne-Jones. Cartoon for Adam and Eve, 1857, for Bradfield College, Berks. Victoria and Albert Museum.

14 Burne-Jones. Cartoon for the Building of the Tower of Babel, 1857, for Bradfield College, Berks. Victoria and Albert Museum.

15 Burne-Jones. Cartoon for Solomon and the Queen of Sheba, 1857, for Bradfield College, Berks. Victoria and Albert Museum.

13

14

15

16

17

18

16 Bradfield College, Berks. Window designed by Burne-Jones and made by James Powell & Sons, 1857, detail, Symbols of the Creation.
17 The same, Adam and Eve.
18 All Saints, Brightwalton, Berks. Window probably made by James Powell & Sons and designed by Michael F. Halliday, ca. 1863, Christ blessing Children.

19

20

21

22

Latin Chapel, Christ Church Cathedral, Oxford

19 St Frideswide window, designed by Burne-Jones and made by James Powell & Sons, 1859.

20 Burne-Jones. Study for St Frideswide window. Aberdeen Art Gallery.

21 Burne-Jones. Study for St Cecilia teaching St Frideswide, for the St Frideswide window. Birmingham City Art Gallery.

22 Detail of St Frideswide window, ship.

23

24

Holy Cross and St Laurence, Waltham Abbey, Essex

23–25 Tree of Jesse window, designed by Burne-Jones and made by James Powell & Sons, 1860–61.
26 Burne-Jones. Study for Tree of Jesse window. Birmingham City Art Gallery.
27 Eastern rose-window designed by Burne-Jones and made by James Powell & Sons, 1860–61, Creation.

25

26

27

28

29

30

31

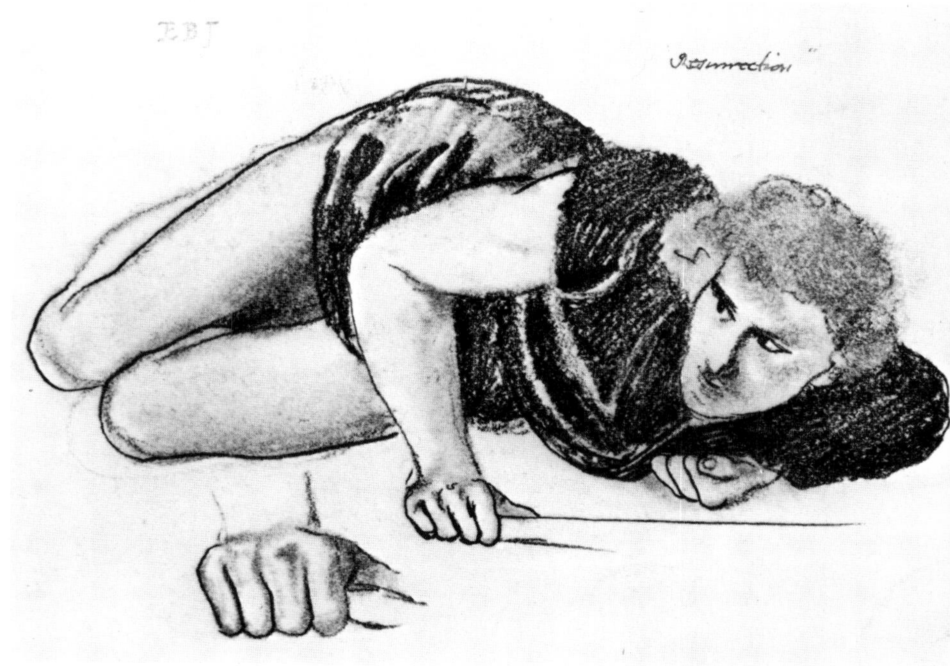

32

All Saints, Selsley, Gloucs.

28–30 Apse windows, 1861–62.
31 Burne-Jones and Philip Webb. Cartoon for Resurrection, for apse window, 1861. Birmingham City Art Gallery.
32 Burne-Jones. Study for a soldier in Resurrection, 1861. Birmingham City Art Gallery.

33

34

All Saints, Selsley, Gloucs.

33 South aisle window, Sermon on the Mount, 1861–62.
34 South aisle window, St Paul Preaching, 1861–62.
35 South aisle window, Christ blessing Children, 1861–62.
36 Dante Gabriel Rossetti. First cartoon for Sermon on the Mount, 1861. Leeds City Art Gallery.
37 William Morris. Cartoon for St Paul Preaching, 1861. William Morris Gallery, Walthamstow.

35

36

37

38

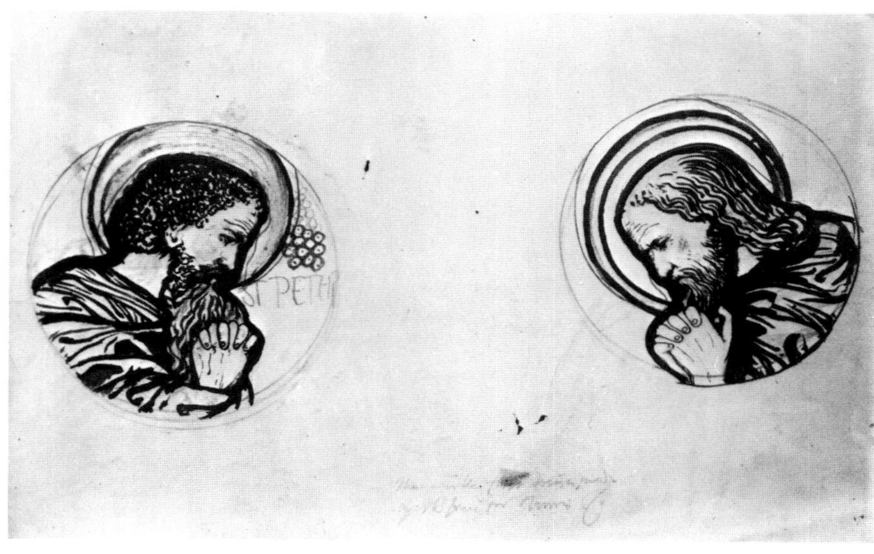

39

All Saints, Selsley, Gloucs.

38 Burne-Jones and Webb. Cartoon for Christ blessing Children, 1861. Birmingham City Art Gallery.

39 Burne-Jones. Cartoons for roundels of Sts Peter and Paul, 1861–62. Birmingham City Art Gallery.

40

41

42

All Saints, Selsley, Gloucs.

40 Chancel south window, Annunciation, 1862.
41, 42 Morris. Cartoons for Annunciation, 1861. Ashmolean Museum, Oxford.

43

44

45

All Saints, Selsley, Gloucs.

43 Vestry window, Adam and Eve, 1862.
44, 45 Burne-Jones. Cartoons for Adam and Eve, 1862. Birmingham City Art Gallery.

46

47

All Saints, Selsley, Gloucs.

46 West window, Isaiah and Moses, 1861–62.
47 West window, Abraham's Sacrifice and Enoch, 1861–62.

48

50

51

49

52

53

All Saints, Selsley, Gloucs.

48 Western rose-window, Creation, 1861–62.
49 Webb. Cartoon for Adam naming the Beasts, 1861. Victoria and Albert Museum.
50 Morris. Study for Ascension. 1861. British Museum.
51 Morris. Cartoon for Ascension, 1861. Birmingham City Art Gallery.
52, 53 North aisle windows, Emblems of the Evangelists.

54

55

56

57

St Michael and All Angels, Brighton

54, 55 Eastern chapel south window, Flight into Egypt, 1862.
56 Burne-Jones. Cartoon for two angels in Baptism of Christ, 1862. Birmingham City Art Gallery.
57 Morris. Cartoon for Angel of Resurrection, 1862. Tate Gallery, London.
58 Morris. Cartoon for Archangel Raphael, 1861. William Morris Gallery, Walthamstow.
59 Morris. Cartoon for Archangel Gabriel, 1861. Tate Gallery, London.
60 Burne-Jones. Cartoon for Virgin and Child, 1862. Birmingham City Art Gallery.
61 Peter Paul Marshall. Cartoon for St Michael and the Dragon, 1862. Victoria and Albert Museum.
62 Morris. Cartoon for Annunciation, 1862. William Morris Gallery, Walthamstow.
63 Morris. Study for Virgin of the Annunciation, 1862. Mr Sanford L. Berger, Berkeley, California.

58

59

61

62

60

63

64

65

66

St Martin's-on-the-Hill, Scarborough, Yorks.

64 East window, 1861–62.
65, 66 Rossetti. Cartoons for Parable of the Vineyard, 1861, scenes 5 and 6. William Morris Gallery, Walthamstow.

67

68

St Martin's-on-the-Hill, Scarborough, Yorks.

67, 68 West window, Adam and Eve, 1862.

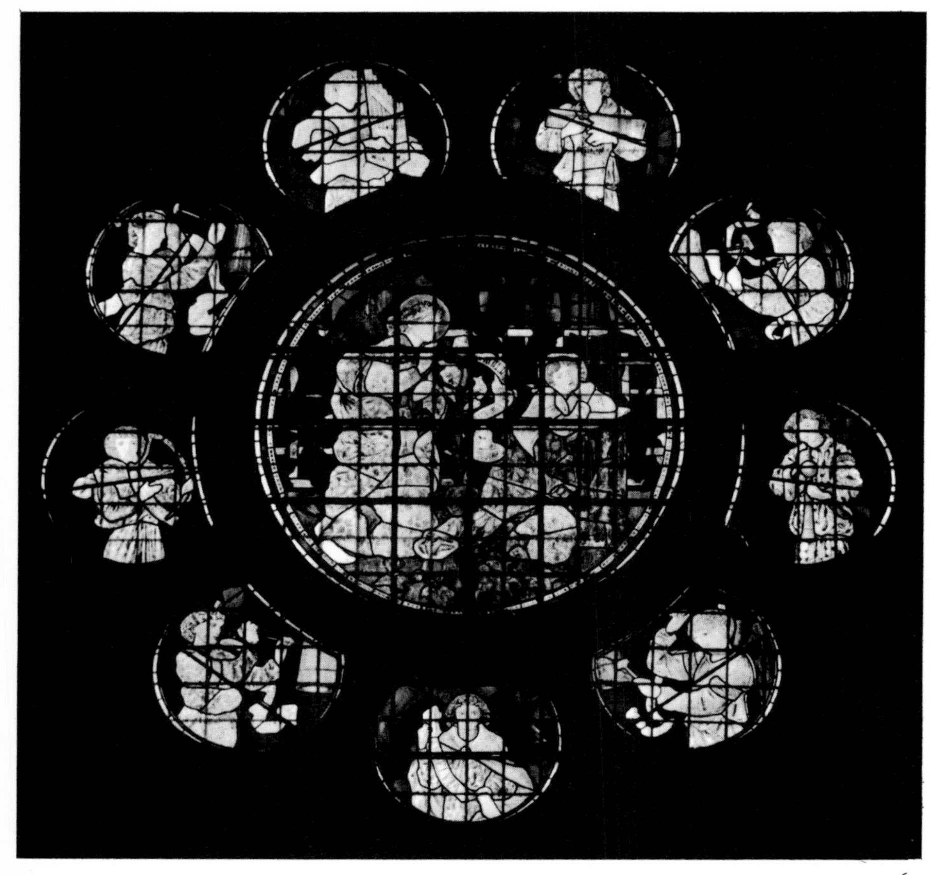

69

71

70

72

73

74

75

St Martin's-on-the-Hill, Scarborough, Yorks.

69 Western rose-window, 1862.
70 Burne-Jones. Cartoon for Annunciation, 1862, adapted for Scarborough. Birmingham City Art Gallery.
71, 72 Burne-Jones. Cartoons for two Angels striking Bells, 1862. Birmingham City Art Gallery.
73 Joshua, St Michael and Gideon window, 1862.
74 Marshall. Cartoon for Joshua, 1862. Victoria and Albert Museum.
75 Ford Madox Brown. Cartoon for Gideon, 1862. Victoria and Albert Museum.

76

77

St Martin's-on-the-Hill, Scarborough, Yorks.

76 St John the Baptist Preaching, 1862.
77 King David window, 1862 (?).

78

80

79

81

The Story of Tristram and Isoude

78 Arthur Hughes. Cartoon for the Birth of Tristram, 1862. Birmingham City Art Gallery.

79 The Fight with Sir Marhaus, 1862. Bradford City Art Gallery.

80 Tristram leaving the King of Ireland, 1862. Bradford City Art Gallery.

81 Burne-Jones. Cartoon for the Madness of Tristram, 1862. Birmingham City Art Gallery.

82

83

84

85

The Story of Tristram and Isoude

82 Morris. Cartoon for King Arthur and Sir Lancelot (the latter after Madox Brown's Gideon, fig. 75), 1862. William Morris Gallery, Walthamstow.

83 Morris. Cartoon for King Howell of Brittany and Isoude his Daughter (?), 1862. National Gallery of Scotland, Edinburgh.

84 Madox Brown. Cartoon for the Death of Tristram, 1862. Fitzwilliam Museum, Cambridge.

85 Burne-Jones. Cartoon for the Tomb of Tristram and Isoude, 1863. Birmingham City Art Gallery.

86

87

88

86–88 Woodbank, Harden near Bingley, Yorks. The Lady of Woodbank and her Daughters.

89 Rossetti. Cartoon for Christ on the Cross between the Virgin and St John, 1861, for Langton Green. Whereabouts unknown. (After Marillier)

90 Rossetti. Cartoon for Joshua, ca. 1862. Stone Gallery, Newcastle-on-Tyne (1969).

89

90

91

92

91–96 The Story of St George, scenes 1–6, 1862. Victoria and Albert Museum.

How the woful Princess was borne to be eaten of the Dragon

93

the joyful Princess was borne home again

95

How the good Knight St George of England slew the dragon and set the Princess free

94

How great rejoicing was made for the wedding of
George and the Princess

96

97

98

99

St Peter's, Cranborne, Berks.

97 West windows, Marriage Feast at Cana, 1862.
98 West windows, Christ setting a little Child in the Midst, 1862.
99 South choir chapel window, 1862.

100

100 Peterborough Cathedral. South transept window, ca. 1862.

101

102

103

104

Christ Church, Southgate, Middlesex

101 St Mark, 1862.
102 St Matthew, 1862.
103 Sts James and Jude, 1862–63.
104 Webb. Cartoon for canopy. William Morris Gallery, Walthamstow.

105

106

105 Attributed to C. Fairfax Murray after Burne-Jones. Cartoon for St James as Bishop of Jerusalem, perhaps redrawn in 1870 for a window in the Chapel Royal, Savoy Hill, London. Victoria and Albert Museum.

106 Holy Rood, Rodbourne, Wilts. Chancel east window, 1862–63.

107

108

109

110

St Helen's, Darley Dale, Derbys.

107 Song of Solomon window, 1862–63.
108–10 The same, details of panels 4, 8 and 12.

111

112

113

114

115

St Helen's, Darley Dale, Derbys.

111 Burne-Jones and Webb. Cartoon for Song of Solomon window, panel 1. Birmingham City Art Gallery.

112–15 Burne-Jones. Cartoons for the Song of Solomon window: panels 2, 6, 7 and 10. Birmingham City Art Gallery.

116

117

118

119

120

St Michael and All Angels, Lyndhurst, Hants.

116 Chancel east window, 1862–63, tracery lights.
117 Chancel east window.
118 Chancel east window, detail.
119 Burne-Jones. Cartoon for Two Angels playing Organs. Birmingham City Art Gallery.
120 Burne-Jones. Cartoon for Two Angels playing Harps. Birmingham City Art Gallery.

121

122

123

124

125

St Michael and All Angels, Lyndhurst, Hants.

121 Burne-Jones. Cartoon for chancel east window, group of Apostles. Fitzwilliam Museum, Cambridge.

122 Burne-Jones. Cartoon for Angel and Man. Fitzwilliam Museum, Cambridge.

123 Burne-Jones. Cartoon for Angel blowing a Curved Horn. Birmingham City Art Gallery.

124 Burne-Jones. Cartoon for Angel playing Double-pipes. Birmingham City Art Gallery.

125 Burne-Jones. Cartoon for Angel with Cymbals. William Morris Gallery, Walthamstow.

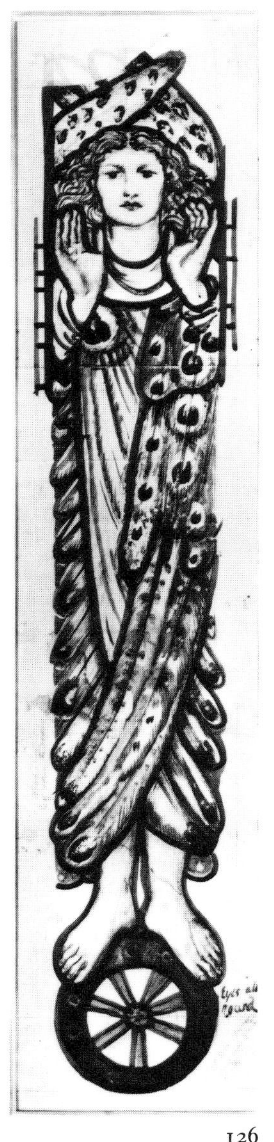

126

127

128

129

130

St Michael and All Angels, Lyndhurst, Hants.

126 Burne-Jones. Cartoon for chancel east window, Seraph. Birmingham City Art Gallery.

127 Burne-Jones. Study for Angel with Lunette Dulcimer. Stanford University Museum of Art (ex Hartnoll & Eyre Gallery, London).

128 Burne-Jones. Cartoon for Angel with Lunette Dulcimer. William Morris Gallery, Walthamstow.

129 Burne-Jones. Cartoon for Angel holding Moon. Birmingham City Art Gallery.

130 Burne-Jones. Cartoon for Angel holding Sun. William Morris Gallery, Walthamstow.

131

St Michael and All Angels, Lyndhurst, Hants.

131 South transept window, 1863.
132–35 Burne-Jones. Cartoons for south transept window, Joshua staying the Sun and Moon, Elijah and the Priests of Baal, Stoning of St Stephen, and Liberation of St Peter. Birmingham City Art Gallery.
136 South transept window, tracery lights.

132

133

134

135

136

138 139

140

137

137 Burne-Jones. Cartoon for Christ in Majesty, 1862, unidentified. Birmingham City Art Gallery.

138, 139 All Saints, Banstead, Surrey. West window, 1863, Ezekiel and St John the Baptist.

140 Rossetti. Cartoon for Ezekiel, 1863, for Banstead. Victoria and Albert Museum.

141 Marshall. Cartoon for Daniel, ca. 1863. Victoria and Albert Museum.

142 Morris. Cartoons for Annunciation, ca. 1863, unidentified. Mr J. A. Ross, Bieldside, Aberdeens.

141

142

143

145

143 St Chad's, Bishop's Tachbrook, Warwicks. North aisle east window, ca. 1863.

144, 145 Morris. Cartoons for Presentation in the Temple, ca. 1863, for Bishop's Tachbrook. William Morris Gallery, Walthamstow.

146

147

148

146 All Saints, Langton Green, Kent. St Mary Magdalene, ca. 1862.
147 Burne-Jones. Cartoon for St Editha, 1863, for Amington. Birmingham City Art Gallery.
148 St Mary's, Coity, Glamorgans. Chancel east window, 1863.
149 All Saints, Dedworth, Berks. Chancel east window, 1863.
150 The same. Annunciation window, 1863.
151 Burne-Jones. Cartoon for Noah building the Ark, for Kentish Town parish church, 1863. Birmingham City Art Gallery.
152 Burne-Jones. Cartoon for the Building of the Temple, for Kentish Town parish church, 1863. Birmingham City Art Gallery.

149

150

151

152

153

154

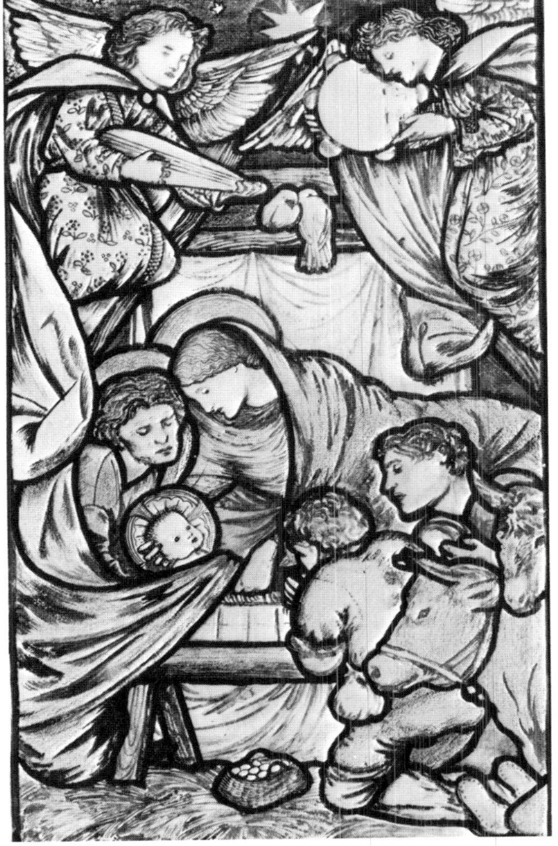

155

153 St Ladoca, Ladock, Cornwall. Chancel east window, 1863.
154 Burne-Jones. Cartoon for St Mary Magdalene anointing Christ's Feet, 1863, for Ladock. Birmingham City Art Gallery.
155 Burne-Jones. Cartoon for Nativity, 1863, for Dedworth. Birmingham City Art Gallery.

156

157

158

159

160

156–59 Burne-Jones. Cartoons for roundels, 1863: Constance, Dorigen, Griselda, and Creside. Birmingham City Art Gallery.

160 Victoria and Albert Museum. Penelope, 1863.

161

F.P. 189

162

ARS
REX EDWARDVS
SANCTVS GEORGIVS
REX HENRICVS
SCIENTIA

163

164

165

166

161 Morris & Co. Sketch-design for a proposed window for Brasenose College Chapel, Oxford, 1862. Birmingham City Art Gallery.
162 Morris. Cartoon for Josiah for Guernsey, ca. 1865. William Morris Gallery, Walthamstow.
163 Morris & Co. Sketch-design for an unidentified window, ca. 1863. Birmingham City Art Gallery.
164 Morris. Drapery study for St Paul, 1864, for Camberwell. Mr Sanford L. Berger, Berkeley, California.
165 Morris. Cartoon for St Paul, 1864, for Camberwell. William Morris Gallery, Walthamstow.
166 Morris. Cartoon for St John the Baptist, 1864, for Camberwell. William Morris Gallery, Walthamstow.

167

168

167 St Edward the Confessor, Cheddleton, Staffs. Chancel window, St Edward and King Alfred, 1864.

168 St Peter's, Bournemouth, Hants. Keble Chapel south window, 1864.

169

170

St Editha's, Amington, Staffs.

169 East window, 1864.
170 Burne-Jones. Cartoon for Christ on the Cross, 1864. William Morris Gallery, Walthamstow.

171

172

173

St Editha's, Amington, Staffs.

171 East window, detail, Adoration of the Magi.
172 Burne-Jones. Cartoon for Adoration of the Magi, 1864. National Gallery of Scotland, Edinburgh.
173 East window, detail, Annunciation to the Shepherds.

174

Bradford Cathedral, Yorks.

174 Chancel east window, 1863, before removal and division.

175

176

177

178

179

180

Bradford Cathedral, Yorks.

175 Morris & Co. Sketch-design, after Rossetti, for Christ in Majesty. Birmingham City Art Gallery.

176 Marshall. Cartoon for St Peter, ca. 1863. William Morris Gallery, Walthamstow.

177–80 Chancel east window, after removal and before cleaning and restoration, details: Anna Prophetissa, St Elizabeth and the Boy John, Martha, and St Mary Magdalene.

181

182

183

184

185

186

Bradford Cathedral, Yorks.

181–84 Burne-Jones. Cartoons for east window: Mary Virgin, David, and St Mark, all Birmingham City Art Gallery; St Luke, William Morris Gallery, Walthamstow.

185, 186 Madox Brown. Cartoons for east window: Abraham and Isaac, and Isaac. Whereabouts unknown. (After Rathbone)

187

188

189

Bradford Cathedral, Yorks.

187, 188 Morris. Cartoons for east window, 1863: St Joseph, and Isaiah. William Morris Gallery, Walthamstow.

189 Marshall. Cartoon for east window, Moses, 1863. William Morris Gallery, Walthamstow.

190

Bradford Cathedral, Yorks.

190 Chancel south window, ca. 1864, before removal.

191

192

193

194

195

196

197

198

199

Bradford Cathedral, Yorks.

191 Burne-Jones. Cartoon for chancel south window, St Stephen, 1864. Birmingham City Art Gallery.
192 Morris. Cartoon for chancel south window, St Cyprianus, 1864. William Morris Gallery, Walthamstow.
193 Morris. Cartoon for chancel south window, St Barnabas, 1864. William Morris Gallery, Walthamstow.
194 Morris. Cartoon for chancel south window, Two Angels playing Dulcimers, ca. 1864. William Morris Gallery, Walthamstow.
195 Morris. Drapery study for St James the Greater, 1864. Birmingham City Art Gallery.
196 Albert Moore. Cartoon for chancel south window, Salvator Mundi, ca. 1864. Birmingham City Art Gallery.

197 Chaucer Asleep, 1864. Victoria and Albert Museum.
198 Amor and Alcestis, 1864. Victoria and Albert Museum.
199 Cleopatra and Dido, 1864. Victoria and Albert Museum.

200

201

202

203

200–03 Burne-Jones. Cartoons for Ariadne and Lucretia, Hypsiphile and Medea, Phyllis and Hypermnestra, Thisbe and Philomela. Birmingham City Art Gallery.

204

St Stephen's, Guernsey

204 West window, Tree of Jesse, 1864–65.

205

206

St Stephen's, Guernsey

205 West window, detail, Jesse.
206 West window, detail, Eleazar.

207

208

St Stephen's, Guernsey

207 East window.
208 East window, detail, Christ on the Cross.

209

210

211

St Oswald's, Durham

209 West window, 1864–66.

210 Madox Brown. Cartoon for Baptism of St Oswald. Victoria and Albert Museum.

211 Madox Brown. Cartoon for St Oswald Crowned. Victoria and Albert Museum.

212

214

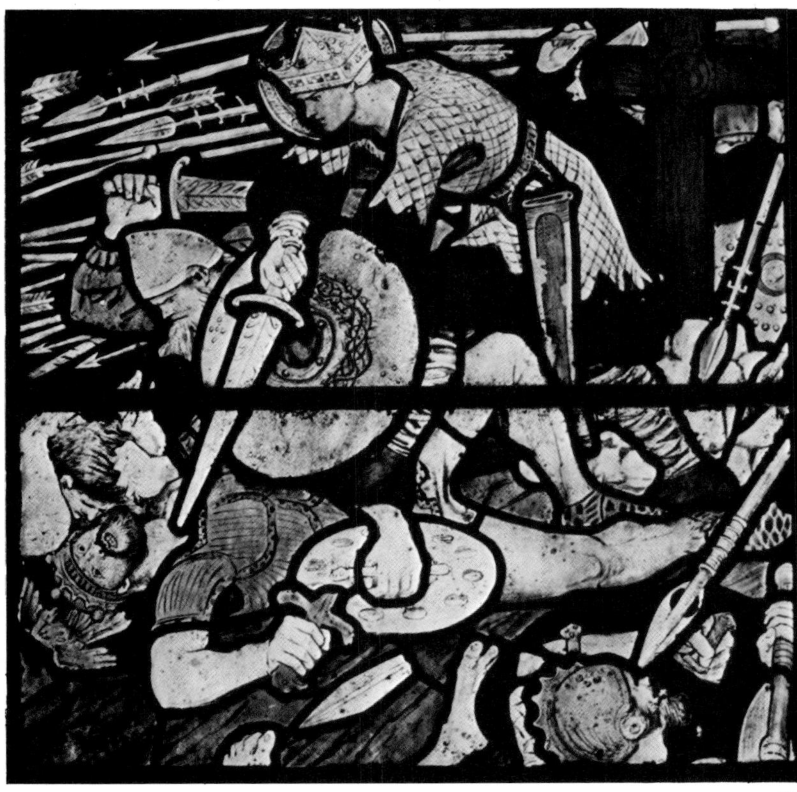

213

215

212–15 West window, details: St Oswald sends Missionaries to Scotland, St Oswald kills Caedwalla, Death of St Oswald, and Enshrining of St Oswald.

216

216 St Mary's, Doddington, Cambs. North aisle east window, ca. 1865.

217

218

219

217 St Nicholas Beaudesert, Henley-in-Arden, Warwicks. Nave south window, Mary Virgin and St Michael, 1865.
218 The same, Sts Nicholas and George, 1865.
219 Christ Church, Sunderland, Co. Durham. East window, 1865.

220

221

220 All Saints, Coddington, Notts. East window, 1865.
221 St Mary's, Antingham, Norfolk. Chancel south window, 1865.

222

223

224

St John the Evangelist, Torquay, Devon.

222 Chancel east window, 1865.
223 Burne-Jones. Cartoon for Angel and Woman, 1865. Fitzwilliam Museum, Cambridge.
224 Burne-Jones. Cartoon for Virgins, Matrons and Children, 1865. Birmingham City Art Gallery.

225

226

227

228

229

St Edmund Hall Chapel, Oxford

225 East window, detail, Last Supper, 1865.
226 Burne-Jones. Cartoon for Last Supper, 1865. Birmingham City Art Gallery.
227 Burne-Jones. Cartoon for Baptism of Christ, 1865. Birmingham City Art Gallery.
228 Burne-Jones. Cartoon for Worship of the Lamb, 1865. Birmingham City Art Gallery.
229 East window, detail, Christ on the Cross between the Virgin and St John, 1865.

230

All Saints, Middleton Cheney, Northants.

230 East window, 1865.

231

232

233

234

235

236

237

238

All Saints, Middleton Cheney, Northants.

231–35 East window, details: the Tribes of Israel, Adam and Noah, David and Isaiah, Sts Peter and Paul, Sts Augustine and Catherine, Abraham and Moses, Eve and Mary Virgin, Sts Mary Magdalene and John, Sts Agnes and Alban.

236 Burne-Jones. Cartoon for Chorus Angelorum, ca. 1864–65, probably intended for Middleton Cheney. Victoria and Albert Museum.

237 Webb. Cartoon for Banners of the Tribes of Israel. Victoria and Albert Museum.

238 Morris. Cartoon for Eve and Mary Virgin. William Morris Gallery, Walthamstow.

239

240

239 St Mary and All Saints, Sculthorpe, Norfolk. South aisle east window, 1865–66.

240 St Edburg's, Bicester, Oxon. South aisle east window, 1866.

241–43 Burne-Jones. Drawings for Faith, Hope, and Charity, ca. 1865. Birmingham City Art Gallery.

244 Burne-Jones. Cartoon for Charity. Toledo Museum of Art, Ohio. (Gift of Edward Drummond Libbey)

St Mary and All Saints, Sculthorpe, Norfolk.

245 Chancel south window, ca. 1865.

246 Madox Brown. Cartoon for Christ walking on the Sea, 1864. Mrs Roderic O'Conor.

241

242

243

244

245

246

247

248

249

St Edward the Confessor, Cheddleton, Staffs.

247 Burne-Jones. Cartoon for the Cleansing of Naaman, 1865. Birmingham City Art Gallery.

248 Burne-Jones. Cartoon for Baptism of Christ, 1865. Birmingham City Art Gallery.

249 North aisle west window, 1866.

250

251

252

253

St Olave's, Gatcombe, Isle of Wight

250–52 Chancel east window, 1865–66, details: Last Supper, Christ on the Cross between the Virgin and St John, and Entombment of Christ.

253 Chancel east window.

254

255

256

St Olave's, Gatcombe, Isle of Wight

254 Chancel north window, 1865–66, Baptism of Christ.
255 Chancel south window, 1865–66, detail, Maries at the Sepulchre.
256 Morris. Cartoon for Ascension, 1865–66. William Morris Gallery, Walthamstow.

257 Church of the Annunciation, Brighton, Sussex. East window, 1866, Annunciation.
258–60 St Wilfrid's, Pool-in-Wharfedale, Yorks. Apse windows, 1866.

257

258

259

260

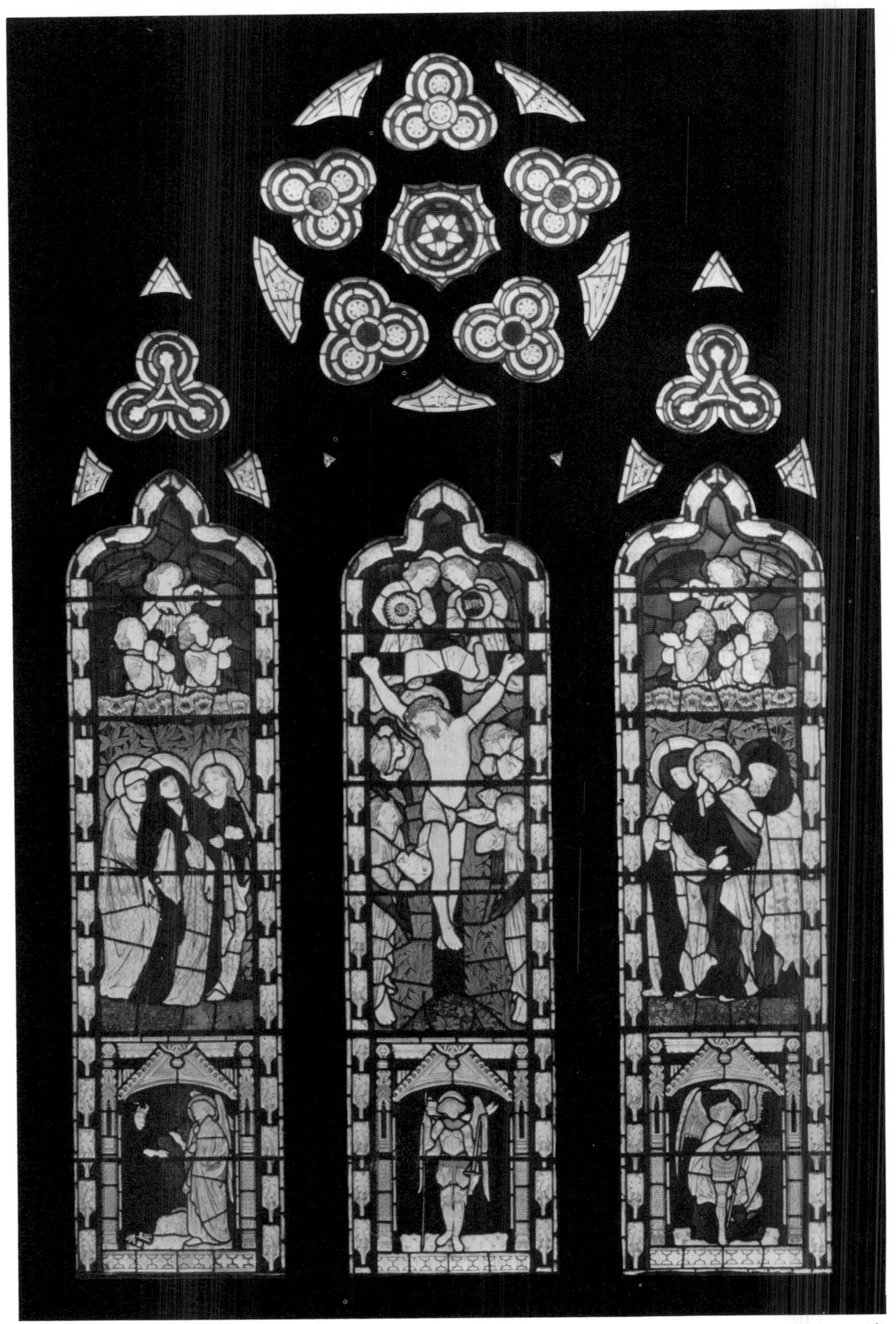

261

261 St Michael's, St Michael Penkevil, Cornwall. Chancel east window, 1866.

262

262 All Saints, Catton, Yorks. East window, 1866.

263

264

265

266

263 All Saints, Cambridge. East window, 1866.
264 The same, detail, St Catherine.
265 Llandaff Cathedral, Glamorgans. South choir east window, 1866.
266 Madox Brown. Cartoon for David and Goliath, 1866, unidentified. Whereabouts unknown. (After Rathbone)

267

268

269

267 Victoria and Albert Museum, Green Dining Room. Garland Weavers, 1867, panels 1 and 2.

268 Burne-Jones. The Garland, 1866. London Borough of Hammersmith Public Libraries (Cecil French Bequest).

269 Victoria and Albert Museum, Green Dining Room. Garland Weavers, 1867, panels 3 and 4.

270

270 Victoria and Albert Museum, Green Dining Room. Garland Weavers, 1867, panels 5 and 6.

271–74 Birmingham City Art Gallery. The Seasons, ca. 1867: Spring, Summer, Autumn, and Winter.

272

273

274

275

276

St John the Baptist, Tuebrook, Liverpool

275 Chancel east window, 1868.
276 Chancel south window, ca. 1868.
277 South aisle west window, 1868.
278 Burne-Jones. Cartoon for St Ursula, ca. 1868. Birmingham City Art Gallery.

277

278

279

280

281

St Wilfrid's, Haywards Heath, Sussex

279 Baptistry window, ca. 1868.
280 East window, 1868 (destroyed).
281 Madox Brown, Cartoon for St Wilfrid, 1866. Whereabouts unknown. (After Rathbone)

282

283

282 St Mary's, Fawley, Berks. Chancel east window, ca. 1868.
283 Morris. Cartoon for St Joseph, 1868, for Fawley. William Morris Gallery, Walthamstow.

284

285

286

287

288

289

290

291

284 Llandaff Cathedral, Glamorgans. Nave north aisle, third window, 1868.
285 St Mary's, Farnham Royal, Berks. North aisle window, 1868.
286 Burne-Jones. Drapery study for Moses, ca. 1868, for Haywards Heath or Llandaff. Birmingham City Art Gallery.
287 Burne-Jones. Drapery study for St John the Baptist, ca. 1868, for Tuebrook or Llandaff. Birmingham City Art Gallery.
288 St Edward the Confessor, Cheddleton, Staffs. Ruth and Boaz window, ca. 1868.
289 All Saints, Wigan, Lancs. St Christopher window, 1868.
290 Burne-Jones. Nude study for St Christopher, for Wigan. Birmingham City Art Gallery.
291 Burne-Jones. Drawing for St Christopher, for Wigan. Birmingham City Art Gallery.

292

293

294

292 Morris. Cartoon for Three Angels in Procession to Right, ca. 1868. Birmingham City Art Gallery.
293 Morris. Cartoon for Three Angels in Procession to Left, ca. 1868. Birmingham City Art Gallery.
294 All Saints, Middleton Cheney, Northants. Chancel south window, ca. 1868.

295

296

297

298

St Mary's, Bloxham, Oxon.

295 East window, 1869, tracery lights.
296 East window.
297 East window, detail, Two Angels swinging Censers, Sts Michael and Raphael.
298 East window, detail, Sts James and Augustine, Sts Cecilia and Catherine.

299

300

301

302

303

304

St Mary's, Bloxham, Oxon.

299 East window, detail, Sts Peter and Paul, Ezekiel and St John the Baptist.
300 Morris. Drapery study for King Alfred, ca. 1868. Mr Sanford L. Berger, Berkeley, California.
301 Morris. Cartoon for King Alfred, 1868. William Morris Gallery, Walthamstow.

St Michael's, Tilehurst, Berks.

302 Burne-Jones. Cartoon for Virgin and Child. Birmingham City Art Gallery.
303 South aisle east window, 1869.
304 The same, detail, Two Minstrel Angels.

305

306

307

308

305 Llandaff Cathedral, Glamorgans. South aisle easternmost window, 1869.
306 The same, detail, Christ blessing Children.
307 Burne-Jones. Drapery study for David, for Llandaff. Birmingham City Art Gallery.
308 St Ladoca, Ladock, Cornwall. St Luke window, 1869–70.

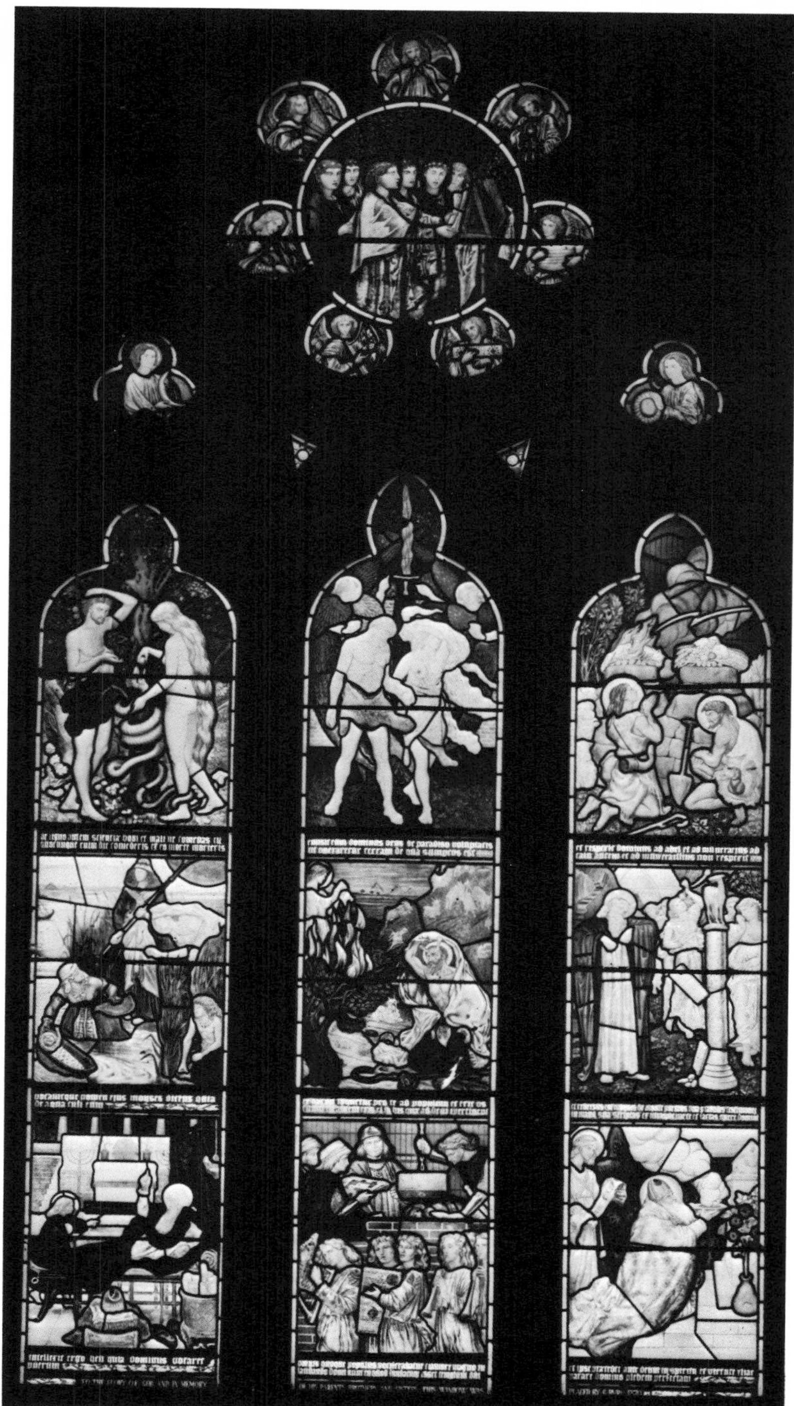

309

310

311

Holy Trinity, Meole Brace, Salop.

309 Apse left window, 1870.

310, 311 Apse left window, details: Expulsion from Eden, Moses and the Burning Bush.

312

313

314

315

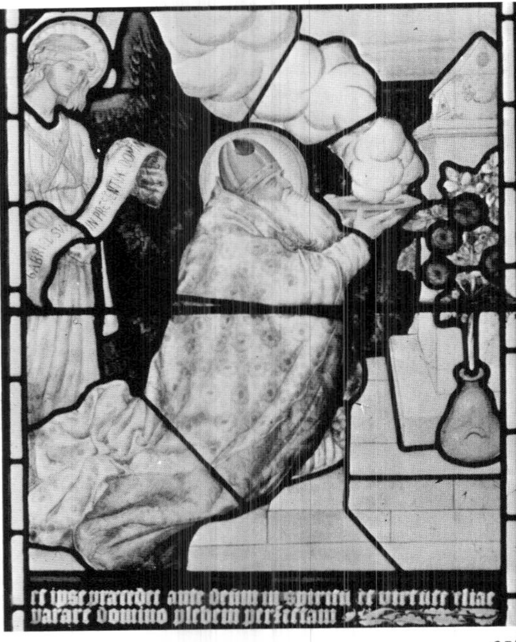

316

Holy Trinity, Meole Brace, Salop.

312–16 Apse left window, details: Finding of Moses, Worship of the Golden Calf, Samuel and Eli, the Building of the Temple, and Sacrifice of Zacharias.

317

318

Holy Trinity, Meole Brace, Salop.

317 Apse centre window, ca. 1871.
318 Apse right window, 1871–72.

319 St Nicholas, Bromham, Wilts. East window, ca. 1870.

320

321

320 Llanllwchaiarn parish church, Montgomerys. Nave south window, ca. 1870.

321 Madox Brown. Cartoon for Liberation of St Peter, 1870. Whereabouts unknown.

322

323

322 All Saints, Middleton Cheney, Northants. West window, 1870.

323 Burne-Jones. Cartoons for Adam and Eve, for Middleton Cheney west window. Victoria and Albert Museum.

324 Christ Church Cathedral, Oxford. South nave aisle west window, 1870–71.

Spes
Caritas
Fides

325

326

327

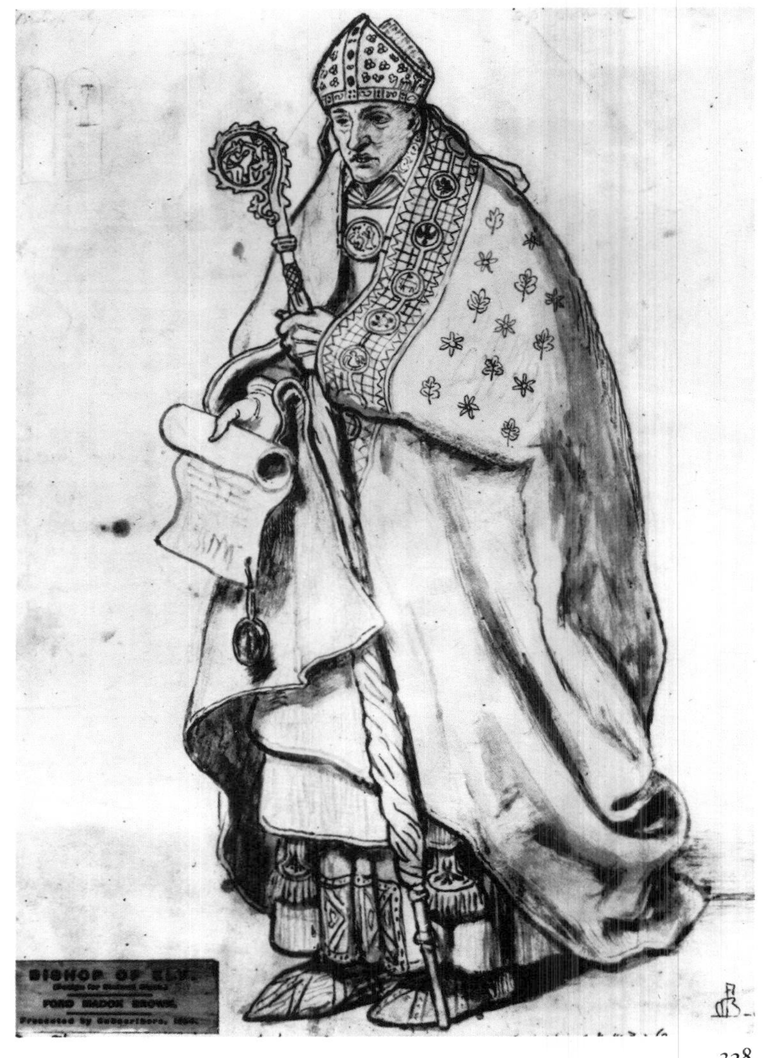

328

329

330

Peterhouse, Cambridge

325 Combination Room window, 1871–74, Spenser and Milton.
326 The same, Edward I and Hugo de Balsham.
327 Burne-Jones. Cartoon for Lucretius, 1873. Private Collection, U.K.
328 Madox Brown. Cartoon for Hugo de Balsham, 1869. Walker Art Gallery, Liverpool.
329 Hall bay window, 1870–71.
330 The same, detail, Homer and Aristotle.

331

333

332

334

335

336

Peterhouse, Cambridge

331 Hall bay window, detail, Cicero, Hugo de Balsham and Roger Bacon.

332 The same, foliage, arms and inscriptions.

333, 334 Madox Brown. Cartoons for Sir Francis Bacon and Sir Isaac Newton. University of Manchester.

335 Hall, left side, first window, 1871–72, Whitgift, Cosin and Crashaw.

336 Madox Brown. Cartoon for John Whitgift, 1871. Whereabouts unknown. (After Rathbone)

337

Peterhouse, Cambridge

337 Hall, left side, second window, 1872–74, Gray, Grafton and Cavendish.

338 Hall, right side, left window, Edward I, Queen Eleanor and Hugo de Balsham.

339 Madox Brown. Cartoon for Queen Eleanor, 1870. Whereabouts unknown. (After Rathbone)

338

339

340

341

Peterhouse, Cambridge

340 Hall, right side, centre window, Sts George, Peter and Etheldreda.

341 Madox Brown. Cartoon for Chancellor Holbrook, 1872. Victoria and Albert Museum.

342

343

Peterhouse, Cambridge

342 Hall, right side, right window, 1872–73, Holbrook, Beaufort and Warkworth.

343 Madox Brown. Cartoon for John Warkworth, 1872. Whereabouts unknown. (After Rathbone)

344

345

346

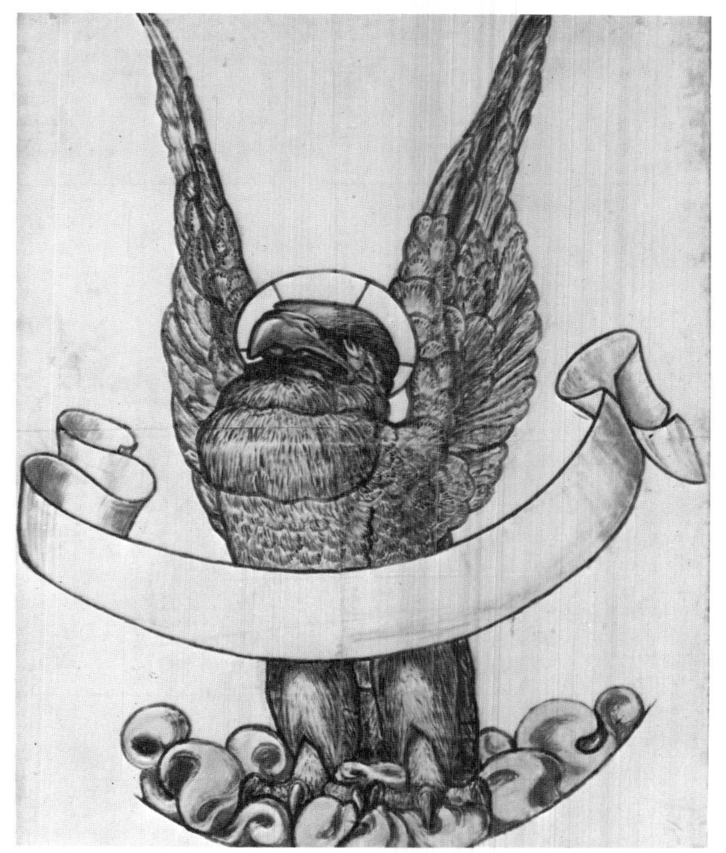
347

348

349

344–47 Webb. Cartoons for Emblems of the Evangelists, 1871, for Scarborough: St Matthew, St Mark, St Luke, and St John. Ashmolean Museum, Oxford.

348 St Saviour's, Leeds, Yorks. South aisle westernmost window, 1872, St Thomas and St Anne.

349 Burne-Jones. Cartoon for Fra Angelico, 1870, for Leeds. Birmingham City Art Gallery.

350

351

350 St John the Evangelist, Knotty Ash, Lancs. Absalom window, 1872, lower half.

Christ Church Cathedral, Oxford

351, 352 Burne-Jones. Cartoons for Lady Chapel east window, (Vyner memorial window): Samuel, and Timothy, 1872. Art Institute of Chicago.

353 Lady Chapel east window (Vyner memorial window), 1872–73.

DABIT TIBI
DOMINUS
IN OMNIBUS
INTELLECTUM

352

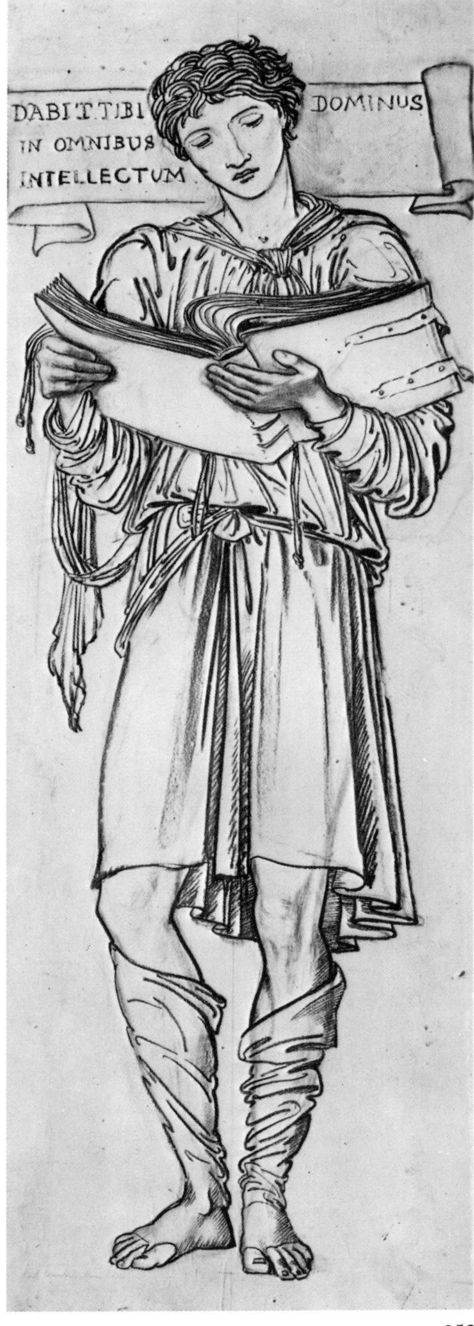

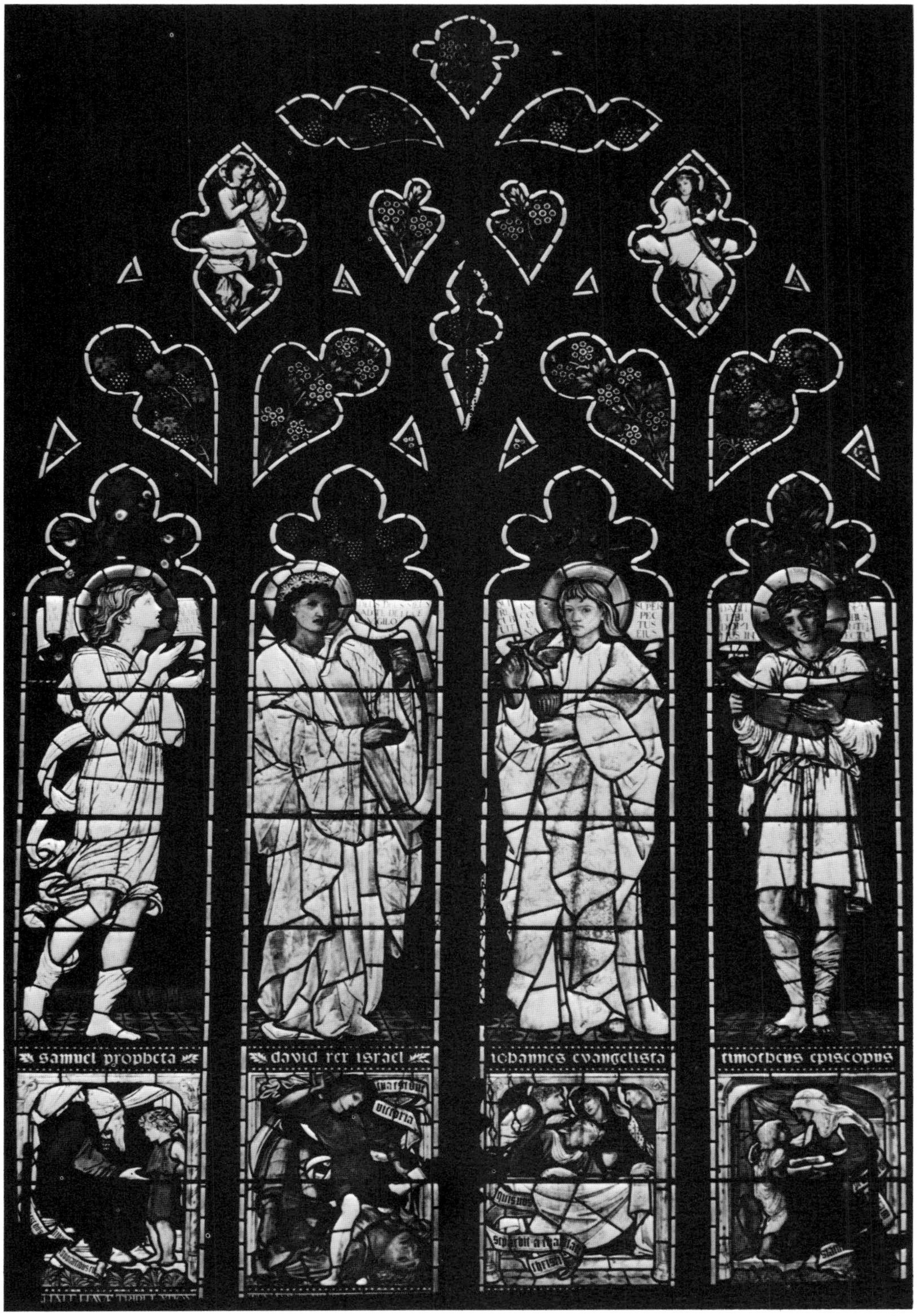
samuel propheta
david rex israel
iohannes evangelista
timotheus episcopus

353

354

355

356

357

358

Christ Church Cathedral, Oxford

354–57 Lady Chapel east window (Vyner memorial window), details: Samuel brought to Eli, David and Goliath, Last Supper, Timothy and Eunice.

358 St Peter's, Kirkbampton, Cumberland. East window, 1871.

359, 360 Victoria and Albert Museum. Aeschylus and Homer, ca. 1872–74.
361, 362 Victoria and Albert Museum. Minstrel Figure with Mandolin, and Minstrel Figure with Harp, ca. 1872–74.
363 Victoria and Albert Museum. Elaine, ca. 1870

364

365

366

367

364–67 Burne-Jones. Cartoons for Emblems of the Evangelists, for Castle Howard Chapel, 1872: St Matthew, St Mark, St Luke, and St John. Victoria and Albert Museum.

368

369

370

371

372

373

368–71 Burne-Jones. Cartoons for Castle Howard Chapel, 1872: Annunciation, Nativity, Adoration of the Magi, and Flight into Egypt. William Morris Gallery, Walthamstow.

372 St James's, Flockton, Yorks. Good Shepherd and St Anne, ca. 1872.

373 Madox Brown, Cartoon for Good Shepherd, 1869, for Flockton. William Morris Gallery, Walthamstow.

374

375

376

374 St Michael's, Waterford, Herts. St Philip, ca 1872.
375 The same. Miriam, ca. 1872.
376 Burne-Jones. Cartoon for Hope, 1872, for Meole Brace. Birmingham City Art Gallery.

377

378

377 Madox Brown. Cartoon for Abraham's Sacrifice (Isaac bearing wood), 1872, for Holy Cross, Haltwhistle. Mrs Roderic O'Conor.

378 Madox Brown. Cartoon for the Brazen Serpent, 1872, for Holy Cross, Haltwhistle. Stone Gallery, Newcastle-on-Tyne.

379

380

381

382

Royal National Hospital Chapel, Ventnor, Isle of Wight

379 North window, 1873 (removed).
380–82 The same, details: Raising of Jairus's Daughter, Woman with an Issue of Blood, and Raising of Lazarus.

Church of Jesus, Troutbeck, Westmorland

383 East window, 1873.
384–87 East window, details: Baptism of Christ, Christ blessing Children, Christ's Charge to St Peter, and Supper at Emmaus.

383

384

385

386

387

388

389

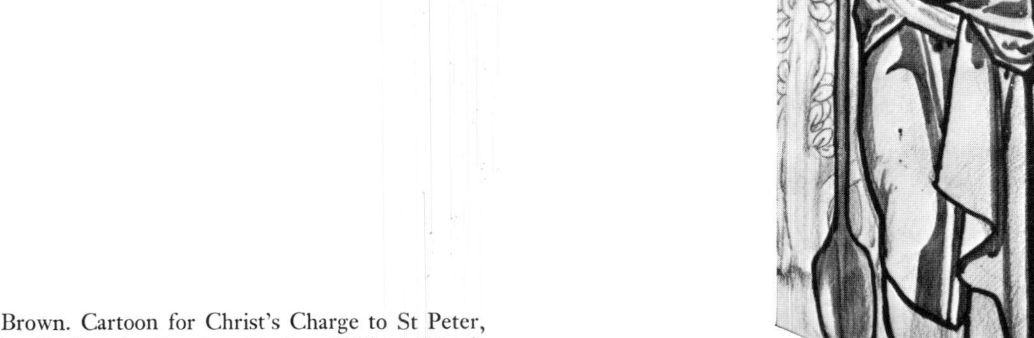

390

388 Madox Brown. Cartoon for Christ's Charge to St Peter, 1870, for St Peter's, London Docks. William Morris Gallery, Walthamstow.
389 After Madox Brown. Cartoon for Christ's Charge to St Peter, reduced version with background of trees, 1873, for Troutbeck. William Morris Gallery, Walthamstow.
390 Burne-Jones. Cartoons for Christ and St Mary Magdalene in the Garden, 1872, for Troutbeck. Victoria and Albert Museum.

391

392

St Martin's-on-the-Hill, Scarborough, Yorks.

391 North aisle westernmost window, 1872.
392 North aisle fourth window, 1873.

393

394

St Martin's-on-the-Hill, Scarborough, Yorks.

393 South aisle second window, 1873.
394 South aisle third window, 1873.

396

395 St Martin's, Marple, Cheshire. South window, 1873.
396 Morris. Cartoon for background of Mary Virgin, ca. 1873, for Marple. Victoria and Albert Museum.

395

397

398

399

397 St Chad's, Rochdale, Lancs. Tower west window, 1873.

398 St Peter and St Paul, Over Stowey, Somerset. St Mary Magdalene at the Sepulchre, 1873.

399 St Nicholas, Whiston, Lancs. South aisle east window, ca. 1873, detail, Minstrel Angel with Cymbals, 'gothic tree' background.

400

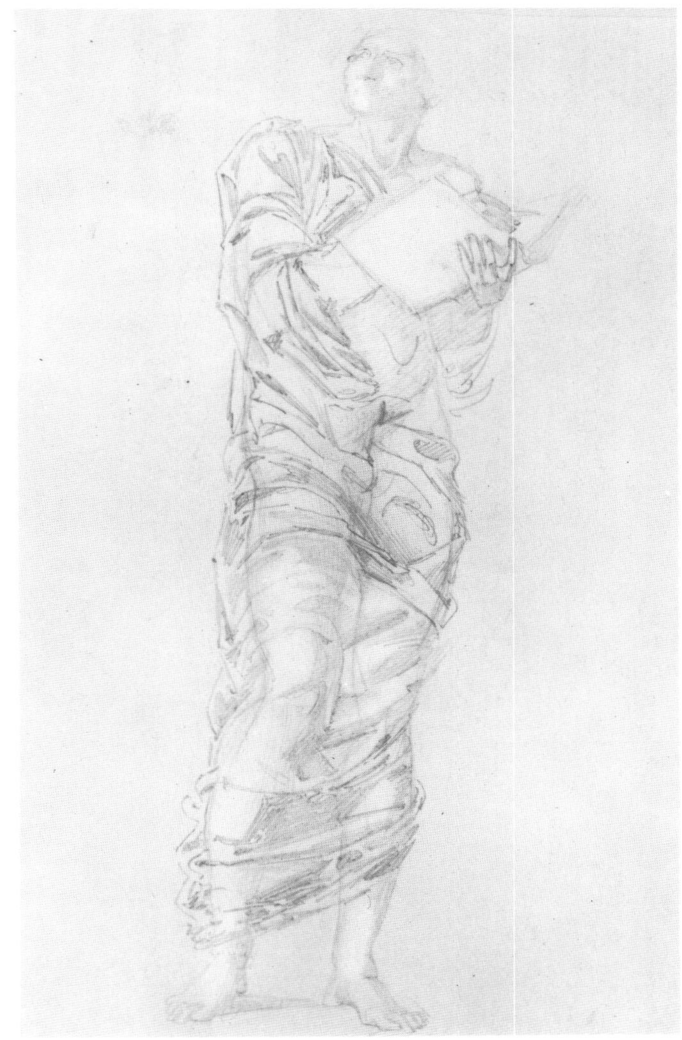

402

401

400 St John the Divine, Frankby, Cheshire. Abel and Enoch, 1873.
401 The same. Abraham and Moses, 1873.
402 Burne-Jones. Drawing for Enoch, 1872, for Frankby. A. C. Sewter, Esq.

403

404

405

403 All Saints, Madeley, Staffs. South-west window, ca. 1873.
404 Burne-Jones. Cartoon for St Bernard, 1873, for Margam. Whitworth Art Gallery, University of Manchester.
405 Burne-Jones. Cartoon for St David, 1873, for Margam. Whitworth Art Gallery, University of Manchester.

406

407

406 St Mary's, Edge Hill, Liverpool. North aisle westernmost window, 1873.
407 Attributed to Charles Fairfax Murray after Morris. Cartoon for Mary Virgin, probably redrawn ca. 1870 from a design of 1862. William Morris Gallery, Walthamstow.

408

409

410

408 Attributed to Charles Fairfax Murray after Morris. Cartoon for Mary, wife of Cleophas, redrawn from a design of 1862, probably for St Mary's, Edge Hill, Liverpool. William Morris Gallery, Walthamstow.

409 Morris. Cartoon for foliage background, unidentified. Ashmolean Museum, Oxford.

410 Morris. Cartoon for foliage background of Minstrel Figure with Harp, ca. 1876. National Trust, Wightwick Manor, Wolverhampton.

411 Bieldside, Aberdeen. Minstrel Figure with Long Pipe. J. A. Ross, Esq.

412 Bieldside, Aberdeen. Minstrel Figure with Cymbals. J. A. Ross, Esq.

411

412

413

Jesus College Chapel, Cambridge

413 South transept window, 1873, Angels of the Hierarchy and Saints.

414

415

416

420

421

422

417

418

419

423

Jesus College Chapel, Cambridge

414–23 Attributed to Charles Fairfax Murray after Burne-Jones. Cartoons for Angels of the Hierarchy, 1873: Seraphim, Cherubim, Throni, Potentates, Dominationes, Principates, Virtutes, Arcangeli, Angeli, and Imago Dei. Birmingham City Art Gallery.

sanctus lucas

425

426

427

Jesus College Chapel, Cambridge

424 St Luke window, 1873.

425 Burne-Jones. Cartoon for St Luke, 1872. Tate Gallery, London.

426 Burne-Jones. Cartoon for Cimmerian Sibyl, 1872. Tate Gallery, London.

427 Madox Brown. Cartoon for Flagellation, 1872. Whereabouts unknown. (After Rathbone)

428

429

430

Jesus College Chapel, Cambridge

428 Nave south window, Adam, Enoch, Noah, Abraham.
429 Burne-Jones. Cartoon for Adam and Eve, 1874. Victoria and Albert Museum.
430 Burne-Jones. Cartoon for Noah building the Ark, 1874. Birmingham City Art Gallery.
431 Hope, Faith and Charity window, 1873.
432 St Matthew window, 1873–74, upper part.
433 Burne-Jones. Nude study for St Matthew. Birmingham City Art Gallery.
434 Burne-Jones. Drapery study for St Matthew. Birmingham City Art Gallery.

431

432

433

434

435

436

Jesus College Chapel, Cambridge

435 St Mark window, 1874.
436 Burne-Jones. Cartoon for St Mark, 1874. Birmingham City Art Gallery.

437

438

Jesus College Chapel, Cambridge

437 St John window, 1873–75, upper part.
438 Burne-Jones. Cartoon for Tiburtine Sibyl, 1875. Birmingham City Art Gallery.

439

440

441

442

Jesus College Chapel, Cambridge

439 Burne-Jones. Cartoon for Injustice, 1875. Victoria and Albert Museum.
440 Burne-Jones. Cartoon for Vision of St Stephen, 1875. A.C. Sewter, Esq.
441 Burne-Jones. Cartoon for Fear, 1875. Victoria and Albert Museum.
442 Morris. Cartoon for panel of dense foliage and fruit, ca. 1875. William Morris Gallery, Walthamstow.

443

Jesus College Chapel, Cambridge

443 North transept window, 1876, Patience, Obedience and Docility.

444

445

446

St Mary's, Speldhurst, Kent

444 North aisle window, 1873, Sts Ursula and Nicholas.
445 North aisle window, Sts Gregory and Augustine.
446 Burne-Jones. Cartoon for St Gregory, 1873. Victoria and Albert Museum.
447 South aisle window, 1874, Mary Virgin and St Elizabeth.
448 Burne-Jones. Cartoon for Mary Virgin, 1874. Victoria and Albert Museum.
449 Burne-Jones. Cartoon for Christ blessing Children, 1874. Leeds City Art Gallery.

sancta
maria virgo
sancta
elisabeth
IN LOVING MEMORY OF A LITTLE CHILD
C.M.B. WHO WAS MADE GOD'S CHILD IN

447

448

449

450

451

452

450 St John the Baptist, Knaresborough, Yorks. South aisle west window, 1873.
451 Madox Brown. Cartoon for Zacharias, 1872, for Knaresborough. Birmingham City Art Gallery.
452 Madox Brown. Cartoon for Simeon, 1873, for Knaresborough. Whereabouts unknown. (After Rathbone)
453 Holy Trinity, Meole Brace, Salop. South aisle centre window, 1873.
454 St Michael's, Forden, Montgomerys. Chancel east window, 1873.
455 Madox Brown. Cartoons for the Marriage of St Editha, 1873, for Tamworth. Whitworth Art Gallery, University of Manchester.

453

454

455

456

457

458

459

460

461

462

456, 457 Cragside, Rothbury, Northumberland. Two quarries, with moth and bird, 1873.
458 Morris. Design for two quarries for Red House, Bexley Heath, Kent. William Morris Gallery, Walthamstow.
459–61 Cragside, Rothbury, Northumberland. The Seasons: Autumn and Winter; Virgil and Horace, all 1873.
462 Madox Brown. Cartoons for the young Milton and Edmund Spenser, 1874. Whereabouts unknown. (After Rathbone)

463

464

465

Llandaff Cathedral, Glamorgans.

463 Nave north aisle second window, 1874.
464 Madox Brown. Cartoon for St Simon, 1874. Birmingham City Art Gallery.
465 Madox Brown. Cartoon for St Jude, 1874. Birmingham City Art Gallery.

466

467

468

469

470

466–68 Llandaff Cathedral, Glamorgans. Nave north aisle second window, details: Miraculous Draught of Fishes, Christ Walking on the Water, and Shipwreck of St Paul.

469, 470 St James's, Brighouse, Yorks. Chancel north window, 1874, details: St Anne teaching the Virgin, and Repose in Egypt.

471

472

471 St Anne's, Brown Edge, Staffs. East window, 1874.
472 St Philip's, Alderley Edge, Cheshire. South aisle centre window, 1874.

473

474

473 All Saints, Ruskington, Lincs. South aisle east window, 1874.

474 St Mary Magdalene, Monkton, Devon. Chancel east window, 1874.

475

476

477

St Peter's, Woolton, Lancs.

475 South aisle window, 1874.
476 Burne-Jones. Cartoon for Ascension, 1874. National Gallery of Victoria, Melbourne, Australia.
477 Baptistry south window, Noah building the Ark, 1876.

478

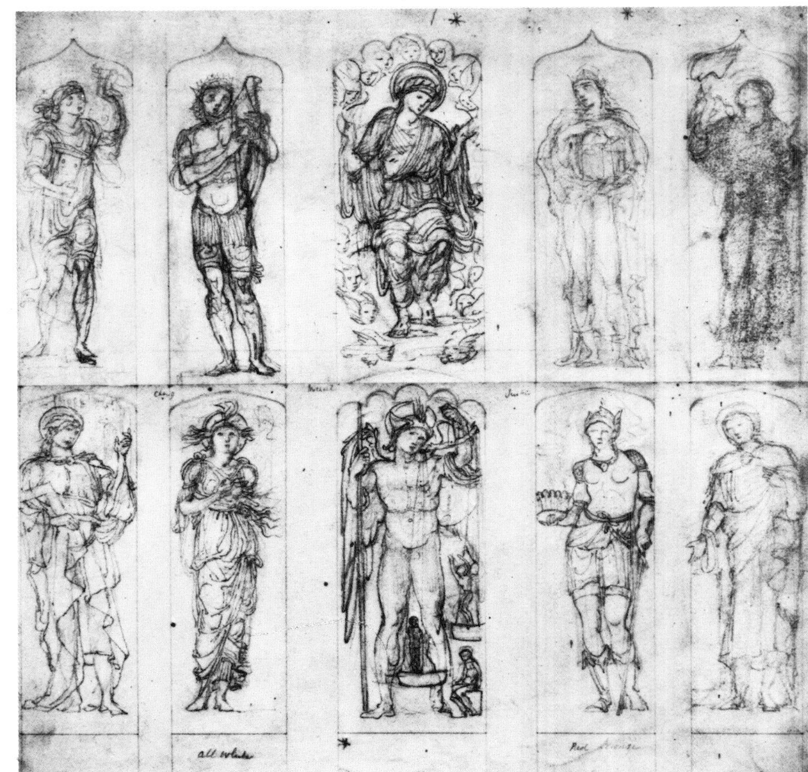

479

478 Trinity Church, Saugerties-on-Hudson, New York. Vanderpoel memorial window, 1874.

479 Burne-Jones. Drawing for the main lights of a window for Calcutta Cathedral, 1874. Birmingham City Art Gallery.

480

481

482

480–82 Burne-Jones. Cartoons for tracery lights for All Saints, Leigh, Staffs., 1874: Sacrifice of Abel, Sacrifice of Noah, and Sacrifice of Abraham. Birmingham City Art Gallery.

483

484

485

486

483–85 St Cuthbert's, Lytham, Lancs. Transfiguration window, 1875, details: sleeping apostles.
486 The same. Transfiguration window.

487

488

487 St Peter's, Edgmond, Salop. Chancel south window, 1876.
488 St Mary Magdalene, Westerfield, Suffolk. West window, ca. 1875.

489

490

489 Sacred Heart, Gosforth, Northumberland. South aisle window, ca. 1875, Mary Virgin and St Joseph.
490 The same. Chancel north window, ca. 1875, Sts Mark and Matthew.
491 The same. Chancel east window, 1875, Christ on the Cross.
492 Ponsonby parish church, Cumberland. East window, 1875.
493 Burne-Jones. Cartoon for Nativity, 1875, for Ponsonby. City Museum and Art Gallery, Carlisle.

INRI
qui peccata nostra
ipse pertulit in corpore
suo super lignum
491

INRI
S petrus
S paulus
agnus dei
S iohannes
tollit peccatum mundi
S barnabas
492

493

494

495

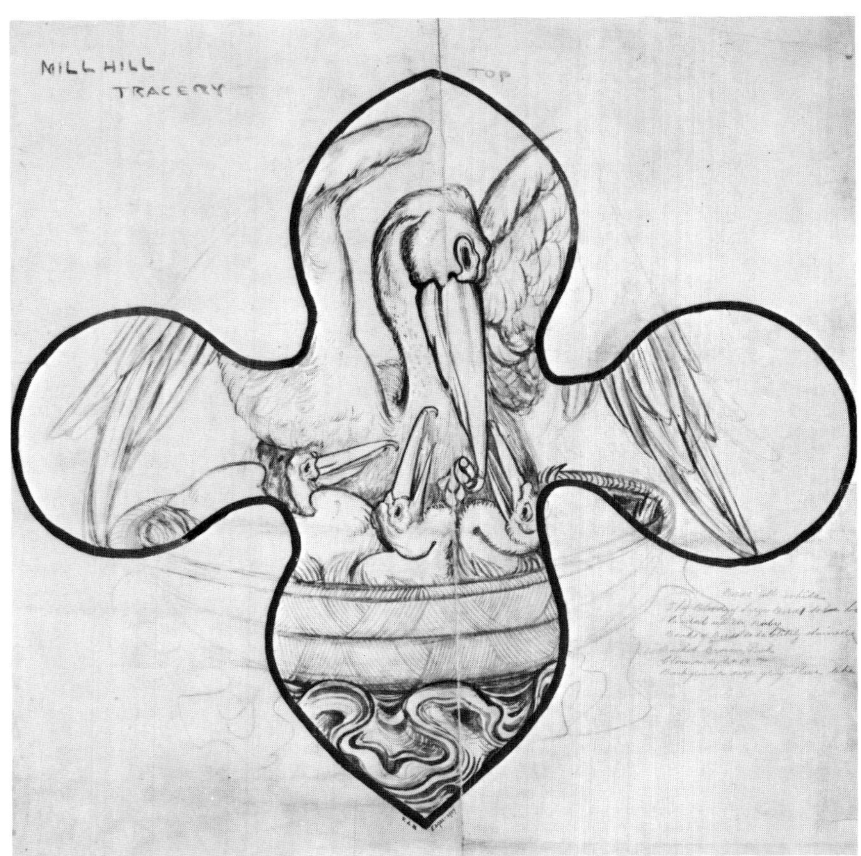

496

Mill Hill Unitarian Chapel, Leeds, Yorks.

494 South aisle window, 1875, upper part.
495 South aisle window, 1875, lower part.
496 Webb. Cartoon for Pelican on Nest. Victoria and Albert Museum.

497

498

499

500

Christ Church Cathedral, Oxford, St George's Chapel

497 East window, 1875.
498 The same, detail, Conversion of Valerian.
499 The same, detail, Valerian and the Angel.
500 The same, detail, Martyrdom of St Cecilia.

501

502

503

504

505

506

507

501 Burne-Jones. Cartoon for the Calling of Sts Peter and Andrew, 1875, for Coats parish church, Coatbridge, Lanarks. Whitworth Art Gallery, University of Manchester.

502 Burne-Jones. Cartoon for St Paul Preaching, 1875, for Coats parish church, Coatbridge, Lanarks. Whitworth Art Gallery, University of Manchester.

503 St Mary the Virgin, Speldhurst, Kent. South aisle middle window, 1875, detail, Christ among the Doctors in the Temple.

504 The same, Christ in the Carpenter's Shop.

505–07 St Peter's, Bramley, Yorks. North transept windows, 1875.

508

508 All Hallows, Allerton, Liverpool. Chancel east window, Rivers of Paradise, 1875.

509

510

509 St Eustachius the Martyr, Tavistock, Devon. North aisle east window, 1876.
510 St Michael and St Mary Magdalene, Easthampstead, Berks. Chancel east window, 1876, Last Judgement.

511

512

513

511–13 Burne-Jones. Cartoons for Last Judgement, 1874–75, for Easthampstead. Birmingham City Art Gallery.

514

516

515

514 Burne-Jones. Cartoon for Baptism of Christ, 1876, for Paisley Abbey. Mr Spencer A. Samuels, New York (ex Hartnoll & Eyre Gallery, London).

515 Burne-Jones. Cartoon for Christ among the Candlesticks, 1876, for Paisley Abbey. Victoria and Albert Museum.

516 Burne-Jones. Cartoon for Eunice, 1876, for Paisley Abbey. Victoria and Albert Museum.

517

518

517 Christ Church, Southgate, Middlesex. Chancel north window, part, Good Samaritan, 1876.
518 St Luke's, Farnworth, Lancs. North aisle window, 1877.

519

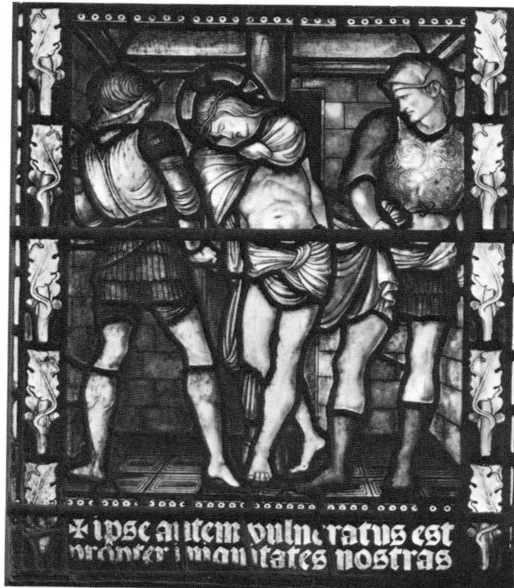

520

521

522

St Martin's, Birmingham

519 South transept window, 1877.
520, 521 South transept window, details: Christ Scourged, and Entombment of Christ.
522 Burne-Jones. Cartoon for Entombment of Christ, 1876. Bristol City Art Gallery.

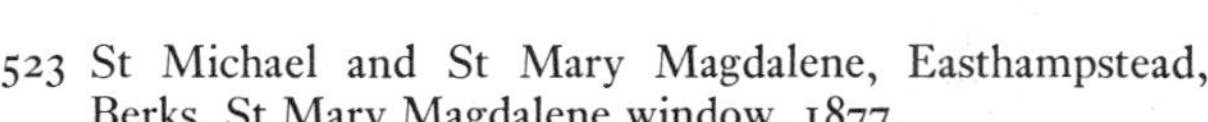

523

524

525

526

523 St Michael and St Mary Magdalene, Easthampstead, Berks. St Mary Magdalene window, 1877.

524 Burne-Jones. Cartoon for Sts Peter and John healing the Cripple at the Beautiful Gate of the Temple, 1877, for Lanercost Priory, Cumberland. William Morris Gallery, Walthamstow.

525 Burne-Jones. Cartoon for Daniel in the Lions' Den, 1877, for Jesus College Chapel, Cambridge. William Morris Gallery, Walthamstow.

526 Burne-Jones. Cartoon for Christ cleansing the Temple, 1877, for St Michael's, Torquay. Birmingham City Art Gallery.

527 St Rule's, Monifieth, Angus. East window, 1877, detail, St John the Baptist Preaching.

528 Gordon Chapel, Fochabers, Morayshire. East window, 1877, detail, Angels at the foot of the Cross.

527

528

529

530

531

532

Christ Church Cathedral, Oxford

529 Regimental Chapel east window, 1877–78, tracery lights.
530 Regimental Chapel east window.
531, 532 Regimental Chapel east window, details: St Catherine in the Temple, and Vision of St Catherine.

533, 534 Burne-Jones. Cartoons for Angeli Laudantes and Angeli Ministrantes, 1878, for Salisbury Cathedral. Fitzwilliam Museum, Cambridge.
535 St John of Beverley, Whatton, Notts. South aisle window, 1878.
536 Castle Howard School Chapel, Welburn, Yorks. East window, 1878.

533

534

535

536

537

538

537 St Etheldreda, Guilsborough, Northants. Lazarus window, ca. 1878.

538 The same. Rachel and Jacob window, ca. 1878.

539

540

539 St Martin's, Brampton, Cumberland. North aisle westernmost window, 1878.

540 The same. North aisle middle window, 1878.

541

542

543

St Helen's, Welton, Yorks.

541 Nave west window, 1879.
542, 543 Burne-Jones. Cartoons for Constantine and St Helena, 1879. Birmingham City Art Gallery.

544

545

546

544 All Hallows, Allerton, Liverpool. North transept window, 1880.

545, 546 Burne-Jones. Cartoons for Ruth and Mary Virgin, 1879, for Allerton. Birmingham City Art Gallery.

547

548

547 St Mary's, Edge Hill, Liverpool. North aisle second window, 1879.

St Martin's, Brampton, Cumberland

548 Chancel east window, 1880.
549 Burne-Jones. Cartoon for Good Shepherd, 1880. City Museum and Art Gallery, Carlisle.
550, 551 Burne-Jones. Cartoons for Two Angels with Scrolls, 1880. City Museum and Art Gallery, Carlisle.
552 Burne-Jones. Cartoon for St Martin, 1880. J. S. Maas & Co. Ltd, London.
553 Burne-Jones, Cartoon for Pelican on Nest, 1880. William Morris Gallery, Walthamstow.
554 Burne-Jones. Cartoon for St George, 1880. City Museum and Art Gallery, Carlisle.

549

550

551

552

553

554

555

557

556

558

559

560

555 All Saints, Middleton Cheney, Northants. North aisle east window, 1880, detail, Annunciation.
556 St Peter and St Paul, Cattistock, Dorset. South aisle window, 1882.
557 St Peter's, Vere Street, Marylebone, London. East window, 1881.
558 St James's, Staveley, Westmorland. Chancel east window, 1881, detail, Christ on the Cross.
559 St Margaret's, Hopton-on-Sea, Norfolk. Chancel east window, 1882.
560 St Peter's, Bramley, Yorks. North aisle window, 1882.

561

562

563

561 St Helen's, Welton, Yorks. West end south window, 1882.
562 Burne-Jones. Cartoon for Viking Ship, 1883, for Miss Catherine Wolfe, Newport, R.I. City Museum and Art Gallery, Carlisle.
563 Burne-Jones. Cartoon for David instructing Solomon in the Building of the Temple, 1882, for Trinity Church, Boston, Mass. Whereabouts unknown. (After Marillier)

564

565

566

564–66 Burne-Jones. Cartoons for Miss Catherine Wolfe, Newport, R.I., 1883: Thor, Odin, and Frey. Birmingham City Art Gallery.

568

567 St Stephen's, Gateacre, Lancs. West window, 1883.
568 All Saints, Harrow Weald, Middlesex. South aisle window, 1883.

569

570

571

569 St Michael and St Mary Magdalene, Easthampstead, Berks. St Maurice window, 1884.

570, 571 Burne-Jones. Cartoons for Adoration of the Magi, 1885, for Easthampstead. City Museum and Art Gallery, Carlisle.

572

572 St Peter's, Vere Street, Marylebone, London. South aisle window, Christ's Entry into Jerusalem, 1884.

573

574

575

576

573 Burne-Jones. Cartoon for Crossing the Red Sea, 1885, for Kirkcaldy old parish church. Municipal Gallery of Modern Art, Dublin.

574 Burne-Jones. Cartoon for Elijah raising the Widow's Son, 1885, for Kirkcaldy old parish church. Municipal Gallery of Modern Art, Dublin.

575 St Andrew and St Paul, Montreal, Quebec. North aisle second window, 1885, detail, Visiting the Prisoners.

576 The same, Clothing the Naked.

577

578

All Hallows, Allerton, Liverpool

577 South aisle easternmost window, Ascension, 1882.
578 North aisle fourth window, Annunciation to the Shepherds, 1883.

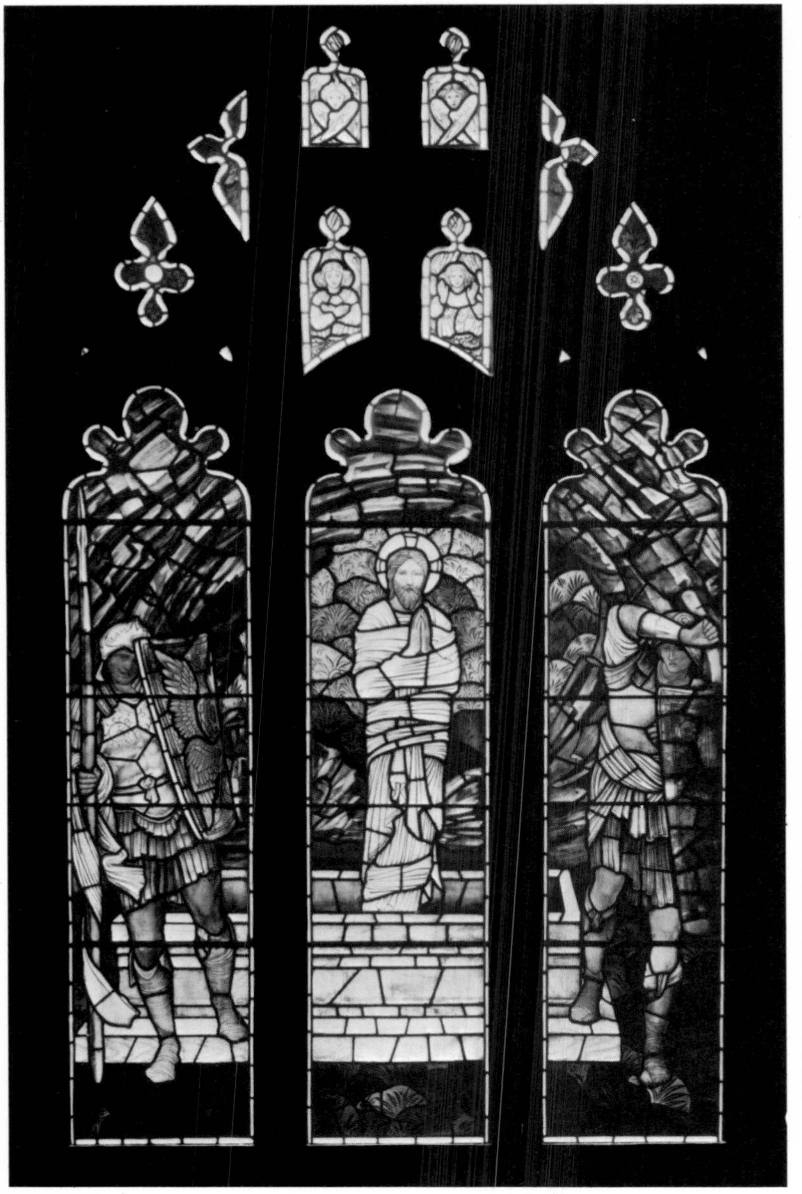

579

580

All Hallows, Allerton, Liverpool

579 South aisle second window, Resurrection, 1885.
580 South aisle westernmost window, Feast in the House of Simon, 1885.

581

582

All Hallows, Allerton, Liverpool

581 South aisle third window, Crucifixion, 1885.
582 North aisle third window, Nativity, 1886.

583

584

All Hallows, Allerton, Liverpool

583 North aisle westernmost window, Baptism of Christ, 1886.
584 North aisle second window, Christ among the Doctors in the Temple, 1886.

585

586

587

585 Burne-Jones. Cartoon for Ascension, 1874, for Woolton, Lancs. National Gallery of Victoria, Melbourne, Australia.

586 St Martin's, Brampton, Cumberland. South aisle window, 1886.

587 Burne-Jones. Cartoons for Jephthah's Daughter, Miriam, and Ruth, 1886, for St Giles' Cathedral, Edinburgh. Whereabouts unknown. (After Marillier)

588

589

588–91 Victoria and Albert Museum. The Quest for the Sangreal, 1886. Four panels.

how galahad sought the sangreal and found it because his
heart was single so he followed it to sarras the city of the spirit

590

how the sangreal abideth in a far country
which is sarras the city of the spirit

591

592

593

594

592–95 Burne-Jones. Studies for a window at the English Church, Berlin, 1886: St Michael, Peace, Justice, and St George. Victoria and Albert Museum.
596 St James, Weybridge, Surrey. North aisle window, 1887.
597 St Martin's, Brampton, Cumberland. South aisle easternmost window, 1888.
598 The same. South aisle second window, 1888.

595

596

597

598

599

600

599, 600 Burne-Jones. Cartoons for Crucifixion and Nativity, 1887, for St Philip's Cathedral, Birmingham. Victoria and Albert Museum.

601

602

603

Dundee Council Chambers

601 Burne-Jones. Cartoon for King Robert Bruce, 1888. Birmingham City Art Gallery.
602 Burne-Jones. Cartoon for David, Earl of Huntingdon, 1888. Birmingham City Art Gallery.
603 James Haliburton, 1889. Before removal.

604

606

605

604 St Brycedale, Kirkcaldy, Fife. Psalm 137, 1889.

605 The same. Moses and the Burning Bush, and Burial of Moses, 1892.

606 St Mary's, Ingestre, Staffs. Nave north window, 1890.

607

608

609

607 Burne-Jones. Cartoon for St Lucia, 1890, for Whitelands College, Putney. National Gallery of Ireland, Dublin.
608 Burne-Jones. Cartoon for St Barbara, 1890, for Whitelands College, Putney. Victoria and Albert Museum.
609 Burne-Jones. Cartoon for St Valentine, 1891, for Ilford Hospital Chapel. Letchworth Museum and Art Gallery.

610

611

610 St Paul's, Morton, Lincs. Stoning of St Stephen, 1892.
611 The same. St Paul preaching at Athens, 1892.
612 Hillhead Church, Glasgow. Chancel apse window, 1893.

612

613

614

615

Bute Hall, University of Glasgow

613 West window, details, Dante and Chaucer, 1893.
614 East window, details, Sts Augustine and Thomas Aquinas, 1900.
615 West window, details, Virgil, Horace, Shakespeare, and Milton, 1893.

616

617

618

St Margaret's, Rottingdean, Sussex

616 East window, 1893.
617 Burne-Jones. Cartoon for Gabriel, 1892. Lady Lever Art Gallery, Port Sunlight.
618 Burne-Jones. Cartoon for Raphael, 1892. Lady Lever Art Gallery, Port Sunlight.

619

620

621

St Margaret's, Rottingdean, Sussex

619 Chancel north window, St Margaret, 1894.
620 Chancel south window, Mary Virgin, 1894.

621 St Leonard's, Loddington, Northants. Chancel south window, 1893, detail.

622

623

622 St Tyfaelog, Llandefeilog, Carmarthen. East window, 1895.
623 Burne-Jones. Cartoons for Faith, Charity and Hope, 1894, for Llandefeilog. Brook Street Gallery, London.

624

624 Albion Congregational Church, Ashton-under-Lyne, Lancs. Chancel east window, 1893.

625

626

627

625 Albion Congregational Church, Ashton-under-Lyne, Lancs. South transept window, 1895.

626, 627 Burne-Jones. Cartoons for Ashton-under-Lyne, 1892: Moses and Abraham. William Morris Gallery, Walthamstow.

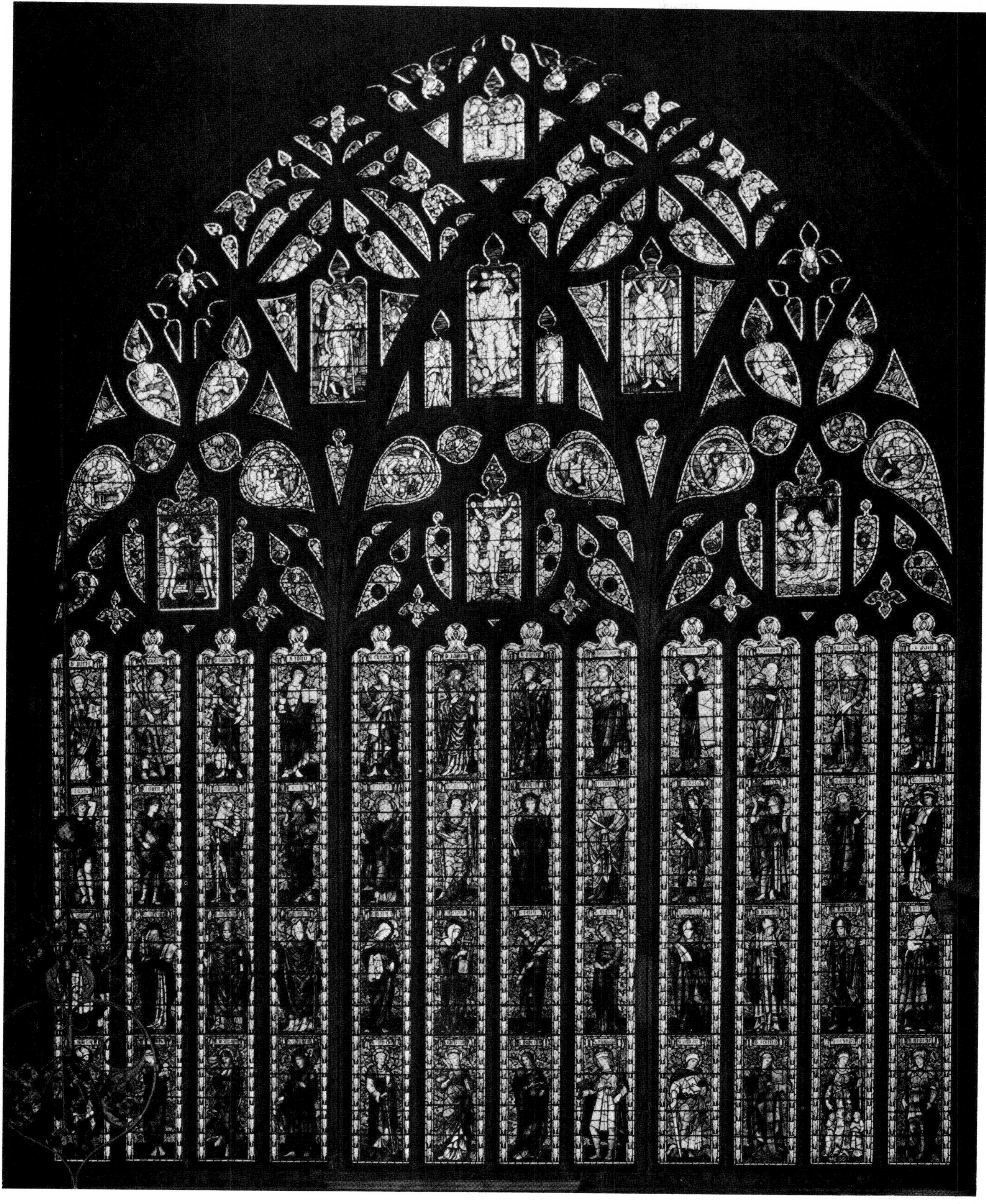

628

628 Holy Trinity, Sloane Street, Chelsea, London. East window, 1894–95.

629

630

631

632

629 Manchester College Chapel, Oxford. Third and fourth Days of Creation, 1895.
630 Holy Saviour, Bitterne, Hants. Salvator Mundi, 1896.
631 Burne-Jones. Cartoons for Jacob's Dream and Tree of Jesse, 1896, for Rottingdean. Brighton Art Gallery – at the Grange, Rottingdean, Sussex.
632 St Paul's, Morton, Lincs. South transept westernmost window, 1896.

633

634

635

633 King's College Chapel, Aberdeen. Chancel north window, 1897.
634 The Duke of Westminster (Saighton Grange, Cheshire). St Francis, 1897.
635 The same. St Veronica, 1901.

636

636 St Deiniol, Hawarden, Flints. West window, 1898.

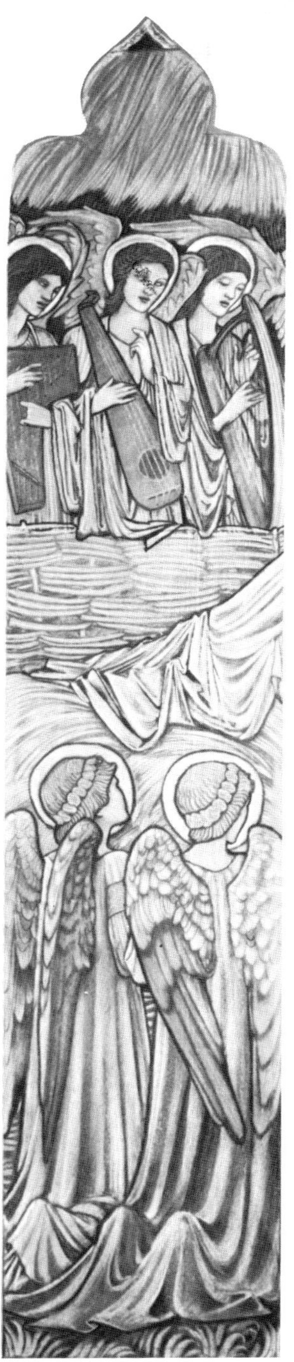
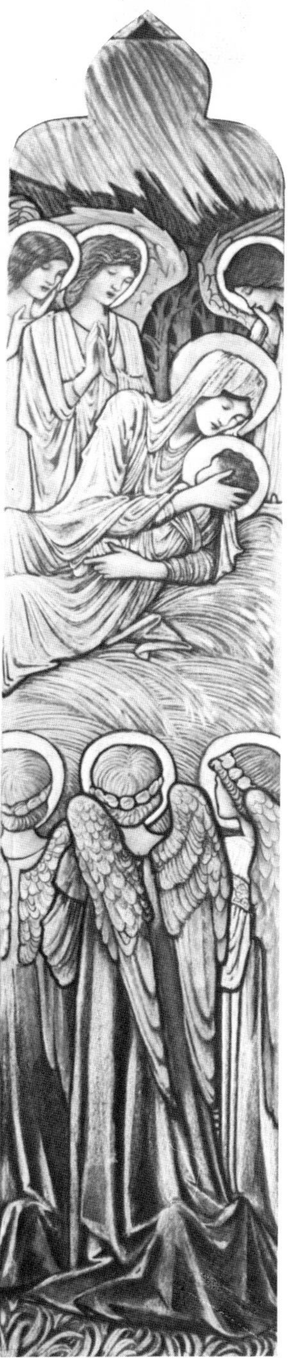

637

637 Burne-Jones. Cartoons for Nativity, 1898, for Hawarden.
Leger Galleries, London.

638

639

638 St John the Baptist, Wolverley, Worcs. 'Consider the Lilies', 1899.
639 Lismore Cathedral, Co. Waterford, Eire. South transept window, 1900.

640

640 Rugby School Chapel, Warwicks. West window, 1902.

641

642

641 Christ Church Cathedral, Montreal, Quebec. North aisle westernmost window, 1902.

642 St Andrew and St Paul, Montreal, Quebec. North aisle third window, 1903.

643

644

643 Queen Elizabeth's Grammar School, Blackburn, Lancs. Window from Wilmar Lodge, 1903.
644 Troon Old Parish Church, Ayrshire. Ascension, 1903.

645

646

645 All Saints, Elton, Hunts. South aisle west window, 1905.
646 Dundonald parish church, Ayrshire. Chancel east window, 1906.

647

648

647 High Pavement Chapel, Nottingham. David and Jonathan, 1907.

648 St Mary the Virgin, Merton, Surrey. South aisle window, 1907.

649

649 Brechin Cathedral, Angus. South transept window, 1907.

650

651

650 St Botolph's, Shenley, Herts. North aisle window, 1908.
651 St Mary the Virgin, Great Brington, Northants. Adoration of the Lamb, 1912.

652

653

St Stephen's, Tonbridge, Kent

652 North aisle west window, Maries at the Sepulchre, 1910.
653 North aisle centre window, Road to Emmaus, 1911.
654 North aisle easternmost window, Resurrection, 1911.
655 North aisle westernmost window, Agony in the Garden, 1911.

TO THE GLORY OF GOD
THIS WINDOW IS PLACED BY
AND IN MEMORY OF WILLIAM
THEIR SON ARTHVR WILLIAM
AND SARAH CHIPPINDALE
ANNO DOMINI 1911

654

655

656

657

656 St Helen's, Isle of Wight. Sermon on the Mount, 1913.
657 St Mary's, Old Swinford, Worcs. Christ rescuing St Peter from the Water, 1915.

658

659

658 St Bartholomew's, Wilmslow, Cheshire. War, 1920.
659 The same. Peace, 1920.

660

660 The stained-glass studios of Morris & Co. at Merton Abbey, ca. 1908.
661, 662 Two left-hand pages from Burne-Jones's account-books. Fitzwilliam Museum, Cambridge.
663 Page from the Minute Book of Morris, Marshall, Faulkner & Co. Mr Sanford L. Berger, Berkeley, California.

263 16 2

To first design of same "on approval" (ye gods.) 20.

1885 July — Small design for Church at Edinburgh 10.

July & August. — 2 windows for Allerton in three lights each.

- Resurrection 60.
- House of Simon 60.

Sept. — Crucifixion 50..

463 16 2

Nov. — 2 subjects for window at Kirkcaldy —

Raising of widow's son 20.

Passage of Red Sea. 20.

On the morning when I began these designs I made a scene which however I my regret, was wholly beyond my control. 503 16 2

661

My Employer Wm. Morris may remember some expressions I made use of, and for which I take this early opportunity of tendering an ample apology. Though, by God, if ill considered subjects like these, entirely unfitted for the space are offered to me again I will not be responsible for the language I use nor the property I smash — and it is not my fault that my apology is thus qualified by menace. 503 16 2

By 4 designs for Bedroom window panels 44

31 Dec " Royalties '85 28

575 16 2

662

Meeting at 8 Red Lion Sq. April 1. 1863.

Present: Rossetti, Jones, Webb, Morris, Marshall, Faulkner.

Marshall elected chairman.

Agreed that the meeting of April 15 be appointed to consider the subject of a deed of partnership and that notice of this be given to members not present at this meeting.

~~Duty~~ The Cartoons for the single figures in Bradford East window allotted as follows:

Rossetti: Jacob, Mary Magdalene, Martha, ~~Joshua~~ at 3£ each
Ned: Virgin Mary, David at 3£ each
Marshall: ~~[illegible]~~ St Peter, Moses, Solomon, Anna at 2£ each
Morris: ~~[illegible]~~ Elijah, Mary sister of Martha, Joseph, ~~[illegible]~~ at 2£ each.
Brown: Abraham, Elizabeth, Isaac, Paul
if he will accept them

Rossetti to do small drawing of Elisha raising the Shunammite's son for Holy Trinity Church, Halifax for 2£.

Ford Madox Brown

663

664

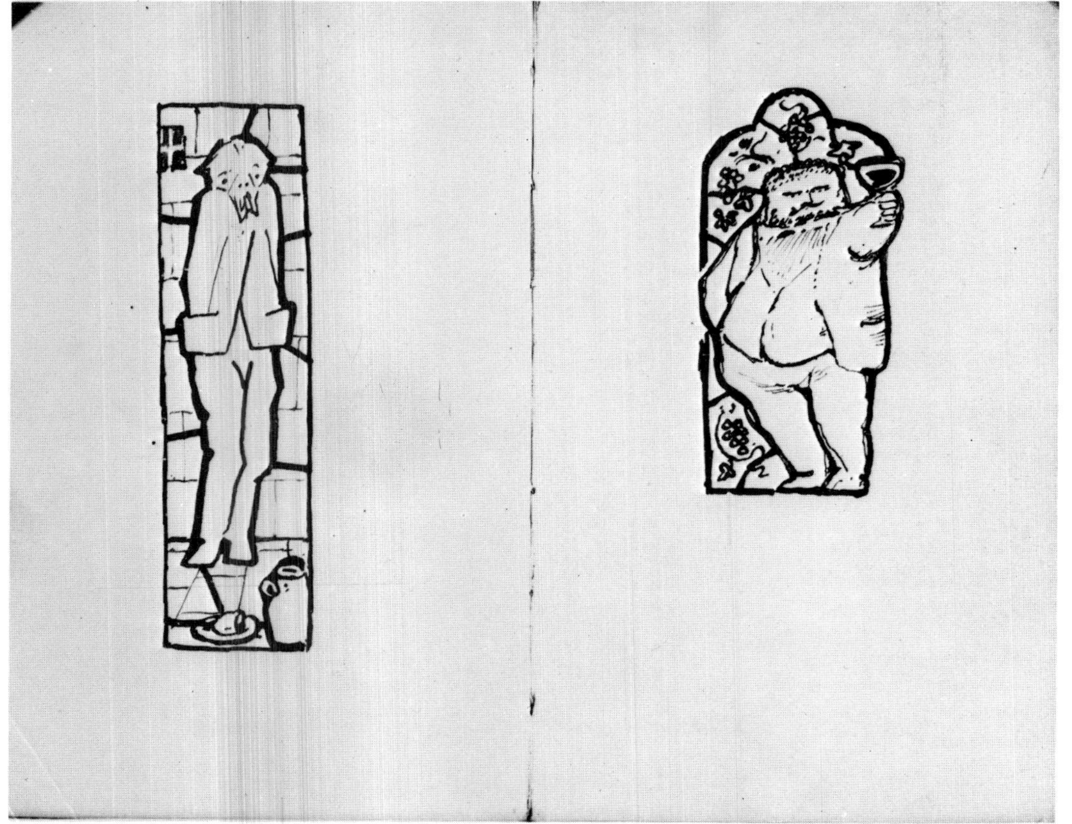

665

664, 665 Burne-Jones. Caricatures of Morris and Burne-Jones, in Burne-Jones's account-books. Fitzwilliam Museum, Cambridge.